The World's Easiest Guide to Using the MLA

A User-Friendly Manual for Formatting Research Papers According to the Modern Language Association Style Guide

Carol J. Amato

STARGAZER Publishing Company

Westminster, CA 92685

For Dylan

Published by Stargazer Publishing Company
PO Box 10084
Westminster, CA 92685-0084
(800) 606-7895
(714) 531-6342
FAX (714) 531-8898
e-mail: stargazer@stargazerpub.com
website: http://www.stargazerpub.com

Edited by Claudia Suzanne

All material in this book corresponds to the Fourth (1995) and Fifth (1999) Editions of the *MLA Handbook for Writers of Research Papers.* This book is intended for high school and undergraduate use only.

ISBN: 0-9643853-6-8 (College Edition, paper, spiral bound)
　　　　0-9643853-7-6 (Library Edition, paper, perfect bound)

Library of Congress Catalog Card Number: 98-89923

Publisher's Cataloging-in-Publication
 (Provided by Quality Books, Inc.)

Amato, Carol J.
   The world's easiest guide to using the MLA : a user-friendly manual for formatting research papers according to the Modern Language Association style guide / Carol J. Amato. -- 1st ed.
    p. cm.
    Includes bibliographical references and index.
    LCCN: 98-89923
    ISBN: 0-9643853-6-8 (paper, spiral)
    ISBN: 0-9643853-7-6 (paper, perfect)

   1. Gibaldi, Joseph, 1942- . MLA style manual and guide to scholarly publishing. 2. Authorship --Style manuals. 3. Humanities--Authorship--Handbooks, manuals, etc. 4. Scholarly publishing --Handbooks, manuals, etc. 5. Academic writing--Handbooks, manuals, etc.   I. Title.

PN147.A63 1999   808'.027
                          QBI98-1767

Table of Contents

Chapter 4 Documenting Your Sources in the Text, Cont'd.

Chapter 5 Creating a Works Cited List

Chapter 5 Creating a Works Cited List, Cont'd.

Chapter 5 Creating a Works Cited List, *Cont'd.*

Chapter 5 Creating a Works Cited List, Cont'd.

List of Figures

List of Tables

Introduction

If you are a high school student or an undergraduate, you probably have asked yourself why you must use a style guide when you write a report. You may not really even understand what a style guide is.

The reason for style guides is simple. Most disciplines require that students' papers be presented in the same manner. Each discipline has a specific way sources must be documented in the text and on the reference page. The books that supply these directions are called style guides. A style guide not only shows how to document sources, but also explains other rules, such as:

- Which font (typestyle) to use

- How to create and place headers and/or footers

- Whether you should single- or double-space the document

- Whether to use upper- or lower-case on certain words, titles, names, etc.

- How to space out such items as mathematical symbols or equations and scientific formulas

- How to document paraphrased material and direct quotations from other sources

- Whether the document should be printed single-sided or double-sided

- How to place figures and tables

There are many style guides. Among the ones commonly used in colleges and universities are:

- APA (American Psychological Association)

- Chicago (The University of Chicago Manual of Style)

- MLA

Most English departments and humanities disciplines use the MLA.

You have probably wondered why using a style guide is generally so difficult. The original sources are more complex than they need to be because often they are geared toward scholars; therefore, some of the guidelines are very confusing and/or may not apply to formatting reports at the high school or college level. Even if the style manuals are geared to undergraduates or high school students, they usually are not written by people knowledgeable in the field of technical writing. For most students, writing a report is formidable enough without having to tackle complicated, poorly written instructions.

Complaints about just this issue from my own students at the University of Phoenix inspired me to apply my skills writing user-friendly software manuals to writing user-friendly versions of style guides. The first result was *The World's Easiest Guide to Using the APA*, and the second is this book, *The World's Easiest Guide to Using the MLA*.

The World's Easiest Guide to Using the MLA gives you a simple, clearcut explanation of how to use the MLA style guide in formatting your reports.

Style guides should be easy-to-use. I hope *The World's Easiest Guide to Using the MLA* proves to be just that for you.

Chapter 1

Setting Up Your Pages

This chapter talks about creating the body pages of a document. It includes specific instructions on the following:

- Using the correct font

- Elements of a report page

  ✓ Setting the margins
  ✓ Formatting the heading
  ✓ Creating body text
  ✓ Formatting the page numbers

Using a Readable Font

With the availability of desktop-publishing programs today, it's easy to feel that one should create fancy covers and use various fonts to make a report look good. As nice as this might appear, you must use *manuscript* style; that is, doublespacing with roughly 25 lines per page. That means just plain type, folks, just plain type.

The MLA style guide states that the font used must be easy to read. The most commonly used fonts for manuscripts are Courier and Courier New. Other easy-to-read fonts include Arial (the font in which this sentence is printed), Times, Times Roman, and Times New Roman. Be sure to ask your instructor which font he/she prefers. If you are not sure, the best solution is to use Courier or Courier New.

Figure 1 shows examples of several fonts.

If you are using older versions of software, such as Microsoft Word 2.0 for Windows or WordPerfect 5.2 or 6.0 for Windows, you may encounter the following:

- *Microsoft Word 2.0*

  Times Roman seems to have a hard time conforming to the margins. When the page is printed, it runs past the right-hand margin. In addition, wherever a word is italicized, it prints over itself, and the result is a very messy page. Test a page out before using this font.

- *WordPerfect 5.2/6.0 for Windows*

  WordPerfect borrows the Courier font names from their old typewriter counterparts. Courier 12 is Elite typesize and Courier 10 is Pica typesize; therefore, Courier 10 is bigger than Courier 12. This is exactly the opposite of other word processors, including Word 2.0, which determine font size by the "point" size (the height of the letter).

Whichever font you select, use 12-point size. If you use a smaller point size, your report will be hard to read. If you use a larger one, your report will look magnified.

```
This is 12 pt. Courier

This is 12 pt. Courier New
```

This is **12 pt. Times**

This is 12 pt. Times Roman

This is 12 pt. Times New Roman

This is **12 pt. Arial**

Figure 1. Examples of Easy-to-Read Fonts.

Elements of a Report Page

Your report's pages will consist of the following elements:

- Margins

- Heading

- Page numbers

- Author information

- Title

- Body text

- Text headings

- Graphics

This section explains how to create the margins, heading, page numbers, author information, title, body text, and text headings. Chapter 2 explains detailed information on how to place graphics.

Setting the Margins

Set the margins of your document to the following:

- Left margin = 1"

- Top margin = 1"

- Right margin = 1"

- Bottom margin = 1"

Refer to Figure 2.

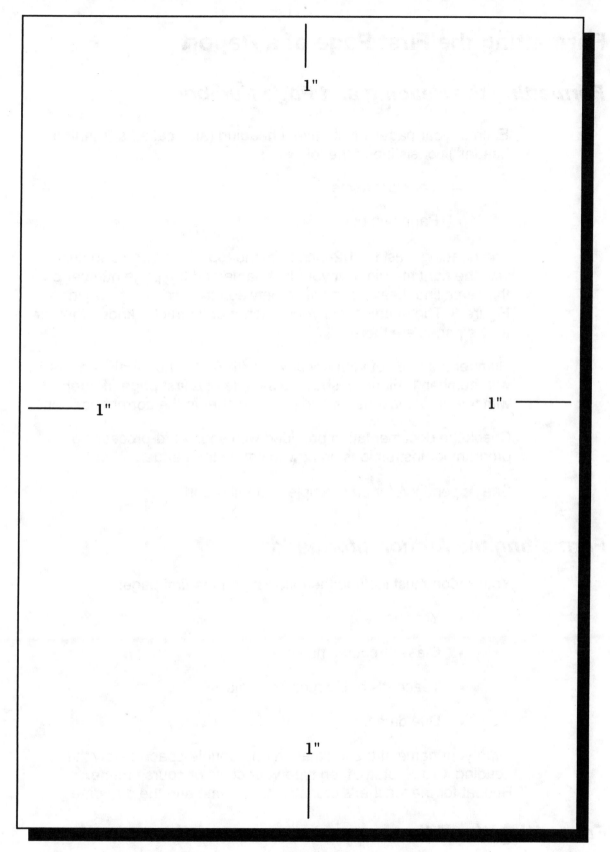

Figure 2. Correct Margin Settings.

Formatting the First Page of a Report

Formatting the Heading and Page Numbers

Each of your pages must have a heading (also called a "running header") consisting of the following:

- Your last name

- Page number

The heading must be 1/2-inch from the top of the page and flush with the right margin. Put your last name and the page number on the same line. Leave one space between the two, as shown in Figure 3. The heading lets your teacher or instructor know whether all the pages are there.

Number the body of your document with Arabic numerals that start with number 1. Figure 6 shows a sample of a first page of a report with the author last name and page number in the correct position.

Check the documentation provided with your word-processing program for instructions on how to set up the header.

See Appendix A for an example of a full report.

Formatting the Author Information

Your report must include the following on the first page:

- Your name

- Class or course name

- Teacher's or instructor's name

- Due date

Type your name at the left margin one double-space below the heading. Press return, then type your class or course name. Repeat for the teacher's or instructor's name and the due date.

Formatting the Title

Center your title one double-space below the last line of your author information. Capitalize the beginning letter of each word.

Johnson 3

Sue Johnson

English 100

Mr. Lockhart

October 29, 1999

An Analysis of Two Classic Authors

The text of your paper starts here. Indent each paragraph one-half inch; that is, to the first tab, or five spaces on a typewriter. Lorem ipsum dolor sit amet, consectetuer adipisci elit, sed diam nonummy nibh eusmod tin cidunt ut loreet dolore magna aliquam erat volutpat. Ut wisi ad minim veniam, quis nostrud exercitation ulcorper suscipit lobortis nisl ut aliquip ex ea commodo consequat.

Duis atem vel eum iriure dolor in hendrerit in putate velit esse molestie consequat, vel illum dolore feugiat nulla facilisis at vero eros et accumsan et odio dignissim qui blandit praesent luptatum zzril del augue duis dolore te feugait nulla facilisi.

Nam liber tempor cum sluta nobis eleifend id congue nihil imperdiet doming id quod mazim placerat possim assum odio dignissim qui blandit praesent luptatum zzril del augue duie dolore te feugait nulla facilisi consectetuer adipisci elit, sed diam nonummy nibh eusmod tin cidunt ut loreet dolore magna aliquam erat volutpat.

Figure 3. Example of a First Page of a Report.

Creating Body Text

Follow these rules when creating the body text:

1. Type your text double-spaced, printed on one side of the page.

CAUTION!

**If you photocopy your document,
do *not* create a double-sided version!**

---

2. Type approximately 25 lines per page. See Appendix A for a sample report.

3. Use a *ragged-right* margin for your pages. A ragged right margin has lines of differing length, as shown in Figure 4. Compare it to the example in Figure 5, which shows a *right-justified* margin.

   A right-justified margin makes the document more difficult to read because the computer adds extra spaces between the words to make the lines end evenly. If you look closely at the text in Figure 5, you can see those extra spaces. The reader's eyes tire easily as they jump from space to space. Ragged-right margins are kinder to your teacher or instructor.

4. Indent the first line of each paragraph one-half inch. Your word processor's tabs should be set automatically in half-inch increments; therefore, one press of the tab key should indent your paragraph one-half inch. If you are using a typewriter, press the space bar five times.

5. Double-space between paragraphs—do not quadruplespace!

    Duis atem vel eum iriure dolor in hendrerit in
vulputate velit esse molestie consequat, vel illum dolore
eu feugiat nulla facilisis at vero eros et accumsan et
iusto odio dignissim qui blandit praesent luptatum zzril
delenit augue duis dolore te feugait nulla facilisi.

Figure 4. Example of Text With Ragged Right Margin.

    Duis atem vel eum iriure dolor in hendrerit in
vulputate velit esse molestie consequat, vel illum
dolore eu feugiat nulla facilisis at vero eros et
accumsan et   usto odio dignissim   qui blandit
prasent lutatum   zril delenit augue duis dolor
terranum feugait nulla facilisi.

Figure 5. Example of Text With Justified Right Margin.

Using Text Headings

If your paper has more than three pages, you might consider using headings to break it up into sections. The MLA allows three ways to accomplish this:

- Numbers (arabic numerals only)

- Headings

- Numbers with headings

If you use numbers only, center them, and do not add extra lines before or after the number. (Your entire paper, including the headings, should be double-spaced only.)

Use numbers for main-level (first-level) headings only. If you need subheadings (second-level headings), use lower-case letters (see Figure 6).

If you use headings, or numbers with headings, place them flush left.

Figure 6 shows an example of headings taken from a paper entitled "Attitudes Toward Evolution in Victorian Literature." See the sample paper in Appendix B for another example.

```
1. Charles Darwin

a. Criticism From Scientists

b. Criticism From Religious Leaders

2. John Tyndall

a. "The Belfast Address"

b. Fragments of Science

3. Sir Edmund Gosse

a. Philip Henry Gosse's Omphalos

b. The Dilemma of the Fundamentalist and Scientist
```

Figure 6. Sample Headings.

Chapter 2

Placing Graphics

Graphics are very important in your document. The saying "A picture is worth a thousand words" is very true. Graphics help your readers understand information that is difficult to get across in words.

Your document can include two types of graphics:

- Figures

- Tables

This chapter explains how to place each of these on the page.

Placing Figures

Figures include diagrams, pictures, photos, line drawings, bar and line graphs, pie charts, etc. They are also called illustrations. While your figure can be narrower than the required margins of the page, it cannot be wider. If you include a figure, refer to it by number in your text:

```
Fig. 1 shows Hemingway's home in Key West.
```

or

```
Hemingway lived in a Spanish-style home in

Key West (see fig. 1).
```

Place the figure as closely as possible to that reference; that means on the same or very next page. When the word "figure" starts a sentence, be sure to abbreviate it as "Fig." with a capital "F," as the first example shows. When you use the word within the sentence, however, be sure to abbreviate it as "fig." with a lower-case "f," as the second example shows.

Each figure must have a sequential number and a caption. Number figures separately from tables; i.e., Figure 1, Figure 2, Figure 3, and Table 1, Table 2, Table 3—*not* Figure 1, Table 2, Figure 3. (For information on table placement, see *Placing Tables*, page 16.) Place the caption below the artwork, beginning at the left margin, as shown in Figure 7.The caption must be a complete sentence and should accurately describe the contents of the artwork. Capitalize all the words in the caption except for the articles and prepositions (unless the first word is an article or preposition).

Notice that in the caption, the word "Figure" is abbreviated as "Fig." but starts with a capital letter. A period follows the figure number. Note that the figure caption immediately follows the figure number and that when the caption goes onto a second line, it is double-spaced.

If you are including a musical illustration, label it "Example," but abbreviate it as "Ex." in the caption and at the beginning of a sentence (but as "ex." within a sentence or phrase):

```
Ex. 3. George Sanders, Symphony no. 4 in B flat,

op. 34 (The White Swan), second movement, opening.
```

Johnson 13

Lorem ipsum dolor sit amet, consectetuer adipiscing,
sed nonummy nibh euismod tin cidunt ut laoreet dolore magna
aliquam volutpat. Ut wisi enim ad minim veniam, quis nostrud exerci tation ullam corper suscipit lobortis nisl ut
aliquip ex ea commodo.

Duis atem vel eum iriure dolor in hendrerit in vulputate velit esse molestie consequat, vel illum dolore eu
feugiat nulla facilisi. Lorem ipsum dolor sit amet, as shown
in Figure 5:

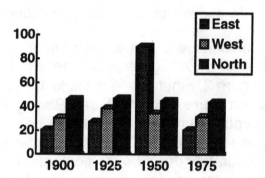

Fig 5. Dist. of Births in Three Major Cities Over a
75-yr. Period.

Dolor sit amet, consectetuer adipiscing, vel illum
sed nonummy nibh euismod tin cidunt ut laoreet dolore magna
aliquam volutpat. Ut wisi enim ad minim veniam.

Figure 7. Example of Figure and Figure Caption Placement.

Placing Tables

Tables compare large amounts of data in columns. You can use a table to compare results in certain categories for test groups, for instance. While your table can be narrower than the required margins of the page, it cannot be wider. Refer to the table number in your text:

```
Table 4 shows the comparisons for the 10

test groups.
```

or

```
The comparisons for the 10 test groups

vary substantially (see table 4).
```

Place the table as closely as possible to that reference; i.e., that means on the same page or the very next page. When the word "table" starts a sentence, be sure to capitalize it, as the first example above shows. When you use the word within the sentence, however, be sure to use a lower-case "t," as the second example above shows.

Each table must have a sequential number and a caption. Number tables separately from figures; i.e., Table 1, Table 2, Table 3, and Figure 1, Figure 2, Figure 3—not Table 1, Figure 2, Table 3. (For information on figure placement, see *Placing Figures*, page 14.) Place the caption at the top of the table, as shown in Figure 8. The caption must start at the left margin, must be a complete sentence, and must accurately describe the contents of the table. Capitalize all the words in the caption except for the articles and prepositions (unless the first word is an article or preposition).

Notice that in the caption, the word "Table" begins with a capital letter. Begin the caption itself on the line below the word "Table" and the table number. Capitalize all the words in the caption. Note also that when the caption goes onto a second line, it is double-spaced, but unlike the second line of a figure caption, the second line of a table caption is indented two spaces.

Cite the source of the table below the table itself. Start at the left margin with the word "Source," followed by a colon and then the source information. If the source information goes onto a second line, double-space it and indent it two spaces.

To add a note to explain information about the table, use a superscripted lower-case letter after the caption. Then, below the source information, indent five spaces, place the same super-scripted letter again, and then include the note information.

Ergonomic Needs of ABC Company   57

Lorem ipsum dolor sit amet, consectetuer adipiscing, sed nonummy nibh euismod tin cidunt ut laoreet dolore magna aliquam volutpat. Table 5 shows comparisons of the ergonomic furniture from four major American manufacturers:

Table 3

Comparisons of the Features of Ergonomic Computer Furniture for Four Major American Manufacturers[a]

COMPANY	FEATURES						
	Adj. Hght.	Kybd Tray	Book-shelf	Cup-brd.	Draw-ers	Chair incl.	Diff. Colors
GERALD	X	X	X	X	X		X
PARTON		X		X	X	X	
ACME	X	X			X		
DOVER		X	X		X		X

Source: Ergonomics Magazine, (New York: Ace Publishing, Nov., 1998) p. 24.

[a]These categories include companies that sold more than $40 million dollars in products.

Nam liber tempor cum soluta nobis eleifend id congue nihil imperdiet doming id quod mazim placerat possim assum.

Figure 8. Example of Table and Table Caption Placement.

Chapter 3

Using Lists and Abbreviations

Creating Lists

No doubt some paragraphs in your text will state a series of items or names. The MLA requires these lists be within the sentence that introduces them.

Figures 9 and 10 show how your sentence should look:

```
Five poets are analyzed: Keats, Shelley, Byron, Burns,

and Coleridge.
```

Figure 9. Example of a List in a Sentence Needing a Colon.

or

```
The poets analyzed include Keats, Shelley, Byron, Burns,

and Coleridge.
```

Figure 10. Example of a List in a Sentence.

Notice that in Figure 9, the first part of the sentence can stand alone. Therefore, a colon is placed after the phrase and before the list of poets. In the second sentence, however, the first part of the sentence cannot stand alone. You cannot use a colon with this sentence construction, but must list the names as part of the sentence.

Using Abbreviations[1]

This section shows you how to abbreviate many kinds of terms and titles from classic literary works. In addition, it shows you how to use acronyms and format plurals of abbreviations.

The only rules to remember are:

1. Avoid using abbreviations in your text except within parentheses.

2. If the abbreviation is all capital letters, don't use periods after or space between the letters.

   EXCEPTION: *Personal names, such as "P. J. Wodehouse."*

3. Always use accepted forms of the abbreviations. Don't make up your own.

4. If you think the abbreviation will confuse your readers, play it safe and spell it out.

Abbreviating Performing Arts Terms

Use the abbreviations in Tables 1 in parenthetical material, in tables, and in the list of works cited only.

Table 1. Performing Arts Terms Abbreviations.

TERM	ABBREVIATION
choreographer, choreographed by	chor.
conductor, conducted by	cond.
director, directed by	dir.
distributor, distributed by	dist.
narrator, narrated by	narr.
new series	ns
old series, original series	os.
orchestra, orchestrated by	orch.
opus (work)	op.
performer, performed by	perf.
producer, produced by	prod.
record, recorded by	rec.
release	rel.
scene*	sc
series	ser.
stanza	st.

*Omit when act and scene numbers are listed together.

[1] The tables in this section are adapted from lists in the *MLA Handbook* (Gibaldi 207-27).

Abbreviating Academic Terms

Use the abbreviations in Tables 2-3 in parenthetical material, in tables, and in the list of works cited only. Be sure to include the periods when indicated. If the example does not show periods, however, do not add any.

Table 2. Academic Terms Abbreviations.

MEANING	ABBREVIATION
academy	acad.
Bachelor of Arts	BA
Bachelor of Education	BEd.
Bachelor of Fine Arts	BFA
Bachelor of Laws *(legum baccalaureas)*	LLB
Bachelor of Science	BS
college	coll.
conference	conf.
department	dept.
dissertation	diss.
Doctor of Arts	DA
Doctor of Education	EdD
Doctor of Fine Arts	DFA
Doctor of Law *(juris doctor)*	JD
Doctor of Laws *(legum doctor)*	LLD
Doctor of Medicine *(medicinae doctor)*	MD
Doctor of Philosophy *(philosophiae doctor)*	PhD
education, educational	educ.
faculty	fac.
Master of Arts	MA
Master of Science	MS

Table 3. Academic Books Abbreviations.

TERM	ABBREVIATION
Dictionary of National Biography	DNB
Dissertation Abstracts	DA
Disseration Abstracts International	DAI
Dictionary of American Biography	DAB
Oxford English Dictionary	OED
A New English Dictionary	NED

Abbreviating Units of Time

Use the abbreviations in Tables 4-6 in parenthetical material, in tables, and in the list of works cited only. Be sure to include periods when indicated.

Table 4. Days of the Week Abbreviations.

MEANING	ABBREVIATION	MEANING	ABBREVIATION
Sunday	Sun.	Thursday	Thurs.
Monday	Mon.	Friday	Fri.
Tuesday	Tues.	Saturday	Sat.
Wednesday	Wed.		

Table 5. Months of the Year Abbreviations.

MEANING	ABBREVIATION	MEANING	ABBREVIATION
January	Jan.	September	Sep., Sept.
February	Feb.	October	Oct.
March	Mar.	November	Nov.
April	Apr.	December	Dec.
August	Aug.		

EXCEPTIONS: May, June, July

Table 6. Other Units of Time Abbreviations.

MEANING	ABBREVIATION
Originally from the Latin phrase, *anno Domini*, which means "in the year of the Lord," it now means "after the birth of Christ." Place the AD before numbers: "AD 325"	AD
Before Christ. Place the BC after numbers: "64 BC"	BC
Before the common era	BCE
circa	c. (ca.)
Common era	CE
Originally from the Latin phrase "*ante meridiem*," which means "before mid-day," it now means "before noon."	a.m.
Originally from the Latin phrase "*post meridiem*," which means "after mid-day," it now means "after noon."	p.m.
second	sec.
minute	min.
hour	hr.
week	wk.
month	mo.
year	yr.
century	cent.

Abbreviating Computing/Electronic Media Terms

Use the abbreviations in Table 7 in parenthetical material, in tables, and in the list of works cited only. Be sure to include periods when indicated. If the example does not show periods, however, do not add any.

Table 7. Computing/Electronic Media Terms Abbreviations.

TERM	ABBREVIATION
Because It's Time Network	BITNET
compact disc	CD
compact disc read-only memory	CD-ROM
electronic mail	e-mail
File Transfer Protocol	FTP
long-playing record	LP
record, recorded by	rec.
revolutions per minute	rpm

Abbreviating Language Terms

Use the abbreviations in Table 8 in parenthetical material, in tables, and in the list of works cited only. Be sure to include periods when indicated. If the example does not show periods, however, do not add any.

Table 8. Language Terms Abbreviations.

TERM	ABBREVIATION	TERM	ABBREVIATION
adjective	adj.	paragraph	para.
adverb	adv.	participle	part.
archaic	arch.	plural	pl.
article	art.	possessive	poss.
colloquial	coll.	preposition	prep.
conjunction	conj.	present	pres.
from	fr.	pronoun	pron.
future	fut.	pronunciation	pronunc.
infinitive	inf.	singular	sing.
irregular	irreg.	subject, subjunctive	subj.
language	lang.	substandard	substand.
nonstandard	nonstand.	synonym	syn.
noun	n.	transitive	trans.
object	obj.	variant	var.

Abbreviating Geographic Names

Use the abbreviations in Tables 9-12 in parenthetical material, in tables, and in the list of works cited only. Be sure to include periods when indicated. If the example does not show periods, however, do not add any.

Table 9. Two-letter Postal Code Abbreviations for American State and Territories.

LOCATION	ABBREVIATION	LOCATION	ABBREVIATION
Alabama	AL	Missouri	MO
Alaska	AK	Montana	MT
American Samoa	AS	Nebraska	NE
Arizona	AZ	Nevada	NV
Arkansas	AR	New Hampshire	NH
California	CA	New Jersey	NJ
Canal Zone	CZ	New Mexico	NM
Colorado	CO	New York	NY
Connecticut	CT	North Carolina	NC
Delaware	DE	North Dakota	ND
District of Columbia	DC	Ohio	OH
Florida	FL	Oklahoma	OK
Georgia	GA	Oregon	OR
Guam	GU	Pennsylvania	PA
Hawaii	HI	Puerto Rico	PR
Idaho	ID	Rhode Island	RI
Illinois	IL	South Carolina	SC
Indiana	IN	South Dakota	SD
Iowa	IA	Tennessee	TN
Kansas	KS	Texas	TX
Kentucky	KY	Utah	UT
Louisiana	LA	Vermont	VT
Maine	ME	Virginia	VA
Maryland	MD	Virgin Islands	VI
Massachusetts	MA	Washington	WA
Michigan	MI	West Virginia	WV
Minnesota	MN	Wisconsin	WI
Mississippi	MS	Wyoming	WY

Table 10. Canadian Provinces and Territories Name Abbreviations.

PROVINCE	ABBREVIATION	PROVINCE	ABBREVIATION
Alberta	AB	Northwest Territories	NT
British Columbia	BC	Ontario	ON
Manitoba	MB	Prince Edward Island	PE
New Brunswick	NB	Quebec	PQ
Newfoundland	NF	Saskatchewan	SK
Nova Scotia	NS	Yukon Territory	YT

Table 11. Country Name Abbreviations.

COUNTRY	ABBREVIATION	COUNTRY	ABBREVIATION
Africa	Afr.	Israel	Isr.
Albania	Alb.	Italy	It.
America	Amer.	Japan	Jap.
Argentina	Arg.	Labrador	LB
Armenia	Arm.	Lebanon	Leb.
Austria	Aus.	Mexico	Mex.
Australia	Austral.	Netherlands	Neth.
Belgium	Belg.	Norway	Norw.
Brazil	Braz.	New Zealand	NZ
Bulgaria	Bulg.	Panama	Pan.
Canada	Can.	Poland	Pol.
Canal Zone	CZ	Portugal	Port.
Denmark	Den.	People's Republic of China	PRC
Ecuador	Ecua.	Russia	Russ.
England	Eng.	Scotland	Scot.
Europe	Eur.	Spain	Sp.
France	Fr.	Sweden	Swed.
Germany	Ger.	Switzerland	Switz.
Greece	Gr.	Turkey	Turk.
Great Britain	Gt. Britain	United Kingdom	UK
Guam	GU	United States	US
Hungary	Hung.	United States of America	USA
Ireland	Ire.	Union of Soviet Socialist Republics	USSR

Table 12. Continent Name Abbreviations.

CONTINENT	ABBREVIATION
North America	No. Amer.
Antarctica	Ant.
South America	So. Amer.
America	Amer.

Abbreviating Latin Terms

Use the abbreviations in Tables 13 in parenthetical material, in tables, and in the list of works cited only. Be sure to include periods when indicated.

Table 13. Latin Term Abbreviations.

TERM	ABBREVIATION
for example	e.g.
and others	et al.
and so forth	etc.
that is	i.e.
take notice	NB

Abbreviating Publishing Terms

Use the abbreviations in Tables 14 in parenthetical material, in tables, and in the list of works cited only. Be sure to include periods when indicated.

Table 14. Publishing Term Abbreviations.

TERM	ABBREVIATION
abridgment, abridged	abr.
adapter, adaptation, adapted by	adapt.
appendix	app.
article	art.
attributed to	attrib.
bibliographer, biography, biographical	biog.
book	bk.
bulletin	bull.
chapter	chap.
column	col.
compare	cf.
compiler, compiled by	comp.
contents	cont.
continued	cont. (contd.)
copyright	©
development, developed by	dev.
document	doc.
editor, edited by, edition	ed.
enlarged	enl.
frontispiece	front.
foreward, foreward by	fwd.
illustrator, illustration, illustrated by	illus.
including	inc.
incorporated	inc.
introduction, introduced by	introd.
journal	jour.
line, lines	line, lines
literature, literary	lit.
magazine	mag.
manuscript, manuscripts	ms., mss.
note, notes	n, nn
no date of publication	n.d.
no place of publication	n.p.
no pagination	n. pag.
number	no.
part	pt.
preface, preface by	pref.
page, pages	p., pp.
proceedings	proc.
postscript	PS
Press	P
pseudonym	pseud.
publisher, publication, published by	pub. (publ.)
quoted	qtd.

Table 14. Publishing Terms Abbreviations, Cont'd.

TERM	ABBREVIATION
report, reported by	rept.
review, reviewed by, revision, revised by	rev. (spell out if meaning unclear)
revised edition	rev. ed.
reprint, reprinted by	rpt.
second edition	2nd ed.
section	sec. (sect.)
series	ser.
stanza	st.
supplement	supp.
Technical Report	Tech. Rep.
translator, translation, translated by	trans. (tr.)
typescript, typescripts	ts., tss.
University	U
University Press	UP
version	vers.
volume	vol.
writer, written by	writ.

Abbreviating Government Terms

Use the abbreviations in Tables 15 in parenthetical material, in tables, and in the list of works cited only. Be sure to include periods when indicated.

Table 15. Government and Legal Terms Abbreviations.

TERM	ABBREVIATION
Congress	Cong.
Congressional Record	*Cong. Rec.*
Constitution	Const.
district	dist.
government	govt.
Government Printing Office, Washington	GPO
House Document	H. Doc.
Her (His) Majesty's Stationery Office, London	HMSO
House of Representatives	HR
House of Representatives Report	H. Rept.
House of Representatives Resolution	H. Res.
Library of Congress	LC
legal	leg.
legislator, legislation, legislature, legislative	legis.
Public Law	Pub. L.
Resolution	Res.
Senate	S
Senate Document	S. Doc.
session	sess.
Senate Report	S. Rept.
Senate Resolution	S. Res.
Statutes at Large	Stat.

Abbreviating Miscellaneous Terms

Use the abbreviations in Table 16 in parenthetical material, in tables, and in the list of works cited only. Be sure to include periods when indicated.

Table 16. Miscellaneous Term Abbreviations.

TERM	ABBREVIATION
abbreviation, abbreviated	abbr.
association	assoc.
associate, associated	assoc.
auxiliary	aux.
born	b.
British Museum, London (now British Library)	BM
died	d.
division	div.
education, educational	educ.
especially	esp.
example	ex.
figure	fig.
flourished	fl.
from	fr.
future	fut.
general	gen.
historian, history, historical	hist.
international	intl.
institution	inst.
junior	jr.
library	lib.
literally	lit.
limited	ltd.
miscellaneous	misc.
modern	mod.
national	natl.
number	no.
numbered	numb.
nonstandard	nonstand.
New Style (calendar)	NS
objective	obj.
obsolete	obs.
Old Style (calendar)	OS
original, originally	orig.
philological	philol.
philosophical	philos.
plate	pl.
reigned	r.
registered, regular	reg.
report, reported by	rept.
respectively	resp.
society	soc.
senior	sr.
Saint, Saints	St., Sts. (S, SS)
subjective	subj.
substandard	substand.
thus in the source	sic
usually	usu.
variant	var.
versus	vs. (v. in legal)

Abbreviating Titles From the Bible

Use the abbreviations in Table 17 in parenthetical material, in tables, and in the list of works cited only. To avoid repeating the full title many times in your text, introduce the abbreviation in parentheses after the first mention of the full title in your text ("In <u>Exodus</u> (<u>Exod.</u>), Moses says . . . ."). Remember to underline the title. If you wish to abbreviate a title not found in this table, the MLA allows you to use one from your source or to make up one of your own.

Table 17. Old and New Testaments Title Abbreviations.

NAME	ABBREVIATION	NAME	ABBREVIATION
OLD TESTAMENT			
Baruch	Bar.	Judith	Jth.
Bel and the Dragon	Bel and Dr.	Lamentations	Lam.
Bible	Bib.	Leviticus	Lev.
biblical	bib.	1 Maccabees	1 Macc.
1 Chronicles	1 Chron.	Malachi	Mal.
Daniel	Dan.	Micah	Mic.
Deuteronomy	Deut.	Nahum	Nah.
Ecclesiastes	Eccles.	Nehemiah	Neh.
Ecclesiasticus (also Sirach)	Ecclus. (also Sir.)	Numbers	Num.
		Obadiah	Obad.
1 Esdras	1 Esd.	Prayer of the Manasseh	Pr. Man.
Esther	Esth.	Psalms	Ps.
Esther (Apocrypha)	Esth.(Apocr.)	Proverbs	Prov.
Exodus	Exod.	1 Samuel	1 Sam.
Ezekiel	Ezek.	Song of Solomon (also Canticles)	Song Sol. (also Cant.)
Genesis	Gen.		
Habakkuk	Hab.	Song of the Three Children	Song 3 Childr.
Haggai	Hag.	Susanna	Sus.
Hosea	Hos.	Tobit	Tob.
Isaiah	Isa.	Wisdom of Solomon (also Wisdom)	Wisd. Sol. (also Wisd.)
Jeremiah	Jer.		
Jonah	Jon.	Zechariah	Zech.
Joshua	Josh.	Zephaniah	Zeph.
Judges	Judg.		
NEW TESTAMENT			
Colossians	Col.	1 Peter	1 Pet.
1 Corinthians	1 Cor.	Philemon	Philem.
Ephesians	Eph.	Philippians	Phil.
Galatians	Gal.	Revelation (also Apocalypse)	Rev. (also Apoc.
Gospel of Thomas			
Gospel of the Hebrews		Romans	Rom.
Gospel of Peter		1 Thessalonians	1 Thess.
Hebrews	Heb.	1 Timothy	1 Tim.
James	Jas.	Titus	Tit.
Matthew	Matt.		

Abbreviating Titles From Classic Literary Works

Use the abbreviations in Tables 18-20 in parenthetical material, in tables, and in the list of works cited only. Use periods where indicated. To avoid repeating the full title many times in your text, introduce the abbreviation in parentheses after the first mention of the full title in your text ("In <u>A Midsummer Night's Dream</u> (<u>MND</u>), Puck asks . . . ."). Remember to underline the title. If you wish to abbreviate a title not found in this table, the MLA allows you to use one from your source or to make up one of your own.

Abbreviating Titles From Shakespearean Works

Use the abbreviations in Table 18 when abbreviating titles from Shakespearean works in parenthetical material, in tables, and in the list of works cited.

Table 18. Shakespearean Works Abbreviations.

NAME	ABBREVIATION	NAME	ABBREVIATION
All's Well That Ends Well	AWW	A Midsummer Night's Dream	MND
Antony and Cleopatra	Ant.	Much Ado About Nothing	Ado
As You Like It	AYL	Othello	Oth.
The Comedy of Errors	Err.	Pericles	Per.
Coriolanus	Cor.	The Phoenix and the Turtle	PhT
Cymbeline	Cym.	The Passionate Pilgrim	PP
First Folio ed. (1623)	F1	Quarto ed.	Q
Hamlet	Ham.	The Rape of Lucrece	Luc.
Henry IV, Part 1	1H4	Richard II	R2
Henry IV, Part 2	2H4	Richard III	R3
Henry V	H5	Romeo and Juliet	Rom.
Henry VI, Part 1	1H6	Second Folio ed. (1632)	F2
Henry VI, Part 2	2H6	The Taming of the Shrew	Shr.
Henry VI, Part 3	3H6	Sonnets	Son.
Henry VIII	H8	The Tempest	Tmp.
Julius Caesar	JC	Timon of Athens	Tim.
King John	Jn.	The Two Gentlemen of Verona	TGV
King Lear	Lr.		
A Lover's Complaint	LC	Titus Andronicus	Tit.
Love's Labor Lost	LLL	Troilus and Cressida	Tro.
Macbeth	Mac.	Twelfth Night	TN
Measure for Measure	MM	The Two Noble Kinsmen	TNK
The Merchant of Venice	MV	Venus and Adonis	Ven.
The Merry Wives of Windsor	Wiv.	The Winter's Tale	WT

Abbreviating Titles From Chaucerean Works

Use the abbreviations in Table 19 when abbreviating titles from Chaucerean works in parenthetical material, in tables, and in the list of works cited.

Table 19. Chaucerean Works Abbreviations.

NAME	ABBREVIATION	NAME	ABBREVIATION
The Canterbury Tales	CT	The Nun's Priest's Tale	NPT
The Canon's Yeoman's Tale	CYT	The Pardoner's Tale	PardT
Chaucer's Retraction	Ret	The Parson's Tale	ParsT
The Clerk's Tale	ClT	The Physician's Tale	PhyT
The Cook's Tale	CkT	The Prioress's Tale	PrT
The Franklin's Tale	FranT	The Reeve's Tale	RvT
The Friar's Tale	FrT	The Shipman's Tale	ShT
The General Prologue	GP	The Second Nun's Tale	SNT
The Knight's Tale	KnT	The Squire's Tale	SqT
The Manciple's Tale	ManT	The Summoner's Tale	SumT
The Merchant's Tale	MerT	The Tale of Melibee	Mel
The Miller's Tale	MilT	The Tale of Sir Thopas	Th
The Monk's Tale	MkT	The Wife of Bath's Tale	WBT
The Man of Law's Tale	MLT		

Abbreviating Titles From Other Classic Literary Works

Use the abbreviations in Table 20 when abbreviating titles from other classic literary works in parenthetical material, in tables, and in the list of works cited.

Table 20. Other Classic Literary Works Abbreviations.

NAME	ABBREVIATION	NAME	ABBREVIATION
Aeneid (Vergil)	Aen.	Moby Dick (Melville)	MD
Agamemnon (Asechylus)	Ag.	Medea (Euripedes)	Med.
Antigone (Sophocles)	Ant.	Le misanthrope (Molière)	Mis.
Bacchae (Eripides)	Bac.	Nibelungenlied	Nib.
Beowulf	Beo.	Odyssey (Homer)	Od.
Candide (Voltaire)	Can.	Oedipus Rex (Sophocles) also called (Oedipus	OR
Decameron (Boccaccio)	Dec.	Tyrannus)	OT
Don Juan (Byron)	DJ	Oresteia (Aeschylus)	Or.
Don Quixote (Cervantes)	DQ	Paradise Lost (Milton)	PL
Epic of Gilgamesh	Gil.	Paradiso (Dante)	Par.
Eumenides (Aeschylus)	Eum.	The Prelude (Wordsworth)	Prel.
The Faerie Queen (Spenser)	FQ	Purgatorio (Dante)	Purg.
Gulliver's Travels (Swift)	GT	Republic (Plato)	Rep.
Heptaméron (de Navarre)	Hept.	Samson Agonistes (Milton)	SA
Hippolytus (Euripides)	Hip.	Sir Gawain and the Green Knight	SGGK
Iliad (Homer)	Il.		
Inferno (Dante)	Inf.	Symposium (Plato)	Sym.
Lyrical Ballads (Wordsworth)	LB		
Lysistrata (Aristophanes)	Lys.	Tartuffe (Molière)	Tar.

Using an Acronym

Acronyms are words formed from the initials of long terms, such as "TQM" for "Total Quality Management." Plan to use acronyms only for long, well-known terms. Spell out the phrase completely the first time you use it. Put the acronym in parentheses, as shown in Figure 11. The next time you refer to this term, use the acronym by itself.

```
Total Quality Management (TQM) is a company-wide

approach dedicated to improving the company's

processes, products, and services.
```

Figure 11. Example of the First Use of an Acronym.

Formatting Plurals

To create a plural of an acronym or abbreviation, just add "s." Do not include an apostrophe. Table 21 shows some examples.

Table 21. Examples Plurals of Abbreviations.

EXPLANATION	ABBREVIATION
Intelligence quotients	IQs
editors	eds.
volumes	vols.

EXCEPTION: "pp." (plural for "pages")

Chapter 4

Documenting Your Sources in the Text

During the course of writing your report, you will research many books, magazine articles, and other publications, and perhaps conduct interviews with experts in your topic. Any time you use that material in your report, you must credit the source; otherwise, you are committing plagiarism (i.e., using another's work as though it were your own).

The MLA uses a specific method for documenting sources. You must first cite the source in the text, where the borrowed material appears. This not only shows the readers that the information is from a specific source, but gives them data that will point them to the full reference in the Works Cited list, which follows the last page of your report. (See Chapter 5 for complete instructions on creating the list of works cited.)

This chapter explains how to create the in-text citations. There are three types:

- *Paraphrased material*

  Perhaps you have read a book or article, or even several books or articles, and you are discussing the idea or ideas contained therein. You have not used any of the author's wording, but have explained the concepts in your own words.

- *Quotes of up to four lines*

  An author's words say what you want to say, so you use those exact words. Your quotation takes no more than four double-spaced lines in your report.

- *Quotes of five lines or more*

    Here again, you use the author's words, but this time, your quotation takes up five double-spaced lines or more in your report.

Because the ideas in paraphrased material and quotations are not your own, you must credit their sources. The MLA style credits sources by using what are called "parenthetical citations."

NOTE: *The citations contained in this section are not necessarily real; some have been created for example purposes.*

Citing Paraphrased Material

You can paraphrase a specific passage from a work in two different ways:

- You do not name the author in your sentence

- You name the author in your sentence

Paraphrasing Material Without Naming the Author in the Sentence

If you are paraphrasing material from a specific page of a book or magazine article, and you do not wish to state the author's name in the sentence, cite the source of the information as shown in Figure 12. Type the opening parenthesis, the author's name, a space, the page number, and the closing parenthesis, followed by a period.

NOTE: *Cite a range of pages as shown in Figure 13. When the numbers are more than two digits, only the first number in the range contains the total number of digit(s).*

Compare these citations to those in which the author's name appears in the text of the sentence (see page 36).

As society continues to undergo rapid technological

change, people will be unable to adapt (Toffler 24).

Figure 12. Example In-Text Citation of Paraphrased Material Without Using the Author's Name in the Sentence.

By the year 2000, 95% of all offices will use PCs

(Smith 124-30).

Figure 13. Example In-Text Citation of Paraphrased Material Without Using the Author's Name in the Sentence and Covering a Range of Pages.

Paraphrasing Material and Naming the Author in the Sentence

If you are paraphrasing material from a specific page of a book or magazine article, and you use the author's name in your sentence, cite the source of the information as shown in Figure 14. At the end of the sentence, type an opening parenthesis, then the page number, then a closing parenthesis, then a period. (Do not include the author's name again in the parenthetical citation.)

NOTE: Cite a range of pages as shown in Figure 15. When the numbers are more than two digits, only the first number in the range contains the total number of digit(s).

Compare these citations to those in which the author's name does not appear in the text of the sentence (see page 34).

```
Toffler believes that as society continues to undergo

rapid technological change, people will be unable to

adapt (24).
```

Figure 14. Example In-Text Citation of Paraphrased Material Using the Author's Name in the Sentence.

```
According to Jones, the two authors oppose one another's

viewpoints (146-58).
```

Figure 15. Example In-Text Citation of Paraphrased Material Using the Author's Name in the Sentence and Showing a Range of Page Numbers.

Citing Quotes

Citing Quotes From Prose

When you use direct quotations from prose works, how you cite them depends on their length:

- Prose that takes up to four lines of manuscript text

- Prose that takes five lines or more of manuscript text

Citing Prose That Takes Up to Four Lines of Manuscript Text

Cite direct quotes from prose that are up to four lines of manuscript text as part of the regular double-spaced text, as shown in Figure 16. Introduce the quotation with words of your own. Whether the material is a complete sentence or a word or phrase, place it in quotation marks to indicate that it is indeed a quote, rather than a paraphrase.

Place the quotation anywhere in your sentence. You may divide the quotation with your words, if you wish. Note that the page number of the original source goes in parentheses between the ending quotation mark and the comma or period.

```
In his book Innovation and Entrepreneurship, Peter

Drucker defines innovation as "the specific tool

of entrepreneurs, the means by which they exploit

change as an opportunity for a different business

or a different service" (20).
```

or

```
Toffler believes that as society continues to undergo

rapid technological change, "people will suffer from

future shock" (24), the inability to adapt.
```

Figure 16. Correct Way to Quote Up to Four Lines of Prose Manuscript Text.

Citing Prose That Takes Five Lines or More of Manuscript Text

When a quote takes five lines or more of manuscript text, follow these steps:

1. Introduce the quote with a sentence of your own and end it with a colon.

2. Begin a new line. Indent it one inch (ten spaces if using a typewriter) from the left margin, and double-space it, as shown in Figure 17. Do not use quotation marks.

3. Place the page number from which you took this quote in parentheses *after* the period.

4a. If you are quoting two or more paragraphs from a work and the first line of the first paragraph begins a paragraph in the original work, indent it an additional .25 inch (three spaces if using a typewriter) as shown in Figure 18.

b. If the first line of the first paragraph does not begin a paragraph in the original work, however, just indent the first lines of the succeeding paragraphs (see Figure 19).

Try to limit your quotations. Find a way to paraphrase the material rather than lifting too much from the original work. Your report should reflect *your* ideas, not someone else's.

```
Drucker states that:

     Innovation is the specific tool of entrepreneurs,

     the means by which they exploit change as an

     opportunity for a different business or a

     different service. Entrepreneurs need to search

     purposefully for the sources of innovation, the

     changes and their symptoms that indicate

     opportunities for successful innovation. (20)
```

Figure 17. Correct Way to Quote Five Lines or More of Manuscript Text.

```
Drucker has a specific definition:

        Innovation is the specific tool of entrepre-

    neurs, the means by which they exploit

    change as an opportunity for a different

    business or a different service.

        Entrepreneurs need to search purposefully

    for the sources of innovation, the changes

    and their symptoms that indicate oppor-

    tunities for successful innovation. (20)
```

Figure 18. Correct Way to Quote Two or More Paragraphs of Manuscript Text When Both Paragraphs are Complete Paragraphs in the Original Work.

```
Drucker has a specific definition of innovation:

        the specific tool of entrepreneurs, the

    means by which they exploit change as an

    opportunity for a different business or a

    different service.

        Entrepreneurs need to search purposefully

    for the sources of innovation, the changes

    and their symptoms that indicate oppor-

    tunities for successful innovation. (20)
```

Figure 19. Correct Way to Quote Two or More Paragraphs of Manuscript Text When the First Line of the First Paragraph Does Not Begin a New Paragraph in the Original Work.

Citing Quotes From Plays

Books and magazine articles aren't the only sources for quotable material. You may wish to quote text from a play or movie script. In this case, you will be quoting dialogue from two or more characters. Your quotation will closely resemble the way the dialogue appears in the play or script.

1. Referring to Figure 20, introduce the dialogue with a sentence of your own and end it with a colon.

2. Begin a new line and indent it one inch from the left margin (ten spaces if using a typewriter).

3. Type the character's name in capital letters, then type a colon and a space.

4. Type the dialogue. If the dialogue continues onto a second line, indent that line and all subsequent lines of that piece of dialogue .25 of an inch (three spaces if using a typewriter).

5. When you start a new character's dialogue, indent the first line of the dialogue one inch (ten spaces if using a typewriter) from the character's name.

6. Repeat Steps 2 through 5 for each character's dialogue.

7. At the end of the last line of dialogue, you must cite the source. Include the act number, scene number, and page number(s):

   a. Type an opening parenthesis.

   b. Type the act number, then a period.

   c. Type the scene number, then a period.

   NOTE: DO NOT skip a space between the period and the next number.

   d. Type the page number(s).

   NOTE: When the numbers are more than two digits, only the first number in the range contains the total number of digit(s).

   e. Type a closing parenthesis.

Lady MacBeth sleepwalks and doesn't realize she is
overheard confessing to her crime:

        LADY MACBETH: Out, damned spot! out, I

            Say!— One: two: why, then 'tis time to do

            't.—Hell is murky!—Fie, my lord, fie! A

            soldier, and afeard? What need we fear

            who knows it, when none can call our

            power to account?—Yet who would have

            thought the old man to have had so much

            blood in him.

        DOCTOR: Do you mark that?

        LADY MACBETH: The thane of Fife had a wife:

            where is she now?—What, will these hands

            ne'er be clean?—No more o'that, my lord,

            no more o' that: you mar all with this

            starting.

        DOCTOR: Go to, go to; you have

            known what you should not.

        GENTLEWOMAN: She has spoke what she

            should no, I am sure of that: heaven knows

            what she had known. (5.1.1002-03)

*Figure 20. Correct Way to Quote Dialogue of Two or More Characters From
a Play or Script.*

Citing Quotes From Poetry

When you use direct quotations from poetry works, the way you cite them depends on their length:

- Poetry of up to three lines

- Poetry of four lines or more

Quoting Up to Three Lines of Poetry

To quote up to three lines of poetry, follow these steps.

1. Introduce the quotation with words of your own. If your introductory phrase is a complete sentence, end it with a colon (see the first example in Figure 21); if it is not a complete sentence, end it with a comma (see the second example in Figure 21).

2. Type an opening quotation mark, the verse, then a closing quotation mark and a space.

3. Type an opening parenthesis, the line number(s), a closing parenthesis, followed by a period and a space.

4. If the verse is two or three lines, separate them using a slash with a space on either side as shown in Figure 22.

Johnson discusses the poem with sadness: "For the innocence of the children is forever lost" (12).

Johnson says sadly, "For the innocence of the children is forever lost" (1).

Figure 21. Example Quotations From Poetry That are Introduced by a Complete and Partial Sentences.

In the poem, Byard discusses her feelings about having to choose sides in the conflict: "The choice was not mine / It was never mine" (6-7).

Figure 22. Example Quotation From Poetry That is Two or Three Lines and Separated by a Slash Between Lines.

Quoting Four Lines or More of Poetry

When quoting poems of four lines or more, follow these steps:

1. Introduce the quotation with words of your own and end the sentence with a colon (see Figure 23).

2. Start the quotation itself on a new line and double-space it.

3. Indent the quotation one inch (ten spaces if using a typewriter) from the left margin.

   EXCEPTION: *If the line of the poem will not fit on one line of your manuscript text, you may reduce the size of the margin.*

   NOTE: Do not include any quotation marks unless they are already in the poem.

4. Just as with prose, place the line number(s) in parentheses after the last line of text as shown in Figures 23 and 24. If the last line of the poem you are quoting ends in a period, place the citation after the period.

5a. If a line of a poem will not fit on one line of your manuscript text even with a reduced margin, continue it to a new line that is indented .25 of an inch (three spaces if using a typewriter) as shown in Figure 25.

   b. If the reference will not fit on the line, go to the next line and place the reference flush with the right margin as shown in Figure 25.

Anne Ewing's "Eulogy" is a lament for a dear friend:

Don't leave us now—

there's more,

one more story

one last smile…

just one more dance.

No, don't leave us now

—it's as if

we've just begun. (1-8)

Figure 23. Example Quote of Four Lines or More of Poetry.

Although the author of "Sir Gawain and the Green Knight" is
unknown, scholars consider his work reminiscent of Chaucer's, who
was certainly his contemporary:

When the siege and assault ceased at Troy, and the City

Was broken, and burned all to brands and to ashes,

The warrior who wove there the web of his treachery

Tried was for treason, the truest on earth. (1-4)

Figure 24. Example Lines of a Poem That Fit When the Margin is Reduced.

The author of "Sir Gawain and the Green Knight" discusses
King Arthur and the Knights of the Round Table:

Yet of all kings who came there was Arthur most

comely;

My intention is, therefore, to tell an adventure

Strange and surprising, as some men consider,

A strange thing among all the marvels of Arthur.

(25-28)

*Figure 25. Example of a Line Continued to a Second Line and Placement of
a Parenthetical Reference That Does Not Fit on the Same Line
as the Last Line of the Poem.*

Quoting Four Lines or More of Poetry, Cont'd.

6. If your quotation begins in the middle of a line, position the partial line where it is in the original work, as shown in Figure 26. Do not start it at the left margin.

8. If the poem itself is arranged in an unusual order, reproduce as closely as possible to the original (see Figure 27).

```
Shelley thought of the west wind as a spirit:

                                  O thou,

        Who chariotest to their dark wintry bed

        The winged seeds, where they lie cold and low,

        Each like a corpse within its grave, until

        Thine azure sister of the Spring shall blow . . . .

                                            (5-9)
```

Figure 26. Example Quotation of a Partial Line Whose Location in the Quotation is the Same as in the Original Poem.

```
In "Discipline," George Herbert disclaims all independence,

describing himself as an actor who speaks only "by the

book":

            Throw away thy rod,

          Throw away thy wrath:

                    O my God,

          Take the gentle path.

            For my heart's desire

          Unto thine is bent:

                    I aspire

          To a full consent.

            Not a word or look

          I affect to own,

                    but by book,

          And thy book alone.
```

Figure 27. Example Quotation of a Poem That Has Unusual Spacing.

Omitting Material From Your Quotation

You can omit words, phrases, sentences, or paragraphs from your quotation, but be sure it still reads grammatically correctly and that you have not changed the meaning of the original work.

Omitting Material From a Prose Quotation

To indicate that material has been omitted within a sentence or paragraph, use an *ellipsis*. An ellipsis is three periods with a space before each and after the last as shown in Figure 28. You can place the ellipsis in the middle of your quotation as shown in Figure 28 or at the end of a sentence or sentences as shown in Figure 29.

NOTE: *If the ellipsis is at the end of your quotation, do not add a space before the first period. Add a fourth period to end the sentence. Notice that when your quotation does not have a parenthetical page reference, the final period goes just before the ending quotation mark (see the first example in Figure 29).*

In Godel, Escher, Bach, Douglas R. Hofstadter
writes of King Frederick the Great of Prussia,
"Frederick was an admirer not only of pianos,
but also of . . . Bach."

or

In Godel, Escher, Bach, Douglas R. Hofstadter
writes of King Frederick the Great of Prussia,
"Frederick was an admirer not only of pianos,
but also of . . . Bach" (3).

Figure 28. Examples of Material Omitted From the Middle of a Sentence in a Prose Quotation.

Hofstadter adds, "In those days, being an organist
not only meant being able to play, but also to
extemporize. . . . The King let it be known how
pleased he would be to have the elder Bach come
and pay him a visit. . . ."

or

Hofstadter adds, "In those days, being an organist
not only meant being able to play, but also to
extemporize . . ." (3).

Figure 29. Examples of Material Omitted From the End of a Prose Quotation.

Omitting Material From a Poetry Quotation

To indicate that material has been omitted from within a poetry quotation, use an *ellipsis*. An ellipsis is three periods with a space before each and after the last one as shown in Figure 30. You can place the ellipsis in the middle of your quotation as shown in Figure 30 or at the end of your quotation as shown in Figure 31. Remember that your sentences must still read grammatically correctly.

NOTE: *If the ellipsis is at the end of your quotation, do not add a space before the first period. Add a fourth period to end the sentence. And notice that when your quotation does not have a parenthetical page reference, the final period goes just before the ending quotation mark (see the first example in Figure 31).*

```
Tennyson's words "Sweet and low, sweet and

low . . . While my little one, while my pretty one,

sleeps" became well-known in a children's lullaby.
```

Figure 30. Example of Material Omitted From Within a Poetry Quotation.

```
Tennyson's words became well-known in a children's

lullaby: "Sweet and low, sweet and low. Wind of

the Western Sea. . . ."
```

or

```
Tennyson's words became well-known in a children's

lullaby: "Sweet and low, sweet and low. Wind of

the Western Sea . . ." (1-2).
```

Figure 31. Examples of Material Omitted From the End of a Poetry Quotation.

If your quotation is set off from the text because it is four lines or more, use a line of ellipses to indicate a missing line or lines as shown in Figure 32. Make the line of ellipses as long as a line of the quoted part of the poem. The missing line(s) can be in the middle of the quotation as shown in Figure 32 or at the end of the quotation as shown in Figure 33. Include only the line numbers actually quoted, as shown in Figure 32.

```
Gilbert and Sullivan parodied Tennyson's "Sweet

and Low," from "Songs From The Princess," in their

play, "Princess Ida":

          Sweet and low, sweet and low.

          Wind of the western sea,

          Low, low breathe and blow,

          Wind of the western sea!

          . . . . . . . . . . . . .

          While my little one, while my pretty one,

          sleeps. (1-4, 8)
```

Figure 32. Example Quotation of a Poem That Uses an Ellipsis to Represent Lines Missing in the Middle.

```
Gilbert and Sullivan parodied Tennyson's "Sweet

and Low," from "Songs From The Princess," in their

play, "Princess Ida," because it reflected the role

of modern women in society:

          Sweet and low, sweet and low.

          Wind of the western sea,

          Low, low breathe and blow,

          Wind of the western sea. . . . (1-4)
```

Figure 33. Example Quotation of a Poem Omitting Material at the End.

Citing a Publication With Two or Three Authors

If two or three people have written the book or article, cite it as shown in Figure 34. List the authors' last names only. Use the word "and" between the two authors' names or between the second and third author's name whether they appear in the text or in the parenthetical citation.

Smith and Jones state that "by the year 2000, 95% of offices will use PCs" (54).

or

"By the year 2000, 95% of offices will use PCs" (Smith and Jones 54).

or

Others feel that automation will dominate by the turn of the century (Smith and Jones 54-56).

Thompson, Ford, and Rodriguez state that "the world is currently in a complete state of moral decay" (182).

or

"The world is currently in a complete state of moral decay" (Thompson, Ford, and Rodriguez 182).

or

Others feel that moral decay has permeated societies throughout the world (Thompson, Ford, and Rodriguez 182).

Figure 34. Example Citations of a Publication With Two or Three Authors.

Citing a Publication With Four or More Authors

If the work has four or more authors, you can cite it in two ways:

- By listing all the authors' names

- By listing the first author's last name followed by "et al.," which means "and everyone."

Figure 35 shows examples.

```
The author chose the South for the novel's setting

because he wanted to deal with the issue of racism

(Everett, Sanders, Ford, and Green 256).
```

or

```
The author chose the South for the novel's setting

because he wanted to deal with the issue of racism

(Everett et al. 256).
```

Figure 35. Example Citations With Four or More Authors.

Citing Multiple Authors With the Same Name

You will no doubt encounter a situation in which you have source documents by different authors with the same last name. The MLA has a solution to this problem so that your readers can easily determine which citation belongs to which full reference in the Works Cited list.

This shouldn't be a problem In the text, because you can use the author's first and last name in the text itself as shown in the first example in Figure 36. In your parenthetical citation, however, include the first initial with the author's name as shown in the second example in Figure 36.

```
Michael Everett chose the South for the novel's

setting because he wanted to deal with the issue of

racism (256).
```

or

```
The author chose the South for the novel's setting

because he wanted to deal with the issue of racism

(M. Everett 256).
```

Figure 36. Example Citations for an Author With the Same Last Name as Another Author Cited.

Citing an Entire Work

With some material, you may just state the concept; for example, perhaps you want to explain Alvin Toffler's concept of our technological future without paraphrasing or directly quoting material from his book. Instead, you cite the entire book itself. The preferable way to credit this information source is to use the author's name in the sentence, rather than in the parenthetical citation, as shown in Figure 37.

If you use the title of the work in the sentence, use the author's last name only (see Figure 37). If you do not use the title of the work in the sentence, however, use the author's full name, as shown in Figure 38. Then use the last name by itself after that.

```
In his book Future Shock, Toffler discusses his belief

that as society continues to undergo rapid techno-

logical change, people will be unable to adapt.
```

Figure 37. Example Citation of an Entire Work Using the Work's Title in the Sentence.

or

```
Alvin Toffler discusses his belief that as society

continues to undergo rapid technological change, people

will be unable to adapt.
```

Figure 38. Example Citation of an Entire Work Without using the Work's Title in the Sentence.

Citing Multiple Works

Cite several works that all have the same common thread, philosophy, concepts, or conclusions as shown in Figure 39. Use a semicolon between each of the citations.

```
Several scholars (Chan and Jefferson 56; Gomez 42-46;

Thompson, Jones, and Sanders 258-274) disagree with this

viewpoint.
```

Figure 39. Example Citation of Multiple Works.

Citing Part of a Work

For information on citing part of a work, see *Citing Paraphrased Material*, pages 34-36, and *Citing Quotes*, pages 37-47.

Citing Titles

Titles are underlined or placed within quotation marks depending on their type. Cite the title of a work exactly as it is on the *title page* of the work. Type it using initial caps and lower-case letters on all words except for articles, prepositions, conjunctions, and the "to" in an infinitive (unless the first word is one of these), as shown in Figure 40. If the title includes a subtitle, type a colon and a space between the title and the subtitle.

```
The Three-Cornered Hat

The Personal Efficiency Program: How to Get Organized

to Do More Work in Less Time

"An Analysis of Three Victorian Authors"
```

Figure 40. Example Citations of Titles.

Titles Requiring Underlining

Titles of the works shown in Table 22 should be underlined.

Table 22. *Titles Requiring Underlining.*

TYPE OF MATERIAL	TYPE OF MATERIAL
books	instrumentals
pamphlets	paintings
newspapers	sculptures
magazines	ships
plays	aircraft
ballets	audiocassettes
operas	compact discs
films	record albums
TV shows	

EXAMPLE: The Grapes of Wrath

Titles Requiring Quotation Marks

Cite titles of the works shown in Table 23 in quotation marks.

Table 23. *Titles Requiring Quotation Marks.*

TYPE OF MATERIAL	EXAMPLE
newspaper articles	poems
magazine articles	book chapters
encyclopedia articles	episodes of TV shows
essays	songs
short stories	lectures

EXAMPLE: "Flowers for Algernon"

Citing a Title Within a Title

Sometimes, an article title contains the title of another work; for example, "An Analysis of Who's Afraid of Virginia Wolff?"

Titles within titles are cited in different ways depending on what category the original material falls into:

- Titles normally underlined

- Titles nomally in quotation marks

Citing a Title Normally Underlined

A title normally underlined in a report done in MLA style may appear within a title enclosed in quotation marks. For instance, the title may be for an article about a book, ship, movie, or other material shown in Table 22. Underline the part of the title normally underlined:

EXAMPLE: "Racism in <u>Huckleberry Finn</u>"

A title normally underlined in a report done in MLA style may appear within another underlined title. In this case, do not underline the title that appears within the title. For example, let's say you find a book that discusses Twain's *Huckleberry Finn* and its title is *The Missouri of Huckleberry Finn.* In your report, cite this title as follows:

EXAMPLE: <u>The Missouri of</u> Huckleberry Finn

Citing a Title Normally in Quotation Marks

Appearing Within a Title Enclosed in Quotation Marks

A title normally in quotation marks may appear within a title enclosed in quotation marks. For instance, the title may be for an article about an article, short story, TV episode, song, or other material shown in Table 23. Place single quotation marks around the part of the title normally in quotation marks:

EXAMPLE: "An Analysis of Bioethics in 'Flowers for Algernon'"

Appearing Within an Underlined Title

A title normally in quotation marks may appear within an underlined title. For instance, the title may be for a book about a movie, short · story, TV episode, song, or other material shown in Table 23. Place double quotation marks around the part of the title normally in quotation marks:

EXAMPLE: <u>The Making of "Titanic"</u>

Citing a Quotation Within a Title

If a quotation appears within a title already enclosed in quotation marks, place it in single quotation marks:

EXAMPLE: "Bush Contradicts His 'Read My Lips' Promise"

Citing a Work Listed by Title

Sometimes a source has no author at all or is the result of the efforts of many different authors, such as a magazine, television show, newspaper, book, or other document for which no author is listed. Refer to the work by its title, which remains constant. You can cite this source in two ways:

- By including the title in the sentence

- By including a shortened version of the title in the parenthetical citation

If you include a shortened version of the title in the parenthetical citation, be sure to use its first word or first few words so your readers can correctly look up the work in Works Cited list. Figures 41 and 42 show examples of these citations.

<u>Dr. Quinn, Medicine Woman</u> showed the challenges of practicing medicine in the Old West and how Native American cures could help in the treatment of disease.

<u>Newsweek</u> exposed corruption in the government in an article entitled "Corruption at the Top."

Figure 41. Example Citations of a Work Listed by Title and Including the Title in the Sentence.

Native Americans had many treatments for diseases that Western medicine had yet to discover (<u>Dr. Quinn</u>).

<u>Newsweek</u> exposed the city government officials who were accepting bribes ("Corruption").

The officials who were accepting bribes claimed they were "under financial stress" ("Corruption").

Figure 42. Example Citations of a Work Listed by Title and Placing a Shortened Version of the Title in the Parenthetical Citation.

Citing an Author or Authors with More Than One Publication

What if you cite more than one publication by the same author? Since the reader must be able to determine which work in the Works Cited list matches that particular citation, either state the title of the work in the sentence or add a shortened version of it in the parenthetical citation. Let's say John Jones wrote three books. Cite each in one of the citation styles shown in Figure 43.

In the <u>New Age of Reason</u>, Jones claims that philosophical thought will undergo a radical change in the new century (23-27).

or

John Jones claims that philosophical thought will undergo a radical change in the new century (<u>Reason</u> 23-27).

or

Philosophical thought will undergo a radical change in the new century (Jones, <u>Reason</u> 23-27).

Figure 43. Example Citations of an Author or Authors With More Than One Publication.

Citing a Work by a Corporate Author

A corporate author can be a company, a governmental or non-governmental agency, a commission, or some other entity that is not an individual. You can cite this source in two ways:

- By including the company's/agency's name in the sentence

- By including the company's/agency's name in the parenthetical citation

Place the company's/agency's name in the sentence, as shown in Figure 44. A long name can take up too much space in the parenthetical citation. Compare Figure 44 to Figure 45.

```
The Interagency Arctic Research Policy Committee

explains that the Arctic Research and Policy Act of

1984 outlines the needs and plans for future research

in the Arctic (1-2).
```

Figure 44. Example Citation of a Work by a Corporate Author Using the Author's Name in the Sentence.

```
The Arctic Research and Policy Act of 1984 outlines

the needs and plans for future research in the Arctic

(Interagency Arctic Research Policy Committee 1-2).
```

Figure 45. Example Citation of a Work by a Corporate Author Using the Author's Name in the Parenthetical Citation.

Citing Classic Literary Works

Classic works, such as famous books, plays, or poems, have been published in many different editions by many different publishers. Your readers may already have a copy of the work; therefore, the MLA suggests you provide more information than just the page number in your parenthetical citation so readers can easily refer to the quotation or paraphrased material. The additional information differs according to the type of work.

Citing a Classic Prose Work

The additional information in a parenthetical citation of a classic prose work can include the book, chapter, part, section, scene number, etc. The information then is easily accessible in any version of the work.

To cite a classic prose work, follow these steps:

1. Type an opening parenthesis.

2a. If you used the author's name in the sentence, refer to Figure 46 and go to Step 3.

  b. If you have not used the author's name in the sentence, refer to Figure 47, then type the author's last name followed by a space.

3. Type the page number.

4. Type a semicolon and a space.

5. Type the next division in abbreviated form with its number (see Table 14 on pages 26-27 for the correct form of the abbreviations).

> REMEMBER: 1. *Use lowercase letters only.*
> 2. *Use arabic numerals numerals for volume, part, book, section, chapter, and page numbers, even if your source shows roman numerals.*

> EXCEPTION: *Your teacher or instructor requires you to use roman numerals for acts and scenes in plays.*

6. Repeat Steps 4 and 5 for any other elements.

7. Type the closing parenthesis and a period.

In Tolkien's <u>The Fellowship of the Rings</u>, Frodo was
one of the few mortals who had seen Arwen, Elrond's
daughter, and he had never seen anyone so lovely (239;
bk. 2; ch. 1).

*Figure 46. Example Classic Prose Work Citation Using the Author's
Name in the Sentence and Including Additional Information in
the Parenthetical Citation for Easier Reference.*

When Huckleberry Finn first encounters Jim after
running away from home, he is surprised to discover
that Jim thinks he is a ghost (Twain 777; ch. 8).

*Figure 47. Example Classic Prose Work Citation Using the Author's Name
in the Parenthetical Citation and Additional Information for
Easier Reference.*

Citing a Classic Poem or Play

The additional information in a parenthetical citation of a classic poem or play can include the act, scene, canto, book, or part number and the line number. Then the information is easily accessible in any version of the work (see Figure 48).

To cite a classic poem or play, follow these steps:

1. Type an opening parenthesis.

2a. If you used the title of the work in the sentence, refer to Figure 49, then go to Step 3.

 b. If you have not used the title of the work in the sentence, refer to Figure 50, and type the shortened version of the title, followed by a space.

3. Type the act (or scene, canto, book, or part) number, followed by a period.

4. Type the next division in abbreviated form with its number (see Table 14 on pages 26-27 for the correct form of the abbreviations).

NOTE: Do not include page numbers.

NOTE: If you are citing only line numbers, use the word "line" or "lines" in the first citation, then just the numbers alone in any further citations from that work (see Figure 48).

REMEMBER: Use arabic numerals numerals for volume, part, book, section, chapter, and page numbers even if your source shows roman numerals.

EXCEPTIONS: 1. Pages of a preface.
2. Your teacher or instructor requires you to use roman numerals for acts and scenes in plays.

5. Repeat Steps 3 and 4 for any other elements.

6. Type the closing parenthesis and a period.

Some literary works are abbreviated, such as *Troilus* for *Troilus and Criseyde* (see Figure 50), "Nightingale" for Keats's "Ode to a Nightingale," etc.

In <u>MacBeth</u>, Lady MacBeth sleepwalks and doesn't realize she is overheard confessing to murder: "What
need we fear who knows it, when none can call our
power to account?——Yet who would have thought the old
man to have had so much blood in him" (5.1.42-45).

or

Lady MacBeth sleepwalks and doesn't realize she is
overheard confessing to her crime: "What need we fear
who knows it, when none can call our power to account?
——Yet who would have thought the old man to have had
so much blood in him"   (MacBeth 5.1.22-90).

Figure 48. Example Classic Play Citation Using Additional Information
for Easier Reference.

In the prologue to <u>The Canterbury Tales</u>, Chaucer
points out that it is early in the year because the
sun has run only halfway though its course in Aries,
the Ram: ". . . and the yonge sonne / hath in the
Ram his halve cours yronne . . ." (7-8).

Figure 49. Example Classic Work Citation Using Line Numbers Only.

Most of the best ballads have a tragic accident as
their subject: "Since my love died for me today, /
I'll die for him tomorrow" ("Barbara" 35-36).

Figure 50. Example Classic Work Citation Using An Abbreviated
Form of the Title.

Citing Volume and Page Numbers of a Multivolume Work

Some works are so large they comprise several volumes, such as encyclopedias, anthologies of literature, history books, etc. How you cite these sources depends on whether you:

- Cite an entire volume

- Cite a specific passage in a volume of the work

Citing an Entire Volume

You can cite an entire volume in two ways:

- Place the citation the text of your sentence

- Place the citation in parentheses

Placing the Citation in the Text of the Sentence

If you place the citation in the text of your sentence, you must spell out the word "volume" and use an arabic numeral for the volume number, as shown in Figure 51.

NOTE: Do NOT capitalize the "v" in "volume" nor abbreviate the word.

```
In volume 4, Danielson deals with the social issues

facing the South during Reconstruction.
```

Figure 51. Example of One Volume of a Multivolume Work Cited in the Text of the Sentence.

Placing the Citation in Parentheses

1. Referring to Figure 52, type an opening parenthesis.

2. Type the author's name, followed by a comma and a space.

3. Type the abbreviation "vol." for "volume," followed by a space. Use a lower-case "v."

4. Type the volume number itself. Do not include page numbers.

5. Type a closing parenthesis and then a period.

```
The South faced many social issues during Reconstruc-

tion (Danielson, vol. 4).
```

Figure 52. Example of an Entire Volume of a Multivolume Work Cited in Parentheses.

Citing a Specific Passage

When you cite a specific passage in a volume in a multivolume work, follow these steps:

1. Type an opening parenthesis.

2a. If you used the author's name in the sentence, go to Step 3 and refer to the first example in Figure 53.

  b. If you have not used the author's name in the sentence, type the name, followed by a space, as shown in the second example in Figure 53.

3. Type the volume number. Do not type the word "volume" nor its abbreviation.

4. Type a colon and then a space.

5. Type the page number(s). Do not type the word "page" nor its abbreviation.

> *NOTE: When the numbers are more than two digits, only the first number in the range contains the total number of digits.*

6. Type a closing parenthesis and then a period.

```
Danielson discusses the problems the carpetbaggers

caused when they arrived in the South (4: 113-15).
```

```
The carpetbaggers exploited people when they arrived

in the South (Danielson 4: 113-15).
```

Figure 53. Example Citations of a Specific Passage of a Multivolume Work.

Citing Indirect (Secondary) Sources

Sometimes a quotation you use will come from an indirect, or secondary, source; that is, Author 1 will cite Author 2, and you want to use Author 2's words. If possible, look up the original source yourself and cite that. If citing the secondary source is necessary, and the material you are paraphrasing or quoting is a quotation itself, add the phrase "qtd. in" (for "quoted in") in your parenthetical citation as shown in Figure 54. If you think your readers need more information about where this source came from, document the original source in a content note (see *Creating Content Notes* on page 82).

Joseph Garretson, claimed that the leader of the
group, Terence Brown, said he would "take back the
city house by house" (qtd. in Lazinsky 113).

The southern senators told the newspapers exactly how
they felt about carpetbaggers coming to the south
(qtd. in Danielson 2: 148).

Figure 54. Example Citations of an Indirect (Secondary) Source.

Citing Legal Material

Your citations may include legal material. Like many other style manuals, the MLA uses *The Bluebook: A Uniform System of Citation*, published by the Harvard Law Review Association, as its guideline for creating legal citations.

Legal material falls into eight categories:

- Court cases

- Statutes

- Testimony at hearings

- Full hearings

- Unenacted federal bills and resolutions

- Enacted bills and resolutions

- Federal reports and documents

- Adminstrative and executive materials

As with books and magazine articles, you must cite legal material in the text; however, it is documented in a slightly different way.

Citing Court Cases

You can cite several types of court cases:

- Court decisions

- Unpublished cases

- Court cases at the trial level

- Court cases at the appellate level

All court cases are cited in the same manner, as shown in Figure 55. Be sure to underline the case title. Note that "v." is used, not the word "versus" or the abbreviation "vs.," and that the "v" is lower case.

The case of <u>Smith v. Jones</u> (1992) set a major legal precedent regarding sexual harrassment in the workplace.

or

Apple Computer Company charged Microsoft Corporation with patent infringement, saying that Microsoft appropriated the code for their graphic interface and used it in their development of their Windows program (<u>Apple Computer v. Microsoft</u> 1993).

Figure 55. Example Citations of a Court Decision in the Text.

Citing Statutes

When you cite a statute in the text, you must give the:

- Name of the act

- Year it was passed

You can do this in two ways, as shown in Figure 56. Be sure to use initial caps on each word of the statute.

```
To prevent people with disabilities from being
discriminated against in the workplace and in
society at large, the U.S. Congress passed the
Americans With Disabilities Act (1990).
```

or

```
To prevent people with disabilities from being
discriminated against in the workplace and in
society at large, the U.S. Congress passed the
Americans With Disabilities Act of 1990.
```

Figure 56. Example Citations of a Statute in the Text.

Citing Testimony at Hearings

When you cite testimony from a hearing in the text of your document, you must:

- Indicate that it is testimony

- Include the name of the person testifying

- Include the year in which the testimony took place

Figure 57 shows two examples. Note that the words "Testimony of John Smith" are underlined.

```
As stated in the Testimony of John Smith (1990), ut wisi

enim ad minim veniam, quis nostrud exerci tation

ullamcorper suscipit lobortis nisl ut aliquip.
```

or

```
"Lorem ipsum dolor sit amet, consectetuer adipiscing

elit, sed diam nonummy nibh euismod tin cidunt ut laoreet

dolore magna aliquam erat volutpat"  (Testimony of John

Smith, 1990).
```

Figure 57. Example Citations of Testimony at a Hearing.

Citing Full Hearings

When you cite information from a full hearing in the text of your document, you must include the:

- Name of the hearing

- Year in which the hearing took place

Figure 58 shows two examples.

Note that the title of the hearing is underlined.

In the hearing <u>RU486: The Import Ban and Its Effect on Medical Research</u> (1990), ut wisi enim ad minim veniam, quis nostrud exerci tation ullamcorper suscipit lobortis nisl ut aliquip.

or

Lorem ipsum dolor sit amet, consectetuer adipiscing elit, sed diam nonummy nibh euismod tin cidunt ut laoreet dolore magna aliquam erat volutpat (<u>RU486: The Import Ban and Its Effect on Medical Research</u>, 1990).

Figure 58. Example Citations of a Full Hearing.

Citing Unenacted Federal Bills and Resolutions

When you cite an unenacted federal bill or resolution in the text of your document, you must include the:

- Name of the bill or resolution

- Year in which the bill or resolution was introduced

Figure 59 shows two examples. When the citation is completely within the parentheses, as shown in the second example in Figure 59, use only the initials and type a space between the "H." and the "J."

NOTE: *The correct abbreviation for a House Joint Resolution, when used in parentheses, is "H. J. Res."*

House Joint Resolution 504 (1986), introduced by Rep. Robert Badham, the Republican congressman from Newport Beach, California, sought to authorize establishment of a memorial in Washington, DC, or its environs to honor the Challenger astronauts.

or

In 1986, Congressman Robert Badham of Newport Beach, California, sought to pass a resolution authorizing the building of a memorial to the Challenger astronauts on federal land in the District of Columbia or its environs (H. J. Res. 504, 1986).

Figure 59. Example Citations of an Unenacted Federal Resolution.

Citing Enacted Federal Bills and Resolutions

When you cite an enacted federal bill or resolution in the text of your document, you must include the:

- Name of the bill or resolution

- Year in which the bill or resolution was passed

Bear in mind that enacted federal bills and resolutions are really laws and, therefore, should be cited as statutes, if possible (see page 74).

Figure 60 shows two examples.

When the citation is completely within the parentheses, as shown in the second example in Figure 60, use only the initials and type a space between the "S." and the "B."

NOTE: The correct abbreviation for a Senate Resolution when used in parentheses is "S. Res."

```
Lorem ipsum dolor sit amet, consectetuer adipiscing elit,

sed diam nonummy nibh euismod tin cidunt ut laoreet

dolore magna aliquam erat volutpat as stated in Senate

Bill 345 (1993).
```

or

```
Ut wisi enim ad minim veniam, quis nostrud exerci tation

ullamcorper suscipit lobortis nisl ut aliquip ex ea

commodo consequat (S. B. 345, 1993).
```

Figure 60. Example Citations of an Enacted Bill.

Citing Federal Reports and Documents

When you cite a federal report or document in your report, you must include the:

- Number of the report or document

- Year in which the report or document was issued

Figure 61 shows two examples.

When using the citation as part of your text, as shown in the first example in Figure 61, the words of the title are completely spelled out, with the exception of "Number," which is abbreviated as "No."

When the citation is completely within the parentheses, as shown in the second example in Figure 61, all the words of the title are abbreviated; i.e., (S. Rep. No. 1234, 1993).

NOTE: *The correct abbreviation for a federal document, when used in parentheses, is "Doc"; i.e., (S. Doc. No. 1234, 1992).*

```
Lorem ipsum dolor sit amet, consectetuer adipiscing

elit, sed diam nonummy nibh euismod tin cidunt ut

laoreet dolore magna aliquam erat volutpat as stated

in Senate Report No. 123 (1991).
```

or

```
Ut wisi enim ad minim veniam, quis nostrud exerci

tation ullamcorper suscipit lobortis nisl ut aliquip

ex ea commodo consequat (S. Rep. No. 123, 1991).
```

Figure 61. Example Citations of a Federal Report or Document.

Citing Administrative and Executive Materials

There are two types of administrative and executive materials:

- Federal rules and regulations
- Executive orders and advisory opinions

Citing a Federal Rule or Regulation

You'll find federal rules and regulations in both the *Code of Federal Regulations* and in the *Federal Register*. They are generally published first in the *Federal Register*, then codified in the *Code of Federal Regulations*.

When you cite a federal rule or regulation in the text of your document, you must include the:

- Title of the rule or regulation
- Year in which the rule or regulation was passed

Figure 62 shows two examples.

NOTE: *If the rule is contained in both the Code and the Register, cite the title from both sources. Put the title of the second citation in parentheses as a cross-reference.*

```
Lorem ipsum dolor sit amet, consectetuer adipiscing

elit, sed diam nonummy nibh euismod tin cidunt ut

laoreet dolore magna aliquam erat volutpat as stated

in the FTC Credit Practices Rule (1991).
```

or

```
Ut wisi enim ad minim veniam, quis nostrud exerci

tation ullamcorper suscipit lobortis nisl ut aliquip

ex ea commodo consequat (FTC Credit Practices Rule,

1991).
```

Figure 62. Example Citations of a Federal Regulation.

Citing an Executive Order or Advisory Opinion

You'll find executive orders in Volume 3 of the *Code of Federal Regulations*. They may also be listed in the United States Code (U.S.C.).

When you cite an executive order or advisory opinion in the text of your document, you must include the:

- Title (which includes the number) of the order or opinion

- Year in which the rule or regulation was passed

If the executive order is contained in both the *Code of Federal Regulations* and the United States Code, cite the title from both sources. Put the title of the second citation in parentheses as a cross-reference.

Figure 63 shows two examples.

```
Lorem ipsum dolor sit amet, consectetuer adipiscing

elit, sed diam nonummy nibh euismod tin cidunt ut

laoreet dolore magna aliquam erat volutpat as stated

in Executive Order No. 12804, 1992).
```

or

```
Ut wisi enim ad minim veniam, quis nostrud exerci

tation ullamcorper suscipit lobortis nisl ut aliquip

ex ea commodo consequat (Executive Order No. 12804,

1992).
```

Figure 63. Example Citations of an Executive Order.

Using Notes

Use notes to explain information in greater detail than the scope of your paper allows. You can create notes of two types:

- Content notes
- Bibliographic notes

Number both types chronologically in your report.

Creating Content Notes

Perhaps you want to tell your readers why you worked from secondary sources or to explain other information that does not necessarily fit in the text of your paper. Do so with what is called a "content note." There are two types: footnotes and endnotes.

Footnotes go at the bottom of the page; endnotes go on a page at the end of your report. Endnotes are easier to create, especially if you are using a typewriter, since determining how far down the page to start a footnote can be tricky. If you are using a word-processing program, creating footnotes can be easier; however, endnotes are still simpler to use. Before deciding whether to create footnotes or endnotes, check with your teacher or instructor to see which type he or she prefers.

To mark a passage for either a footnote or an endnote, place a superscripted number by the passage to which your footnote or endnote applies (see Figure 64). Then follow the steps in one of the two following sections.

Creating Footnotes

1. At the bottom of the page, allow enough room for your footnote(s). On a new line, center the word "Note" (or "Notes," if there is more than one). (See Figure 64.)

2. Indent the first line of the footnote text of the note one-half inch (five spaces if using a typewriter).

3. Type the superscripted number that matches the first superscripted passage on that page.

4. Doublespace the footnote; begin the second and any subsequent lines back at the left margin.

5. Repeat Steps 2-4 for any other footnote(s). Remember to number each footnote and the passage to which it refers with the next chronological number.

Johnson 3

Lorem ipsum dolor sit amet, ex ea commodo consequat consectetuer adipisci elit, sed diam nonummy nibh eusmod tin cidunt ut loreet dolore magna aliquam erat volutpat. Ut wisi ad minim veniam, quis nostrud exercitation ulcorper suscipit lobortis nisl ut aliquip ex ea commodo consequat.

Duis atem vel eum iriure dolor in hendrerit in putate velit esse molestie consequat, vel illum dolore feugiat nulla facilisis at vero eros et accumsan et odio dignissim qui blandit praesent luptatum zzril del augue duis dolore te feugait nulla facilisi.[1]

Nam liber tempor cum sluta nobis eleifend id congue nihil imperdiet doming id quod mazim placerat possim assum odio dignissim qui blandit praesent luptatum zzril del augue duie dolore te feugait nulla facilisi consectetuer adipisci elit, sed diam nonummy nibh eusmod tin cidunt ut loreet dolore magna aliquam erat volutpat.[2] Ut wisi ad minim veniam, quis nostrud exercitation

Lorem ipsum dolor sit amet, ex ea commodo consequat consectetuer adipisci elit, sed diam nonummy nibh eusmod tin dolore magna aliquam erat volutpat. Ut wisi ad minim veniam,

Notes

[1] A complete description of the author's earlier works is contained in Josefson. See "The Early Years" 108-150.

[2] See Kennedy for further examples.

Figure 64. Example Marked Passages and Corresponding Footnotes.

Creating Endnotes

To create a content note as an endnote, follow these steps:

1. Referring to Figure 65, center the word "Note" (or "Notes," if there is more than one) on a new page following the last page of report text and before the Works Cited list.

2. Indent the first line of the endnote text one-half inch (five spaces if using a typewriter).

3. Type a superscripted number 1 to match that of the first superscripted passage.

4. Doublespace the endnote; begin the second and any subsequent lines back at the left margin.

5. Repeat Steps 2-4 for any other endnotes. Remember to number each endnote and the passage to which it refers with the next chronological number.

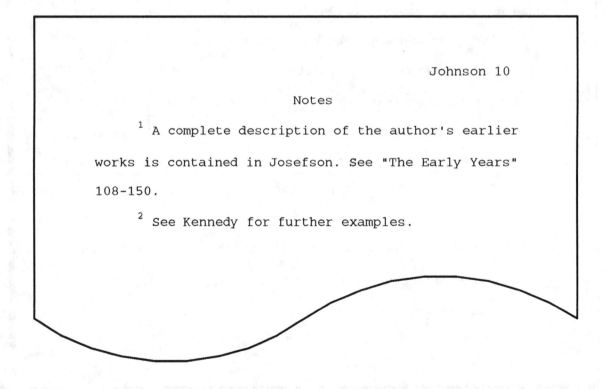

```
                                              Johnson 10

                         Notes

        1 A complete description of the author's earlier

   works is contained in Josefson. See "The Early Years"

   108-150.

        2 See Kennedy for further examples.
```

Figure 65. Example Endnotes Page.

Using Bibliographic Notes

Use bibliographic notes on your Works Cited page to provide additional comments about your sources and to list references that have multiple citations.

In the text of your report, mark the passage(s) to which the bibliographic note(s) refer by placing a superscripted character after each. Just as with endnotes and footnotes, mark them in chronological order (see Figure 64 on page 83 for an example).

To create a bibliographic note, follow these steps:

1. Referring to Figure 66, center the word "Note" (or "Notes" if there is more than one) at the top of your Works Cited page.

2. Indent the first line of bibliographic-note text one-half inch (five spaces if using a typewriter).

3. Type a superscripted number 1 to match that of the first superscripted passage.

4. Double-space the bibliographic note; begin the second and any subsequent lines back at the left margin. Include the author's last name and the page number(s) for each reference.

5. Repeat Steps 2-4 for any other bibliographic notes. Remember to number each bibliographic note and the passage to which it refers with the next chronological number.

6. Center "Works Cited" below the last bibliographic note and start your works cited list below that. Include full references for any authors or works mentioned in your notes.

See Appendix B for a sample works cited list.

Johnson 10

Notes

[1] Toffler has written two more books since writing *Future Shock* in 1970: *The Third Wave* in 1980, which also introduces new ways to think about change, and *Power Shift* in 1990, which focuses on shifts in power at the local level of our everyday world.

[2] Several other authors follow this same line of thought: Galbraith 60-71; Redfield 67-90; Stine 11-26; and Ferguson 145-188.

Works Cited

Adams, Perry. "The Turn of the Millenium." *Future* (Dec. 1998): 20-23.

Ferguson, Marilyn. *The Aquarian Conspiracy: Personal and Social Transformation in the 1980s*. Los Angeles: Tarcher, 1980.

Galbraith, John Kenneth. *The New Industrial State*. Boston: Houghton, 1967.

Redfield, James. *The Celestine Prophecy*. New York: Warner, 1993.

Rogers, Jeffrey. *The Coming Revolutio* York: Ace, 1998.

Stine, G. Harry. *The Third In* New York: Putnam's, 1

Toffler, Alvin. *The Thir* Morrow, 1980.

Figure 66. Example of Bibliographic Notes on the Works Cited Page.

Chapter 5

Creating a Works Cited List

A Works Cited list contains the complete citation information your readers will need to find the original sources you used in your report. You may use many different sources, such as:

- Journal articles

- Magazine articles and editorials

- Newspaper articles and editorials

- Books

- Conference proceedings

- Encyclopedias, dictionaries, and reference books

- Academic material

- Government publications

- Book, movie, and video reviews

- Manuscripts or typescripts

- Graphical materials

- Letters and memos

- Legal sources

- Audio-visual materials and personal interviews

- Electronic media

This chapter shows how to create all these references.

When you create your Works Cited list, follow these rules:

- Start the Works Cited list on a new page.

- Continue page numbering from the last page of your text.

- Center "Works Cited" an inch from the top of the page.

- Create the list in alphabetical order by author last name.

- Include only those sources for which you have citations in the text of your report.

- Follow the layout and punctuation exactly as shown in this chapter.

NOTE: *Many of the examples shown in this section are not real; they have been created for example purposes.*

For an example of a Works Cited list, please see Appendix B.

Citing Authors' Names

Many works have one author; others have two or more. In addition, writers may list their names in various ways. For example, some use:

- First and last names

- First, middle, and last names

- First name, middle initial, and last name

- First initial, middle name, and last name

- First and middle initials and last name

- First name, maiden name, and last name

- Pen name in any of the above formats

Cite each author's name exactly as it appears on the work. Follow the rules in this section for doing so, no matter which type of work.

Citing One Author's Name

Figure 67 shows the correct way to cite one author's name:

1. At the left margin, type the author's last name followed by a comma and a space.

2a. If only the first name or initial is available, follow it with a period and a space.

b. If the author's middle name or initial is available, however, type the first name, followed by a space. Then type the middle name or initial, followed by a period and then a space.

NOTE: Type the authors' names exactly as listed on the work; i.e., if the work lists the names in full, you should, too. If the work lists initials, use those.

```
Matthews, Yolanda.
```

or

```
Matthews, Yolanda S.
```

Figure 67. Correct Way to Cite One Author's Name.

NOTE: If the author goes by initials, put a period and a space between each initial:

```
T. S. Eliot
```

Citing Two Authors' Names

Figure 68 shows the correct way to cite two authors' names:

1. At the left margin, type the first author's last name, followed by a comma and a space.

2a. Type the first name of the first author. If the author does not have a middle name or initial, follow the first name with a comma and a space. If only the first initial is available, follow it with a period, a comma, and a space.

b. If the author's middle name or initial is available, however, type the first name, followed by a space. Then type the middle name, followed by a comma and a space, or the middle initial, followed by a period, a comma, and a space.

3. Type "and," followed by a space.

4a. Type the second author's first name, followed by a space. If only the first initial is available, follow it with a period and a space.

b. If the author's middle name is available, follow it with a space. If only the author's middle initial is available, follow it with a period and a space.

5. Type the second author's last name, followed by a period and a space.

NOTE: *Notice that the first author's name is in reverse order, while the second author's name is not.*

NOTE: *Type the authors' names exactly as listed on the work; i.e., if the work lists the names in full, you should, too. If the work lists initials, use those.*

```
Spetch, Mark L., and Alan Dean Jensen.
```

```
Jones, Mary Ann, and John M. Smith.
```

Figure 68. Correct Way to Cite Two Authors' Names.

Citing Three Authors' Names

Figure 69 shows the correct way to cite three authors' names:

1. At the left margin, type the first author's last name, followed by a comma and a space.

2a. Type the first name of the first author. If the author does not have a middle name or initial, follow the first name with a comma and a space. If only the first initial is available, follow it with a period, a comma, and a space.

 b. If the author's middle name or initial is available, however, type the first name, followed by a space. Then type the middle name, followed by a comma and a space, or the middle initial, followed by a period, a comma, and a space.

3a. Type the second author's first name, followed by a space. If only the first initial is available, follow it with a period and a space.

 b. If the author's middle name is available, follow it with a space. If only the author's middle initial is available, follow it with a period and a space.

4. Type the second author's last name, followed by a comma and a space.

5. Type the word "and," followed by a space.

6a. Type the third author's first name, followed by a space. If only the first initial is available, follow it with a period and a space.

 b. If the author's middle name is available, follow it with a space. If only the author's middle initial is available, follow it with a period and a space.

7. Type the third author's last name, followed by a period and a space.

```
Spetch, Mark L., Darryl M. Wilkie, and John Smith.
```

Figure 69. Correct Way to Cite Three Authors' Names.

Citing Four or More Authors' Names

Cite a book with four or more authors in two ways :

- By listing all the authors' names

- By listing the first author's name, followed by "et al."

Figure 70 shows examples of both of these ways. Follow these steps:

1.   At the left margin, type the first author's last name, followed by a comma and a space.

2a. Type the first name of the first author. If the author does not have a middle name or initial, follow the first name with a comma and a space. If only the first initial is available, follow it with a period, a comma, and a space.

  b. If the author's middle name or initial is available, however, type the first name, followed by a space. Then type the middle name, followed by a comma and a space, or the middle initial, followed by a period, a comma, and a space.

      NOTE: *Type the author's name exactly as listed on the work; i.e., if the work lists the name in full, you should, too. If the work lists initials, use those.*

3.   If you want to list just the first author's name, type the phrase "et al.," which means "and everyone." Make sure it ends in a period and a space.

     To list all the authors' names, however, skip this step and go to Step 4.

4a. Type the second author's first name, followed by a space. If only the first initial is available, follow it with a period and a space.

  b. If the author's middle name is available, follow it with space. If only the author's middle initial is available, follow it with a period and a space.

5.   Type the second author's last name, followed by a comma and a space.

6.   Repeat Steps 4 and 5 for all remaining authors except the last.

7. After the second-to-the-last author's last name, type the word "and," followed by a space.

8a. Type the last author's first name, followed by a space. If only the first initial is available, follow it with a period and a space.

b. If the author's middle name is available, follow it with a space. If only the author's middle initial is available, follow it with a period and a space.

9. Type the last author's last name, followed by a comma and a space.

10. If the names continue to a second line, double-space the second line and indent it one-half inch (five spaces on a typewriter).

```
Sanders, Thomas J., et al.
```

```
Sanders, Thomas J., Gerald Smith, Mary Lou Adams Rosen,

     Peter Jones, and Abigail A. Turner.
```

Figure 70. Correct Way to Cite Four or More Authors' Names.

Citing an Author Who Uses a Pen Name (Pseudonym)

Some writers do not write under their own names; for example, Samuel Clemens wrote under the name Mark Twain. Some current writers who are well-known under their real names for a particular type of writing (for example, mystery novels) may use a pen name when writing a work that falls into a different genre or category. Figure 71 shows the correct way to cite a work for which the author uses a pen name.

1. At the left margin, type the author's last name as it appears on the work (i.e., the pen name), followed by a comma and a space.

2a. Type the author's first name. If the author does not have a middle name or initial, follow the first name with a comma and a space. If only the first initial is available, follow it with a period, a comma, and a space.

b. If the author's middle name or initial is available, however, type the first name, followed by a space. Then type the middle name, followed by a comma and a space, or the middle initial, followed by a period, a comma, and a space.

3. Type an opening bracket, then the author's real first name followed by a space or first initial followed by a period and a space. (The brackets indicate that you supplied the real name.)

4. Type the author's real middle name, if available, followed by a space, or the author's middle initial, followed by a period and a space.

5. Type the author's last name, followed by a closing bracket, a period, and a space.

NOTE: *Type the author's names exactly as listed on the work; i.e., if the work lists the names in full, you should, too. If the work lists initials, use those.*

```
Twain, Mark [Samuel Langhorne Clemens].
```

Figure 71. Example Citation of the Real Name of an Author for a Work on Which the Author Uses a Pen Name.

Citing an Author Who Uses Initials for Whom You Supply the Full Name

You may know or find out the complete name of a writer who uses first and/or middle initials and wish to supply this information for your readers. Figure 72 shows the correct way to cite an author's name in this manner.

1.   At the left margin, type the author's last name, followed by a comma and a space.

2a. Let's say that the author uses both first and middle initials. Type the first initial, then an opening bracket. Then type the rest of the first name followed by closing bracket. (The brackets indicate that you supplied this information yourself, and that the work does not list the name in this manner.)

b.   Type the middle initial, then an opening bracket. Then type the rest of the first name followed by closing bracket and a period.

NOTE: If the writer just uses one initial (either first or middle; such as "J. Thomas Reed" or "Roger K. Benson,") the brackets would, of course, go only around the part of the name you are supplying for the initial.

```
Sanders, E[lizabeth] A[nn].
```

Figure 72. Example Citation of an Author Who Uses Initials for Whom You Supply the Full Name.

Citing Editors' Names

When you cite a work by the editor's/editors' names, use the same formats as for citing a work by the author's/authors' names. Simply indicate that the person is the editor rather than the author. Use the abbreviation "ed." for one editor, "eds." for more than one. Figure 73 shows examples.

```
Martin, Judy Allen, ed.
```

```
Jones, Mary Ann, and John M. Smith, eds.
```

```
Lopez, Raul, et al., eds.
```

Figure 73. Correct Way to Cite Editors' Names.

Citing Titles

Cite titles as shown in Chapter 4, *Citing Titles*, pages 57-59.

Citing Periodicals

This section shows you how to cite:

- Journal articles

- Magazine articles

- Microform articles

- Articles in looseleaf collections

- Newspaper articles

- Abstracts

Citing Journal Articles

Many professional associations publish journals that present scholars' research and interpretations of data. These journals are slanted toward an audience professional in those fields.

Most journals are published quarterly. Some form the four issues for the year into a volume, which is paginated from page 1 on. Therefore, the second issue in a set might start on page 235, for example, rather than page 1. This is called a journal with "continuous" pagination. Other journals paginate each issue separately; in other words, each issue begins on page 1.

When you cite a journal article, you must cite both the article and the journal it is in. This section shows you how to cite an:

- Article in a journal with continuous pagination

- Article in a journal that pages each issue separately

- Article in a journal that uses only issue numbers

- Article in a journal with more than one series

All of the following examples are shown with one author. If you need to cite two or more authors, refer to the instructions on pages 90-93.

Citing an Article in a Journal with Continous Pagination

A citation for an article in a journal with continuous pagination appears as shown in Figure 74 and consists of the following elements:

- Author's last name

- Author's first name or initial (and middle name or initial, if available)

- Title of article

- Title of journal

- Volume number, if available

- Year of publication

- Page number(s) of article

To create this citation, follow these steps:

1. At the left margin, type the author's last name, followed by a comma and a space.

2a. If only the first name or initial is available, follow it with a period and a space.

  b. If the author's middle name or initial is available, however, type the first name, followed by a space. Then type the middle name or initial, followed by a period and a space.

    NOTE: Type the authors' names exactly as listed on the work; i.e., if the work lists the names in full, you should, too. If the work lists initials, use those.

    NOTE: If the article has more than one author, follow the rules for that number of authors.

3. Type an opening quotation mark, then the title of the article. Capitalize the first letter of all words except articles and prepositions (unless the first word is an article or preposition). Type a period, a closing quotation mark, and a space.

4. Type and underline the journal title. Capitalize the first letter of all words except prepositions and articles. Delete the first word if it is an article (e.g., "The"). After the title, type a space.

5. Type the volume number, if available, and another space.

6. Type an opening parenthesis, the copyright year, then a closing parenthesis, followed by a colon and a space.

7. Type the page number(s), followed by a period.

   NOTE: Do not include "p." or "pp." in the page number.

   NOTE: If you are including a range of page numbers that has three digits or more, include only two digits in the second half of the range, as shown in Figure 73.

8. If your citation continues to a second or subsequent line, double-space that line and indent it one-half inch (five spaces on a typewriter).

See Appendix B for a complete sample works cited list.

```
Matthews, Yolanda S. "Racism in Contemporary

    Novels." Journal of Higher Education 39 (1993):

    360-65.
```

Figure 74. Example Citation of an Article With One Author in a Journal With Continuous Pagination.

Citing an Article in a Journal That Paginates Each Issue Separately

A citation for an article in a journal that paginates each issue separately appears as shown in Figure 75 and consists of the following elements:

- Author's last name

- Author's first name or initial (and middle name or initial, if available)

- Title of article

- Title of journal

- Volume (and issue) number, if available

- Year of publication

- Page number(s) of article

To create this citation, follow these steps:

1. At the left margin, type the author's last name, followed by a comma and a space.

2a. If only the first name or initial is available, follow it with a period and a space.

  b. If the author's middle name or initial is available, however, type the first name, followed by a space. Then type the middle name or initial, followed by a period and a space.

     NOTE: Type the authors' names exactly as listed on the work; i.e., if the work lists the names in full, you should, too. If the work lists initials, use those.

     NOTE: If the article has more than one author, follow the rules for that number of authors.

3. Type an opening quotation mark, then the title of the article. Capitalize the first letter of all words except articles and prepositions (unless the first word is an article or preposition). Type a period, a closing quotation mark, and a space.

4. Type and underline the journal title. Capitalize the first letter of all words except prepositions and articles. Delete the first word if it is an article (e.g., "The"). After the title, type a space.

5. Type the volume number followed by a period.

   NOTE: Do not include the word "Volume" or "Vol."

6. Type the issue number(s), followed by a space.

7. Type an opening parenthesis, the year of publication, then a closing parenthesis, followed by a colon.

9. Type the page number(s), followed by a period.

   NOTE: Do not include "p." or "pp." in the page number.

   NOTE: If you are including a range of page numbers that has three digits or more, include only two digits in the second half of the range, as shown in Figure 75.

10. If your citation continues to a second or subsequent line, double-space that line and indent it one-half inch (five spaces on a typewriter).

   See Appendix B for a sample Works Cited list.

   NOTE: If the article has more than one author, follow the rules for that number of authors.

```
Fye, Walter.  "The origin of the full-time faculty

    system."  JAMA 265.1 (1991):  138-49.
```

Figure 75. Example Citation of an Article with One Author in a Journal That Paginates Each Issue Separately.

Citing an Article in a Journal That Uses Only Issue Numbers

Some journals number their issues only and do not use volume numbers. A citation for an article in a journal that uses only issue numbers is shown in Figure 76 and consists of the following elements:

- Author's last name

- Author's first name or initial (and middle name or initial, if available)

- Title of article

- Title of journal

- Issue number

- Year of publication

- Page number(s) of article

To create this citation, follow these steps:

1. At the left margin, type the author's last name, followed by a comma and a space.

2a. If only the first name or initial is available, follow it with a period and a space.

  b. If the author's middle name or initial is available, however, type the first name, followed by a space. Then type the middle name or initial, followed by a period and a space.

   NOTE: Type the authors' names exactly as listed on the work; i.e., if the work lists the names in full, you should, too. If the work lists initials, use those.

   NOTE: If the article has more than one author, follow the rules for that number of authors.

3. Type an opening quotation mark, then the title of the article. Capitalize the first letter of all words except articles and prepositions (unless the first word is an article or preposition). Type a period, a closing quotation mark, and a space.

4. Type and underline the journal title. Capitalize the first letter of all words except prepositions and articles. Delete the first word if it is an article (e.g., "The"). After the title, type a space.

5. Type the issue number, followed by a space.

6. Type an opening parenthesis, the year of publication, then a closing parenthesis, followed by a colon and a space.

7. Type the page number(s), followed by a period.

    NOTE: Do not include "p." or "pp." in the page number.

    NOTE: If you are including a range of page numbers that has three digits or more, include only two digits in the second half of the range, as shown in Figure 76.

8. If your citation continues to a second or subsequent line, double-space that line and indent it one-half inch (five spaces on a typewriter).

See Appendix B for a sample Works Cited list.

NOTE: If the article has more than one author, follow the rules for that number of authors.

```
Johnson, Thomas. "Native American Fishing Rights in

    Oregon." Journal of Ethnic Studies 53 (1991):

    143-47.
```

Figure 76. Example Citation of an Article with One Author in a Journal That Uses Only Issue Numbers.

Citing an Article in a Journal That Appears in More Than One Series

Some journals are published in more than one series. A citation for an article in a journal that appears in more than one series is as shown in Figure 77 and consists of the following elements:

- Author's last name

- Author's first name or initial (and middle name or initial, if available)

- Title of article

- Title of journal

- Series number

- Abbreviation "ser."

- Volume (and issue) number, if available

- Year of publication

- Page number(s) of article

To create this citation, follow these steps:

1. At the left margin, type the author's last name, followed by a comma and a space.

2a. If only the first name or initial is available, follow it with a period and a space.

   b. If the author's middle name or initial is available, however, type the first name, followed by a space. Then type the middle name or initial, followed by a period and a space.

   NOTE: Type the authors' names exactly as listed on the work; i.e., if the work lists the names in full, you should, too. If the work lists initials, use those.

   NOTE: If the article has more than one author, follow the rules for that number of authors.

3. Type an opening quotation mark, then the title of the article. Capitalize the first letter of all words except articles and prepositions (unless the first word is an article or preposition). Type a period, a closing quotation mark, and a space.

4. Type and underline the journal title. Capitalize the first letter of all words except prepositions and articles. Delete the first word if it is an article (e.g., "The"). After the title, type a space.

5. Type the series number using an arabic digit followed by its ordinal suffix (e.g., 1st, 2nd, 3rd, 4th, etc.) and a space.

6. Type the abbreviation "ser" followed by a period and a space.

7. Type the volume number followed by a space.

    NOTE: Do not include the word "Volume" or "Vol."

8. Type an opening parenthesis, the year of publication, then a closing parenthesis, followed by a colon.

9. Type the page number(s), followed by a period.

    NOTE: Do not include "p." or "pp." in the page number.

    NOTE: If you are including a range of page numbers that has three digits or more, include only two digits in the second half of the range, as shown in Figure 77.

10. If your citation continues to a second or subsequent line, double-space that line and indent it one-half inch (five spaces on a typewriter).

    See Appendix B for a sample Works Cited list.

    NOTE: If the article has more than one author, follow the rules for that number of authors.

```
Johnson, Thomas. "Native American Fishing Rights in

     Oregon." Journal of Ethnic Studies 4th ser. 53

     (1991): 143-47.
```

Figure 77. Example Citation of an Article with One Author in a Journal That Appears in More Than One Series.

Citing Magazine Articles

This section shows you how to cite a(n):

- Article in a magazine published every week or two weeks

- Article in a magazine published every month or two months

- Serialized article

- Editorial

- Letter to the editor

- Special issue

Citing an Article in a Magazine Published Every Week or Two Weeks

Some magazines, like *Time* and *Newsweek*, are published every week. Other magazines come out every two weeks. A citation for a magazine published every week or two weeks is as shown in Figure 78 and consists of the following elements:

- Author's last name

- Author's first name or initial (and middle name or initial, if available)

- Title of article

- Title of magazine

- Date

- Year of publication

- Page number(s) of article

To create this citation, follow these steps:

1. At the left margin, type the author's last name, followed by a comma and a space.

2a. If only the first name or initial is available, follow it with a period and a space.

b. If the middle name or initial is available, however, type the first name, followed by a space. Then type the middle name or initial, followed by a period and a space.

> *NOTE:* *If the article has more than one author, follow the rules for that number of authors.*

> *NOTE:* *If the article has no author, begin at the left margin with Step 3.*

3. Type an opening quotation mark, then the title of the article. Capitalize the first letter of all words except articles and prepositions (unless the first word is an article or a preposition). Type a period, a closing quotation mark, and a space.

4. Type and underline the magazine title. Capitalize the first letter of all words except articles and prepositions. Delete the first word if it is an article (e.g., "The"). After the title, type a space.

5. Type the date in day, month, year format. Abbreviate the month using the accepted three-letter abbreviation (see Table 5 on page 22). Follow the abbreviated month with a period and a space or the unabbreviated month with a space.

6. Type the year of publication followed by a colon.

7. Type the page number(s), followed by a period.

> *NOTE: Do not include "p." or "pp." in the page number.*

> *NOTE:* *If you are including a range of page numbers that has three digits or more, include only two digits in the second half of the range, as shown in Figure 78.*

> *NOTE:* *If the article is not printed on consecutive pages, type only the first page number and then a plus sign (e.g., 70+).*

8. If your citation continues to a second or subsequent line, double-space that line and indent it one-half inch (five spaces on a typewriter).

See Appendix B for a sample Works Cited list.

```
Morrison, Howard A. "The Paperless Office." Business

     Talk 21 Dec. 1992: 70-76.
```

Figure 78. Example Citation of an Article With One Author in a Magazine Published Every Week or Two Weeks.

Citing an Article in a Magazine Published Every Month or Two Months

Some magazines are published every month or two months. A citation for a magazine published every month or two months is shown in Figure 79 and consists of the following elements:

- Author's last name

- Author's first name or initial (and middle name or initial, if available

- Title of article

- Title of magazine

- Month of publication

- Year of publication

- Page number(s) of article

To create this citation, follow these steps:

NOTE: If the article has no author, begin at the left margin with Step 3 and refer to the second example in Figure 79.

1. At the left margin, type the author's last name, followed by a comma and a space.

2a. If only the first name or initial is available, follow it with a period and a space.

 b. If the middle name or initial is available for the author of the piece, however, type the first name, followed by a space. Then type the middle name or initial, followed by a period and a space.

NOTE: If the article has more than one author, follow the rules for that number of authors.

3. Type an opening quotation mark, then the title of the article. Capitalize the first letter of all words except articles and prepositions (unless the first word is an article or preposition). Type a period, a closing quotation mark, and a space.

4. Type and underline the magazine title. Capitalize the first letter of all words of the title except prepositions and articles. Delete the first word if it is an article (e.g., "The"). After the title, type a space.

5. Type the month or months. Abbreviate the month(s) using the accepted three-letter abbreviation if applicable (see Table 5 on page 22). Follow the abbreviated month(s) with a period and a space or the unabbreviated month with a space.

6. Type the year of publication followed by a colon.

    NOTE: Do not enclose the year in parentheses.

7. Type the page number(s), followed by a period.

    NOTE: Do not include "p." or "pp." in the page number.

    NOTE: If you are including a range of page numbers that has three digits or more, include only two digits in the second half of the range, as shown in Figure 79.

    If the article is not printed on consecutive pages, type only the first page number and then a plus sign (e.g., 70+).

8. If your citation continues to a second or subsequent line, double-space that line and indent it one-half inch (five spaces on a typewriter).

    See Appendix B for a sample Works Cited list.

```
Morrison, Harold. "The Paperless Office." Business

    Talk Nov. 1992: 70-76.
```

```
Morrison, Harold. "The Paperless Office." Business

    Talk Nov.-Dec 1992: 70+.
```

Figure 79. Example Citations of an Article With One Author in a Magazine Magazine Published Every Month or Two Months.

Citing an Article Serialized in a Magazine

Some articles are serialized over several issues; that is, part of the article appears in one issue and another part or parts appear in another issue or other issues. If the author and title are the same in each installment, you can include all the bibliographic information in one citation. Figure 80 shows an example of this type of citation, which consists of the following elements:

- Author's last name

- Author's first name or initial (and middle name or initial, if available)

- Title of article

- Title of magazine

- Issue number

- Year of publication

- Page number(s) of article

To create this citation, follow these steps:

1. At the left margin, type the author's last name, followed by a comma and a space.

2a. If only the first name is available, follow it with a period and a space.

 b. If the author's middle name or initial is available, however, type the first name, followed by a space. Then type the middle name or initial, folllowed by a period and a space.

    NOTE: If the article has more than one author, follow the rules for that number of authors.

3. Type an opening quotation mark, then the title of the article. Capitalize the first letter of all words except articles and prepositions (unless the first word is an article or preposition). Type a period, a closing quotation mark, and a space.

4. Type and underline the magazine title. Capitalize the first letter of all words except articles and prepositions. Delete the first word if it is an article (e.g., "The"). After the title, type a space.

5. Type issue number for the first issue, followed by a space.

6. Type an opening parenthesis, the year of publication, a closing parenthesis, a colon, and a space.

7. Type the page number(s) for the first installment, followed by a semicolon and a space.

    NOTE: Do not include "p." or "pp." in the page number.

    NOTE: If you are including a range of page numbers that has three digits or more, include only two digits in the second half of the range; e.g., 234-36.

8. Repeat Steps 5-7 for the other issues. Type a period after the last set of page numbers.

9. If your citation continues to a second or subsequent line, double-space that line and indent it one-half inch (five spaces on a typewriter).

See Appendix B for a sample Works Cited list.

```
Morrison, Harold. "Writing a Novel That Sells."

The Writing Life 24 (1998): 79-81; 25 (1998):

70-76.
```

Figure 80. Example Citation of an Article With One Author Serialized in a Magazine.

Citing an Editorial in a Magazine

An editorial is an article, usually written by editor or another staff member of the magazine, that expresses the magazine's official opinion on some issue.

Figure 81 shows an example citation for a magazine editorial with an author, which consists of the following elements:

- Author's last name

- Author's first name or initial (and middle name or initial, if available)

- Title of editorial

- Title of magazine

- Day, month, and year of publication

- Page number(s) of editorial

To create this citation, follow these steps.

NOTE: For an editorial with no author, begin with Step 3 and refer to Figure 82.

1. At the left margin, type the author's last name, followed by a comma and a space.

2a. If only the first name or initial is available, follow it with a period and a space.

b. If the author's middle name or initial is available, however, type the first name, followed by a space. Then type the middle name or initial, followed by a period and a space.

   NOTE: If the editorial has more than one author, follow the rules for that number of authors.

   NOTE: Type the author's name exactly as listed on the work; i.e., if the work lists the name in full, you should, too. If the work lists initials, use those.

3. Type an opening quotation mark, then the title of the article. Capitalize the first letter of all words except articles and prepositions (unless the first word is an article or preposition). Type a period, a closing quotation mark, and a space.

4. Type the word "Editorial" followed by a period and a space.

5. Type and underline the magazine title. Capitalize the first letter of all words of the title except articles and prepositions. Delete the first word if it is an article (e.g., "The"). After the title, type a space.

6. Type the date in day, month format. Abbreviate the month using the accepted three-letter abbreviation (see Table 5 on page 22). Follow the abbreviated month with a period and a space or the unabbreviated month with a space.

7. Type the year of publication followed by a colon and a space.

   NOTE: Do not enclose the year in parentheses.

8. Type the page number(s), followed by a period.

   NOTE: Do not include "p." or "pp." in the page number.

   NOTE: If you are including a range of page numbers that has three digits or more, include only two digits in the second half of the range (e.g., 657-59).

9. If your citation continues to a second or subsequent line, double-space that line and indent it one-half inch (five spaces on a typewriter).

   See Appendix B for a sample Works Cited list.

```
Thompson, John. "To Sue or Not to Sue." Editorial.

     Writing Life 2 Mar. 1998: 4.
```

Figure 81. Example Citation of a Magazine Editorial With an Author.

```
"Tell It to Your Leader." Editorial. Today's News

     20 Mar. 1998: 5.
```

Figure 82. Example Citation of a Magazine Editorial Without an Author.

Citing a Letter to the Editor in a Magazine

Magazines usually have a "Letters to the Editor" section in which they print letters readers have sent in about articles in the magazine. Figure 83 shows an example citation for a letter to the editor, which consists of the following elements:

- Author's last name

- Author's first name or initial (and middle name or initial, if available)

- The word "Letter"

- Title of magazine

- Issue number

- Year of publication

- Page number(s) of article

To create this citation, follow these steps.

1. At the left margin, type the author's last name, followed by a comma and a space.

2a. If only the first name is available, follow it with a period and a space.

  b. If the author's middle name or initial is available, however, type the first name, followed by a space. Then type the middle name or initial, folllowed by a period and a space.

   NOTE: If the article has more than one author, follow the rules for that number of authors.

3. Type the word "Letter" followed by a period and a space.

4. Type and underline the magazine title. Capitalize the first letter of all words of the title except articles and prepositions. Delete the first word if it is an article (e.g., "The"). After the title, type a space.

5. Type the issue number followed by a space.

6. Type an opening parenthesis, the year of publication, and a closing parenthesis, followed by a colon and a space.

7.   Type the page number(s), followed by a period.

   NOTE: Do not include "p." or "pp." in the page number.

   NOTE: If you are including a range of page numbers that has three digits or more, include only two digits in the second half of the range (e.g., 657-59).

8.   If your citation continues to a second or subsequent line, double-space that line and indent it one-half inch (five spaces on a typewriter).

See Appendix B for a sample Works Cited list.

```
Thompson, John. Letter. Writing Life 24 (1998): 6-7.
```

Figure 83. Example Citation of a Letter to the Editor in a Magazine.

Citing an Article on Microfiche or Microfilm

Organizations, such as Newsbank, select articles from periodicals and put them on microfiche. If you are citing one of these reference sources, you must cite the original publication information first, then the information from the reference source. Figure 84 shows an example citation for an article on microfiche, which consists of the following elements:

- Author's last name
- Author's first name
- Title of article
- Title of original periodical
- Day and/or month of publication
- Year of publication

- Page number(s)
- Title of reference source
- Volume number
- Year of publication
- Fiche number
- Grid number(s)

To create this citation, follow these steps.

NOTE: For an article with no author, begin with Step 3.

1. At the left margin, type the author's last name, followed by a comma and a space.

2a. If only the first name is available, follow it with a period and a space.

 b. If the author's middle name or initial is available, however, type the first name, followed by a space. Then type the middle name or initial, followed by a period and a space.

3. Type an opening quotation mark, then the title of the article. Capitalize the first letter of all words except articles and prepositions. Type a period, a closing quotation mark, and a space.

4. Type and underline the magazine title. Capitalize the first letter of all words of the title except articles and prepositions. Delete the first word if it is an article (e.g., "The"). After the title, type a space.

5. Type the date in day, month order or, if the periodical is monthly, type the month. Abbreviate the month using the accepted three-letter abbreviation (see Table 5 on page 22). Follow the abbreviated month with a period and a space or the unabbreviated month (May, June, July) with a space.

6. Type the year of publication followed by a colon and a space.

    NOTE: Do not enclose the year in parentheses.

7. Type the page number(s), followed by a period and a space.

    NOTE: Do not include "p." or "pp." in the page number.

    NOTE: If you are including a range of page numbers that has three digits or more, include only two digits in the second half of the range (e.g., 657-59).

8. Type the name of the reference source and underline it. Capitalize the first letter of all words of the title except articles. Delete the first word if it is an article (e.g., "The"). Type a colon and a space.

9. Type the volume number and a space.

10. Type an opening parenthesis, the year of publication, a closing parenthesis, a colon, and a space.

11. Type the word "fiche" in lowercase letters, a space, then the fiche number, followed by a comma and a space.

12. Type the word "grids" and then a space, then type the grid numbers, followed by a period.

13. If your citation continues to a second or subsequent line, double-space that line and indent it one-half inch (five spaces on a typewriter).

    See Appendix B for a sample Works Cited list.

    NOTE: If the article has more than one author, follow the rules for that number of authors.

Gerritson, Thomas. "Tax Cut Could Make Our Day."

Santa Paula Times 21 Mar. 1997: 23. Newsbank:

Financial News 8 (1998): fiche 5, grids B4-7.

Figure 84. Example Citation of an Article on Microfiche.

Citing an Article Reprinted in a Loose-Leaf Collection

Information services select articles from periodicals and republish them in loose-leaf collections. Each binder contains a specific topic. If you are citing one of these information services, you must cite the original publication information first, then the information from the loose-leaf collection. Figure 85 shows an example citation for an article from a loose-leaf collection, which consists of the following elements:

- Author's last name
- Author's first name
- Title of article
- Title of original periodical
- Day and/or month of publication
- Year of publication
- Page number(s)

- Title of reference source
- Editor's name, if any
- Volume number, if any
- City of publication
- Publisher's name
- Year of publication
- Article number

To create this citation, follow these steps.

NOTE: For an article with no author, begin with Step 3. If the article has more than one author, follow the rules for that number of authors.

1. At the left margin, type the author's last name, followed by a comma and a space.

2a. If only the first name is available, follow it with a period and a space.

  b. If the author's middle name or initial is available, however, type the first name, followed by a space. Then type the middle name or initial, followed by a period and a space.

3. Type an opening quotation mark, then the title of the article. Capitalize the first letter of all words except articles and prepositions. Type a period, a closing quotation mark, and a space.

4. Type and underline the magazine title. Capitalize the first letter of all words of the title except articles and prepositions. Delete the first word if it is an article (e.g., "The"). After the title, type a space.

5. Type the date in day, month order or, if the periodical is monthly, type the month. Abbreviate the month using the accepted three-letter abbreviation (see Table 5 on page 22). Follow the abbreviated month with a period and a space or the unabbreviated month (May, June, July) with a space.

6. Type the year of publication followed by a colon and a space.

7. Type the page number(s), followed by a period and a space.

    NOTE: Do not include "p." or "pp." in the page number.

    NOTE: If you are including a range of page numbers that has three digits or more, include only two digits in the second half of the range (e.g., 657-59).

8. Type and underline the name of the reference source. Then type a period and a space. Capitalize the first letter of all words of the title except articles (unless the first word is an article).

9. If there is an editor, type the word "Ed." followed by a space and the editor's first and last name.

10. Type "Vol." and a space, then the volume number and a period.

11. Type the city of publication followed by a colon and a space.

12. Type the name of the looseleaf source, followed by a comma and a space.

13. Type the year of publication, followed by a period and a space.

14. Type the abbreviation "Art." (for "article") and a space, followed by the article number and a period.

15. If your citation continues to a second or subsequent line, double-space that line and indent it one-half inch (five spaces on a typewriter).

    See Appendix B for a sample Works Cited list.

```
Johnson, Dylan. "Go Dodger Blue!" Sportsweek 22
    Nov. 1990: 8-11. Sports Heroes of the 80s.
    Ed. Mickey Gomes. Vol. 4. Boca Raton: SIRS,
    1993. Art. 17.
```

Figure 85. Example Citation of an Article Reprinted in a Loose-Leaf Collection.

Citing Newspaper Articles

This section shows you how to cite a:

- Newspaper article

- Newspaper editorial

- Letter to the editor

Citing a Newspaper Article

Cite a newspaper article with one author just as you would a magazine article with one author; simply put the newspaper's name in place of the magazine title. Cite the newspaper's title as it appears on the masthead, but omit the first word if it is an article. For example, cite the Los Angeles Times as "Los Angeles Times," not as "The Los Angeles Times." A citation for a newspaper article with one author appears as shown in Figure 86 and consists of the following elements:

- Author's last name

- Author's first name or initial (and middle name or initial, if available)

- Title of article

- Title of newspaper

- Day, month, and year of newspaper issue

- Edition

- Page number(s) of article

To create this citation, follow these steps:

NOTE: If there is no author, begin at the left margin with Step 3.

1. At the left margin, type the author's last name, followed by a comma and a space.

2a. If only the first name or initial is available, follow it with a period and a space.

b. If the author's middle name or initial is available, however, type the first name, followed by a space. Then type the middle name or initial, followed by a period and a space.

NOTE: Type the author's name exactly as listed on the work; i.e., if the work lists the name in full, you should, too. If the work lists initials, use those.

NOTE: If the article has more than one author, follow the rules for that number of authors.

3. Type an opening quotation mark, the title of the article, a period, a closing quotation mark, and a space.

4. Type and underline the newspaper title as it appears on the masthead. Capitalize the first letter of all words except articles and prepositions. Delete the first word of the title if it is an article (e.g., "The"). After the title, type a space.

5. Type the date in day, month order. Abbreviate the month using the accepted three-letter abbreviation (see Table 5 on page 22). Follow the abbreviated month with a period and a space or the unabbreviated month (May, June, July) with a space.

6. Type the year of publication followed by a comma and a space.

7. Type the edition of the newspaper (such as "late," "national," "Metro," etc) in lower case letters (unless it is a proper name), followed by a space. Abbreviate "edition" as "ed." and follow it with a colon and a space.

8. Type the page number, followed by a period and a space. If the article continues onto another page, put a plus sign right after the page number to indicate that. Then type a period.

    NOTE: Do not include "p." or "pp." in the page number.

    NOTE: If the newspaper has section numbers, but the section numbers do not appear in the page numbers, cite as, for example: "late ed., sec. 2: 1+."

9. If your citation continues to a second or subsequent line, double-space that line and indent it one-half inch (five spaces on a typewriter).

See Appendix B for a sample Works Cited list.

```
Jones, John T. "The Truth About Y2K." Los Angeles

     Times 10 Dec. 1998, Orange County ed.: B24+.
```

Figure 86. Example Citation of a Newspaper Article With One Author.

Citing an Article Serialized in a Newspaper

Some articles are serialized over several issues of the newspaper; that is, part of the article appears in one issue and another part or parts appear in another issue or other issues. If the author and title are the same in each installment, you can include all the bibliographic information in one citation. Figure 87 shows an example of this type of citation, which consists of the following elements:

- Author's last name

- Author's first name or initial (and middle name or initial, if available)

- Title of article

- Title of newspaper

- Day, month, and year of publication

- Edition, if applicable

- Page number(s) of article

- Part number of series

- Series title

- Beginning date of series, if not the date of the article referenced

To create this citation, follow these steps:

1. At the left margin, type the author's last name, followed by a comma and a space.

2a. If only the first name or initial is available, follow it with a period and a space.

 b. If the author's middle name or initial is available, however, type the first name, followed by a space. Then type the middle name or initial, followed by a period and then a space.

   NOTE: *Type the authors' names exactly as listed on the work; i.e., if the work lists the names in full, you should, too. If the work lists initials, use those.*

3. Type an opening quotation mark, then the title of the article. Use an initial capital letter on all words except articles and prepositions (unless the the first word is an article or preposition). End the title with a period and a closing quotation mark.

NOTE: If the installments have different titles, list them separately.

4. Type and underline the newspaper title. Capitalize the first letter of all words except articles and prepositions. Delete the first word if it is an article (e.g., "The"). After the title, type a space.

5. Type the date in day, month order. Abbreviate the month using the accepted three-letter abbreviation (see Table 5 on page 22). Follow the abbreviated month with a period and a space or the unabbreviated month (May, June, July) with a space.

6. Type the year of publication followed by a comma and a space.

7. Type the edition of the newspaper (such as "late," "national," "Metro," etc) in lower case letters, unless it is a proper name, followed by a space. Type "edition" as "ed." and follow it with a colon and a space.

8. Type the page number, followed by a period and a space. If the article continues onto another page, put a plus sign immediately after the first page number. Then type a period.

   NOTE: Do not include "p." or "pp." in the page number.

   NOTE: If the newspaper has section numbers, but the section numbers do not appear in the page numbers, cite as, for example: "late ed., sec. 2: 1+."

9. Type "Pt." (for Part) and the part number of the series, followed by a space, then the words "of a series," followed by a comma and a space.

10. Then type the series title, followed by a period.

    NOTE: If this is not the first article in the series, Steps 9 and 10 should read as follows: "Pt. 2 of a series, Lost Cities, begun 20 Mar. 1997."

```
Morrison, Harold. "Where Have All the Cities Gone?"

Los Angeles Times 22 Mar. 1997, morning ed.:

A3+. Pt. 1 of a series, Lost Cities.
```

Figure 87. Example Citation of an Article Serialized in a Newspaper.

Citing a Newspaper Editorial

An editorial is an article, usually written by editor or another staff member of the newspaper that expresses the newspaper's official opinion on some issue. Figure 88 shows an example citation for a newspaper editorial with one author, which consists of the following elements:

- Author's last name

- Author's first name or initial (or middle name or initial, if available)

- Title of editorial

- The word "Editorial"

- Title of newspaper

- Day, month, and year of publication

- Edition, if applicable

- Page number(s) of editorial

To create this citation, follow these steps.

NOTE: If there is no author, begin at the left margin with Step 3.

1. At the left margin, type the author's last name, followed by a comma and a space.

2a. If only the first name or initial is available, follow it with a period and a space.

b. If the author's middle name or initial is available, however, type the first name, followed by a space. Then type the middle name or initial, followed by a period and then a space.

NOTE: Type the authors' names exactly as listed on the work; i.e., if the work lists the names in full, you should, too. If the work lists initials, use those.

NOTE: If the article has more than one author, follow the rules for that number of authors.

3. Type an opening quotation mark, then the title of the editorial. Use an initial capital letter on all words except articles and prepositions (unless the first word is an article or preposition. Type a period, a closing quotation mark, and a space.

4. Type the word "Editorial" followed by a period and a space.

5. Type and underline the newspaper title. Capitalize the first letter of all words except articles and prepositions. Delete the first word if it is an article (e.g., "The"). After the title, type a space.

6. Type the date in day, month order. Abbreviate the month using the accepted three-letter abbreviation (see Table 5 on page 22). Follow the abbreviated month with a period and a space or the unabbreviated month with a space.

7. Type the year of publication followed by a comma and a space.

    NOTE: Do not enclose the year in parentheses.

8. Type the edition of the newspaper (such as "late," "national," "Metro," etc) in lower case letters, unless it is a proper name, followed by a space. Type "edition" as "ed." and follow it with a colon and a space.

9. Type the page number(s), followed by a period.

    NOTE: Do not include "p." or "pp." in the page number.

    NOTE: If the newspaper has section numbers, but the section numbers do not appear in the page numbers, cite as, for example: "late ed., sec. 2: 1+."

10. If your citation continues to a second or subsequent line, double-space that line and indent it one-half inch (five spaces on a typewriter).

    See Appendix B for a sample Works Cited list.

Thompson, John. "To Sue or Not to Sue." Editorial.

Los Angeles Times 2 Mar. 1998, late ed.: 4.

Figure 88. Example Citation of a Newspaper Editorial With One Author.

Citing a Letter to the Editor in a Newspaper

Just as with magazines, newspapers provide space for readers to write letters about articles that have appeared in the publication. These letters usually appear on the "editorial page." Cite a newspaper letter to the editor with one author just as you would a magazine letter to the editor with one author; simply put the newspaper's name in place of the magazine title. A citation for a newspaper article appears as shown in Figure 89 and consists of the following elements:

- Author's last name

- Author's first name (and middle name or initial, if available)

- The phrase "Letter"

- Title of newspaper

- Day, month, and year of newspaper issue

- Page number(s) of article

To create this citation, follow these steps:

1. At the left margin, type the author's last name, followed by a comma and a space.

2a. If only the first name or initial is available, follow it with a period and a space.

b. If the author's middle name or initial is available, however, type the first name, followed by a space. Then type the middle name or initial, followed by a period and then a space.

   NOTE: Type the authors' names exactly as listed on the work; i.e., if the work lists the names in full, you should, too. If the work lists initials, use those.

4. Type the phrase "Letter." Capitalize the "L" on "Letter." End with a period and a space.

5. Type and underline the newspaper title and follow it with a space. Capitalize the first letter of all words except articles and prepositions. Delete the first word if it is an article (e.g., "The").

6. Type the date in day, month order. Abbreviate the month using the accepted three-letter abbreviation (see Table 5 on page 22). Follow the abbreviated month with a period and a space or the unabbreviated month (May, June, July) with a space.

7. Type the year of publication followed by a comma and a space.

    NOTE: Do not enclose the year in parentheses.

8. Type the edition of the newspaper (such as "late," "national," "Metro," etc) in lower case letters, unless it is a proper name, followed by a space. Type "edition" as "ed." and follow it with a colon and a space.

9. Type the page number(s), followed by a period.

    NOTE: Do not include "p." or "pp." in the page number.

9. Type the section number if applicable. Type "sec." followed by a space and the section number, then type a colon and a space.

10. Type the page number, followed by a period.

    NOTE: If the newspaper has section numbers, but the section numbers do not appear in the page numbers, cite as, for example: "late ed., sec. 2: 1."

11. If your citation continues to a second or subsequent line, double-space that line and indent it one-half inch.

    See Appendix B for a sample Works Cited list.

```
Jones, John T. Letter. Los Angeles Times, 10 Dec.

     1993, late ed.: 24.
```

Figure 89. Example Citation of a Letter to the Editor in a Newspaper.

Citing Books

This section shows you how to cite a book with (a/an):

- One author

- Group author (company or agency)

- Editor

- Author and an editor

- No author or editor

- Book with a subtitle

- Multiple publishers

- Multiple volumes

- Brochure or pamphlet

- Proceedings from a conference

- Edition

- Republished book

- Publisher's imprint

and a book

- In a series

- Without stated publication information or pagination

- In a language other than English

- Published before 1900

and

- Two or more books with the same author(s)

- Cross-references

and a/an

- Article in a reference book

- Work in an edited book or anthology

- Translated book

- Introduction, preface, foreward, or afterward

- Book published in a second or subsequent edition

- Presentation in conference proceedings

Citing a Book With One Author

> *NOTE: For citations with more than one author, see the instructions for citing authors' names on pages 89-93.*

A citation for a book with one author appears as shown in Figure 90 and consists of the following elements:

- Author's last name

- Author's first name or initial (and middle name or initial, if available)

- Title of book

- City where publisher is located

- Name of publisher

- Year book was copyrighted

To create this citation, follow these steps:

1. At the left margin, type the author's last name, followed by a comma and a space.

2a. If only the first name or initial is available, follow it with a period and a space.

  b. If the author's middle name or initial is available, however, type the first name, followed by a space. Then type the middle name or initial, followed by a period and a space.

> *NOTE: Type the author's name exactly as listed on the work; i.e., if the work lists the name in full, you should, too. If the work lists initials, use those.*

3. Type and underline the book title. Capitalize the first letter of all words except prepositions and articles (unless the first word is a preposition or an article). Type a period and a space.

4. Type the city of publication, followed by a colon and a space.

5. Type the name of the publisher, followed by a comma and a space. Shorten the publisher's name, if possible; for instance, if the publisher is Harcourt, Brace, Jovanovich, just put "Harcourt."

If the publisher is a university press, or has the word "Press" in its name, just use "U" for "University" and "P" for "Press": "U of Chicago P"; "Oxford UP."

6. Then type the copyright year, followed by a period and a space.

7. If your citation continues to a second or subsequent line, double-space that line and indent it one-half inch (five spaces on a typewriter).

See Appendix B for a sample Works Cited list.

Parris, Crawley A. <u>Mastering Executive Arts and</u>

<u>Skills</u>. New York: Atheneum, 1969.

Figure 90. Example Citation of a Book With One Author.

Citing a Book With a Group Author (Company or Agency)

Some books are published with a company or government agency listed as the author. The American Management Association may publish a book, for instance, and list no author or editor other than itself. On the other hand, the "author" may be a specific group.

A citation for a book with a group author is different from a citation of a book with an author. It appears as shown in Figure 91 and consists of the following elements:

- Name of group

- Title of book

- City where publisher is located

- Name of publisher, if different from the group

- Year book was copyrighted

To create this citation, follow these steps:

1. At the left margin, type the group's name (used in lieu of an author's name), followed by a period and a space.

2. Type and underline the book title. Capitalize the first letter of all words except prepositions and articles (unless the first word is a preposition or an article). Type a space.

3. Type the city of publication, followed by a colon and a space.

4. Type the publisher's name, followed by a comma and a space.

5. Type the copyright year in parentheses, followed by a period.

6. If your citation continues to a second or subsequent line, double-space that line and indent it one-half inch (five spaces on a typewriter).

See Appendix B for a sample Works Cited list.

American Management Association. <u>PCs Today</u>. New York:

American Management Association, 1996.

or

American Management Association. <u>PCs Today</u>. New York:

Adams, 1996.

Figure 91. Example Citations of a Book With a Group Author.

Citing a Book With an Editor

> *NOTE: For citations with more than one editor, see the instructions for citing editors' names on page 96.*

Many times, books are edited rather than authored; that is, they are a collection, such as an anthology or compilation, of articles or stories by other people, that has been put together by another person altogether. The cover and title page of the book will note the editor rather than the writer.

A citation for a book with an editor appears as shown in Figure 92 and consists of the following elements:

- Editor's last name

- Editor's first name or initial (and middle name or initial, if available)

- Phrase "ed."

- Title of book

- City where publisher is located

- Name of publisher

- Year book was copyrighted

To create this citation, follow these steps:

1. At the left margin, type the editor's last name, followed by a comma and a space.

2a. If only the first name or initial is available, follow it with a comma and a space.

b. If the editor's middle name or initial is available, however, type the first name, followed by a space. Then type the middle name followed by a comma and a space, or the initial, followed by a period, a comma, and a space.

   > *NOTE: Type the editor's name exactly as listed on the work; i.e., if the work lists the name in full, you should, too. If the work lists initials, use those.*

3. Type the abbreviation "ed." (for "editor"). Be sure it ends with a period and a space.

4. Type and underline the book title. Capitalize the first letter of all words except prepositions and articles (unless the first word is a preposition or an article). Type a space.

5. Type the city of publication, followed by a colon and a space.

6. Type the name of the publisher, followed by a comma and a space. Shorten the publisher's name, if possible; for instance, if the publisher is Harcourt, Brace, Jovanovich, just put "Harcourt."

    If the publisher is a university press, or has the word "Press" in its name, just use "U" for "University" and "P" for "Press": "U of Chicago P"; "Oxford UP."

7. Type the copyright year in parentheses, followed by a period.

8. If your citation continues to a second or subsequent line, double-space that line and indent it one-half inch (five spaces on a typewriter).

See Appendix B for a sample Works Cited list.

Jones, John Franklin, ed. <u>Authors of the Victorian Age</u>.

New York: Doubleday, 1996.

Figure 92. Example Citation of a Book With an Editor.

Citing a Book With an Author and an Editor

Sometimes, a writer will create new works from those of another author. For instance, a writer might take Shakespeare's plays and put them in a book that has new information or critiques about those plays. In this case, the writer is acting as an "editor," because he or she did not write the original material. The book therefore has an author (the writer of the original material) and an editor (the creator of the new work). Such a book is called an "edition."

When you cite a book with both an author and an editor, the name listed first is the one to which your citations relate. For instance, if you are citing the author's work, cite the author first. If you are citing the editor's notes, critiques, or introduction, for example, cite the editor first.

Citing the Author First

A citation for a book with one author and one editor and citing the author first appears as shown in Figure 93 and consists of the following elements:

- Author's last name

- Author's first name or initials (and middle name or initial, if available)

- Title of book

- Phrase "Ed."

- Editor's first name or initials (and middle name or initial, if available)

- Editor's last name

- City where publisher is located

- Name of publisher

- Year book was copyrighted

To create this citation, follow these steps:

1. At the left margin, type the author's last name, followed by a comma and a space.

2a. If only the first name or initial is available, follow it with a period and a space.

b. If the author's middle name or initial is available, however, type the first name, followed by a space. Then type the middle name or initial, followed by a period and a space.

> *NOTE: Type the author's name exactly as listed on the work; i.e., if the work lists the name in full, you should, too. If the work lists initials, use those.*

3. Type and underline the book title. Capitalize the first letter of all the words except prepositions and articles (unless the first word is a preposition or an article). Then type a period and a space.

4. Type "Ed." followed by a space. Capitalize the "E."

5a. Type the editor's first name, followed by a space, or the first initial, followed by a period and a space.

b. If the editor's middle name or initial is available, type the middle name, followed by a space, or the middle initial, followed by a period and a space.

6. Type the editor's last name, followed by a period and a space.

> *NOTE: Cite two editors as "Eds. Frank G. Taylor and Mary Smith."*

7. Type the city of publication, followed by a colon and a space.

8. Type the name of the publisher, followed by a comma and a space. Shorten the publisher's name, if possible; for instance, if the publisher is Harcourt, Brace, Jovanovich, just put "Harcourt."

   If the publisher is a university press, or has the word "Press" in its name, just use "U" for "University" and "P" for "Press": "U of Chicago P"; "Oxford UP."

9. Type the copyright year, followed by a period.

10. If your citation continues to a second or subsequent line, double-space that line and indent it one-half inch (five spaces on a typewriter).

See Appendix B for a sample Works Cited list.

```
Poe, Edgar Allan. The Murders in the Rue Morgue. Ed.

     Frank G. Taylor. Los Angeles: U of California P,

     1989.
```

Figure 93. Example Book Citation With an Author and an Editor and Citing the Author First.

Citing the Editor First

A citation for a book with both an author and editor and listing the author first appears as shown in Figure 94 and consists of the following elements:

- Editor's last name

- Editor's first name or initials (and middle name or initial, if available)

- Phrase "ed."

- Title of book

- The word "By"

- Author's first name or initials (and middle name or initial, if available)

- Author's last name

- Year author's book was published, if different from that of the current work

- City where publisher is located

- Name of publisher

- Year book was copyrighted

To create this citation, follow these steps:

1. At the left margin, type the editor's last name, followed by a comma and a space.

2a. If only the first name or initial is available, type the first name, followed by a comma and a space, or the first initial, followed by a period and a space.

b. If the editor's middle name or initial is available, however, type the first name, followed by a space, or the first initial, followed by a period, a comma, and a space. Then type the middle name, followed by a comma and a space, or the middle initial, followed by a period, a comma, and a space.

   NOTE: *Type the name exactly as listed on the work; i.e., if the work lists the name in full, you should, too. If the work lists initials, use those.*

3. Type "ed." followed by a space. Make sure the "e" is lowercase.

4. Type and underline the book title. Capitalize the first letter of all the words except prepositions and articles (unless the first word is a preposition or an article). Follow the title with a period and a space.

5. Type the word "By," making sure to capitalize the "B." Follow it with a space.

6a. Type the author's first name, followed by a space, or the first initial, followed by a period and a space.

  b. If the author's middle name or initial is available, however, type the first name, followed by a space, or the first initial, followed by a period and a space. Then type the middle name followed by a space, or the initial, followed by a period and a space.

7. Type the author's last name, followed by a period and a space.

8. Type the city of publication, followed by a colon and a space.

9. Type the year of original publication (if different from that of the current publication), followed by a period and a space.

10. Type the name of the publisher, followed by a comma and a space. Shorten the publisher's name, if possible; for instance, if the publisher is Harcourt, Brace, Jovanovich, just put "Harcourt."

    If the publisher is a university press, or has the word "Press" in its name, just use "U" for "University" and "P" for "Press": "U of Chicago P"; "Oxford UP."

11. Then type the copyright year in parentheses, followed by a period and a space.

12. If your citation continues to a second or subsequent line, double-space that line and indent it one-half inch (five spaces on a typewriter).

See Appendix B for a sample Works Cited list.

```
Taylor, Frank G., ed. The Murders in the Rue Morgue.

     By Edgar Allan Poe. 1841. Los Angeles: U of

     California P, 1996.
```

Figure 94. Example Book Citation With an Author and an Editor Citing the Editor First.

Citing a Book With No Author or Editor

Many books do not list an author or editor at all; they just list the title. Most reference books fall into this category.

A citation for a book with no author is different from one for a book with an author. It appears as shown in Figure 95 and consists of the following elements:

- Title of book

- City where publisher is located

- Publisher's name

- Year book was copyrighted

To create this citation, follow these steps:

1. At the left margin, type and underline the book title, then follow it with a period. Capitalize the first letter of all words except for articles and prepositions (unless the first word is an article or a preposition; i.e., "The").

2. Type the city of publication, followed by a colon and a space.

3. Type the publisher's name, followed by a comma and a space. Shorten the publisher's name, if possible; for instance, if the publisher is Harcourt, Brace, Jovanovich, just put "Harcourt."

    If the publisher is a university press, or has the word "Press" in its name, just use "U" for "University" and "P" for "Press": "U of Chicago P"; "Oxford UP."

4. Type the copyright year, followed by a period.

5. If your citation continues to a second or subsequent line, double-space that line and indent it one-half inch (five spaces on a typewriter).

See Appendix B for a sample Works Cited list.

<u>The Wallace Dictionary</u>. New York: Wallace, 1992.

Figure 95. Example Book Citation With No Author or Editor.

Citing a Book With a Subtitle

What if the book has a subtitle? Figure 96 shows an example citation for a book with a subtitle written by one author. For your citation, follow the rules for the number of authors and/or editors and the type of book per the instructions given in those topics.

Type the title of the book by following these steps:

1. Type the title of the book, followed by a colon and a space.

2. Type the subtitle, followed by a period.

3a. Capitalize the first letter of all words in the title and subtitle, except for articles and prepositions (unless the first word in either the title or the subtitle is an article or preposition; i.e., "The").

 b. Underline all words in the title and subtitle. Do not underline the period.

4. If your citation continues to a second or subsequent line, double-space that line and indent it one-half inch (five spaces on a typewriter).

See Appendix B for a sample Works Cited list.

Bernstein, Thomas M. <u>The Careful Writer: A Modern</u>

<u>Guide to English Usage</u>. New York: Atheneum, 1965.

Figure 96. Example Book Citation With a Subtitle.

Citing a Book in a Series

Books in a series may share the same title but have different sub-titles. For example, the series *Breakthroughs in Science* contains four books: *The Earth*, *Astronomy*, *Inventions*, and *The Human Body*. A citation for a book by one author that is part of a series appears as shown in Figure 97 and consists of the following elements:

- Author's last name

- Author's first name or initial (and middle name or initial, if available)

- Title of book

- Title of series

- The abbreviation "Ser.," if applicable

- Volume number

- City where publisher is located

- Name of publisher

- Year book was copyrighted

To create this citation, follow these steps:

1. At the left margin, type the author's last name, followed by a comma and a space.

2a. If only the first name or initial is available, follow it with a period and a space.

 b. If the author's middle name or initial is available, however, type the first name, followed by a space. Then type the middle name or initial, followed by a period and a space.

 NOTE: *Type the author's name exactly as listed on the work; i.e., if the work lists the name in full, you should, too. If the work lists initials, use those.*

 NOTE: *For citations with more than one author, see the instructions for citing authors' names on pages 89-93.*

3. Type and underline the book title. Capitalize the first letter of all words except prepositions and articles (unless the first word is a preposition or an article). Type a space.

4a. Type the series title, followed by a period and a space. Do not underline the series title.

b. If the word "Series" is part of the name, however, type the series title, followed by a space, then the abbreviation "Ser.," followed by a space. Capitalize the "S" on "Ser."

5. Type the volume number, followed by a period and a space.

6. Type the city of publication, followed by a colon and a space.

7. Type the name of the publisher, followed by a comma and a space. Shorten the publisher's name, if possible; for instance, if the publisher is Harcourt, Brace, Jovanovich, just put "Harcourt."

   If the publisher is a university press, or has the word "Press" in its name, just use "U" for "University" and "P" for "Press": "U of Chicago P"; "Oxford UP."

8. Type the copyright year, followed by a period.

9. If your citation continues to a second or subsequent line, double-space that line and indent it one-half inch (five spaces on a typewriter).

See Appendix B for a sample Works Cited list.

Amato, Carol J. <u>The Earth</u>. Breakthroughs in Science. 3.
    New York: Smithmark, 1992.

or

Crawford, Susan A. <u>Nathaniel Hawthorne</u>. Famous American
    Authors Ser. 24. New York: Adams, 1995.

Figure 97. Example Citations of a Book in a Series.

Citing Two or More Books by the Same Author(s)

As you are creating your Works Cited list, you may discover you have citations from several books by the same author(s). The second and subsequent books follow a slightly different format in your Works Cited list. Such a citation for books by one author appears as shown in Figure 98, and consists of the following elements:

- Three hyphens

- Title of book

- City where publisher is located

- Name of publisher

- Year book was copyrighted

To create this citation, follow these steps:

1. Alphabetize your list by the titles of the books.

2. Assuming the books have only one author, at the left margin, type the citation for the first book according to the rules provided for citing a book with one author.

   NOTE: For citations with more than one author, see the instructions for citing authors' names on pages 89-93.

3. For the second book, at the left margin, type three hyphens, followed by a period and a space.

4. Type and underline the book title. Capitalize the first letter of all words except prepositions and articles (unless the first word is a preposition or an article). Type a space.

5. Type the city of publication, followed by a colon and a space.

6. Type the name of the publisher, followed by a comma and a space. Shorten the publisher's name, if possible; for instance, if the publisher is Harcourt, Brace, Jovanovich, just put "Harcourt."

   If the publisher is a university press, or has the word "Press" in its name, just use "U" for "University" and "P" for "Press": "U of Chicago P"; "Oxford UP."

7.   Type the copyright year, followed by a period.

8.   Repeat Steps 3 through 7 for each subsequent title.

9.   If your citation continues to a second or subsequent line, double-space that line and indent it one-half inch (five spaces on a typewriter).

See Appendix B for a sample Works Cited list.

```
Jones, John. Barrymore the Man. New Haven: Yale UP,

     1992.

---. Crime in the Inner Cities. New York: Adams, 1997.

---. Survival Under Stress. New York: Harcourt, 1995.
```

Figure 98. Example Citations of Two or More Books by the Same Author.

Citing a Work in an Edited Book or Anthology

You may wish to cite an article, essay, poem, short story, or other work within an anthology or book collection. Such a citation appears as shown in Figures 99 and 100 and consists of the following elements:

- Author's last name

- Author's first name or initials (and middle name or initial, if available)

- Title of article, essay, poem, chapter, etc.

- Title of anthology in which the article, essay, etc., appears

- Abbreviation "Ed." For "Edited by"

- Editor's first name or initials (and middle name or initial, if available)

- Editor's last name

- City where publisher is located

- Name of publisher

- Year book was copyrighted

- Pages numbers of article, essay, poem, chapter, etc.

To create this citation, follow these steps:

1. At the left margin, type the author's last name, followed by a comma and a space.

2a. If only the first name or initial is available, follow it with a period and a space.

  b. If the author's middle name or initial is available, however, type the first name, followed by a space. Then type the middle name or initial, followed by a period and a space.

3. Type the title of the cited piece. If it is the first time it has been published, enclose it in quotation marks as shown in Figure 99. If it has been published before as a work of its own, underline it as shown in Figure 100.

4. Type and underline the book title. Capitalize the first letter of all words except prepositions and articles (unless the first word is a preposition or an article). Follow the title with a period and a space.

5. Type the abbreviation "Ed." followed by a space. Capitalize the "E."

6a. Type the editor's first name, followed by a space, or the first initial, followed by a period and a space.

b. If the editor's middle name or initial is available, type the middle name, followed by a space, or the middle initial, followed by a period and a space.

7. Type the editor's last name, followed by a period.

   NOTE: If there are two editors, cite them as "Eds. Frank Taylor and Mary Smith."

8. Type the city of publication, followed by a colon and a space.

9. Type the name of the publisher, followed by a comma and a space. Shorten the publisher's name, if possible; for instance, if the publisher is Harcourt, Brace, Jovanovich, just put "Harcourt."

   If the publisher is a university press, or has the word "Press" in its name, just use "U" for "University" and "P" for "Press": "U of Chicago P"; "Oxford UP."

10. Type the copyright year, followed by a period and a space

11. Type the page number(s), followed by a period.

12. If your citation continues to a second or subsequent line, double-space that line and indent it one-half inch.

See Appendix B for a sample Works Cited list.

Jones, John T. "Lonesome Morning." <u>Anthology of American Literature</u>. Ed. Susan Anderson. New York: Century, 1983. 131-32.

Figure 99. Example Citation of an Original Work in an Anthology.

Poe, Edgar Allan. <u>The Murders in the Rue Morgue</u>. <u>The Unabridged Edgar Allan Poe</u>. Ed. Tam Mossman. Philadelphia: Running Press, 1997. 655-84.

Figure 100. Example Citation of a Reprinted Work in an Anthology.

Citing a Republished Book

Sometimes, books are published more than once. For instance, the book may first be printed as a hardback book, then later as a paperback. The paperback edition is the "republished" book. Usually, but not always, the republication has the same title as the original book. The citations for the two types are different.

Citing a Republished Book With the Same Title as the Original Work

A citation for a republished book with one author that has the same title as the original work appears as shown in Figure 101and consists of the following elements:

- Author's last name

- Author's first name or initial (and middle name or initial, if available)

- Title of book

- Year original book was copyrighted

- City where publisher is located

- Name of publisher

- Year current book was copyrighted

To create this citation, follow these steps:

1. At the left margin, type the author's last name, followed by a comma and a space.

2a. If only the first name or initial is available, follow it with a period and a space.

b. If the author's middle name or initial is available, however, type the first name, followed by a space. Then type the middle name or initial, followed by a period and a space.

   NOTE: *Type the author's name exactly as listed on the work; i.e., if the work lists the name in full, you should, too. If the work lists initials, use those.*

   NOTE: *For citations with more than one author, see the instructions for citing authors' names on pages 89-93.*

3. Type and underline the book title. Capitalize the first letter of all words except prepositions and articles (unless the first word is a preposition or an article). Type a space.

4. Type the copyright year of the original work, followed by a period and a space.

    NOTE: *If you think it is important to include the publication information for the original publication, cite it as shown in Steps 5 through 7.*

5. Type the city of publication, followed by a colon and a space.

6. Type the name of the publisher, followed by a comma and a space. Shorten the publisher's name, if possible; for instance, if the publisher is Harcourt, Brace, Jovanovich, just put "Harcourt."

    If the publisher is a university press, or has the word "Press" in its name, just use "U" for "University" and "P" for "Press": "U of Chicago P"; "Oxford UP."

7. Then type the copyright year, followed by a period and a space.

8. If your citation continues to a second or subsequent line, double-space that line and indent it one-half inch (five spaces on a typewriter).

See Appendix B for a sample Works Cited list.

```
Parris, Crawley A. Mastering Executive Arts and

     Skills. 1990. Englewood Cliffs: Ace, 1993.
```

or

```
Parris, Crawley A. Mastering Executive Arts and

     Skills. New York: Atheneum, 1995. Englewood

     Cliffs: Ace, 1997.
```

Figure 101. Example Citations of a Republished Book With the Same Title as the Original Work.

Citing a Republished Book With a Title Different From the Original Work

A citation for a republished book with one author that has a title different from the original work appears as shown in Figure 102 and consists of the following elements:

- Author's last name

- Author's first name or initial (and middle name or initial, if available)

- Title of book

- City where current publisher is located

- Name of current publisher

- Year current book was copyrighted

- Abbreviation "Rpt. of" ("Reprint of")

- Title of original work

- Year original book was copyrighted

To create this citation, follow these steps:

1. At the left margin, type the author's last name, followed by a comma and a space.

2a. If only the first name or initial is available, follow it with a period and a space.

b. If the author's middle name or initial is available, however, type the first name, followed by a space. Then type the middle name or initial, followed by a period and a space.

   NOTE: *Type the author's name exactly as listed on the work; i.e., if the work lists the name in full, you should, too. If the work lists initials, use those.*

   NOTE: *For citations with more than one author, see the instructions for citing authors' names on pages 89-93.*

3. Type and underline the current book title. Capitalize the first letter of all words except prepositions and articles (unless the first word is a preposition or an article).

4. Type the city of publication for the current work, followed by a colon and a space.

5. Type the name of the current publisher, followed by a comma and a space. Shorten the publisher's name, if possible; for instance, if the publisher is Harcourt, Brace, Jovanovich, just put "Harcourt."

    If the original publisher is a university press, or has the word "Press" in its name, just use "U" for "University" and "P" for "Press": "U of Chicago P"; "Oxford UP."

6. Type the copyright year for the current publication, followed by a period and a space.

7. Type the abbreviation "Rpt. of," followed by a space.

8. Type and underline the original book title. Capitalize the first letter of all words except prepositions and articles (unless the first word is a preposition or an article).

9. Then type the copyright year of the original work, followed by a period.

10. If your citation continues to a second or subsequent line, double-space that line and indent it one-half inch (five spaces on a typewriter.

    See Appendix B for a sample Works Cited list.

Parris, Crawley A. <u>Mastering Executive Arts and Skills</u>. Englewood Cliffs: Ace, 1993. Rpt. of <u>Executive Skills for the 70s</u>. 1974.

Figure 102. Example Citation of a Republished Book With a Title Different From the Original Work.

Citing a Publisher's Imprint

Many publishers have "imprints"; that is, lines of books that fall into the same category. For example, while the publisher itself may publish many types of books, it may group all its textbooks under one imprint, all its mystery books under another imprint, all its westerns under a third, and all its literary books under yet another. Imprint names may sound like publishers' names; consequently, it is easy to mistake them as such. In reality, you must cite both the publisher's and the imprint's name.

A citation for a book with one author published under an imprint appears as shown in Figure 103 and consists of the following elements:

- Author's last name

- Author's first name or initial (and middle name or initial, if available)

- Title of book

- City where publisher is located

- Name of imprint

- Name of publisher

- Year book was copyrighted

To create this citation, follow these steps:

1. At the left margin, type the author's last name, followed by a comma and a space.

2a. If only the first name or initial is available, follow it with a period and a space.

b. If the author's middle name or initial is available, however, type the first name, followed by a space. Then type the middle name or initial, followed by a period and a space.

> *NOTE:* *Type the author's name exactly as listed on the work; i.e., if the work lists the name in full, you should, too. If the work lists initials, use those.*

> *NOTE:* *For citations with more than one author, see the instructions for citing authors' names on pages 89-93.*

3. Type and underline the book title. Capitalize the first letter of all words except prepositions and articles (unless the first word is a preposition or an article). Type a space.

4. Type the city of publication, followed by a colon and a space.

5. Type the imprint name, followed by a hypen.

6. Type the publisher's name, followed by a comma and a space. Shorten the publisher's name, if possible; for instance, if the publisher is Harcourt, Brace, Jovanovich, just put "Harcourt."

    If the original publisher is a university press, or has the word "Press" in its name, just use "U" for "University" and "P" for "Press": "U of Chicago P"; "Oxford UP."

7. Then type the copyright year, followed by a period and a space.

8. If your citation continues to a second or subsequent line, double-space that line and indent it one-half inch (five spaces on a typewriter).

See Appendix B for a sample Works Cited list.

Jones, John. <u>Literary Masterpieces of the 20th Century</u>.

New York: Scribe-Adams, 1995.

Figure 103. Example Citation of a Book With a Publisher's Imprint.

Citing a Book With Multiple Publishers

A book may have more than one publisher. For example, one company may have published a version, then a second may have bought the rights to the book or acquired them by purchasing the first company. Perhaps the first company published a version for sale in the United States, then sold the right to publish another version to a company overseas. When a book has more than one publisher (and don't confuse this with a publishing company that lists more than one office of its own company), you must cite both publishers.

A citation for a book with multiple publishers appears as shown in Figure 104. This example assumes three publishers and consists of the following elements:

- Author's last name

- Author's first name or initial (and middle name or initial, if available)

- Title of book

- Year original book was copyrighted

- City where original publisher is located

- Name of original publisher

- Cities where remaining publishers are located

- Names of remaining publishers

- Year current book was copyrighted

To create this citation, follow these steps:

1. At the left margin, type the author's last name, followed by a comma and a space.

2a. If only the first name or initial is available, follow it with a period and a space.

 b. If the author's middle name or initial is available, however, type the first name, followed by a space. Then type the middle name or initial, followed by a period and a space.

NOTE: *Type the authors' names exactly as listed on the work; i.e., if the work lists the names in full, you should, too. If the work lists initials, use those.*

NOTE: *For citations with more than one author, see the instructions for citing authors' names on pages 89-93.*

3.   Type and underline the book title. Capitalize the first letter of all words except prepositions and articles (unless the first word is a preposition or an article).

4.   Type the copyright year for the original book, followed by a period and a space.

5.   Type the city of publication for the original book, followed by a colon and a space.

6.   Type the name of the original publisher, followed by a semicolon and a space. Shorten the publisher's name, if possible; for instance, if the publisher is Harcourt, Brace, Jovanovich, just put "Harcourt."

   If the original publisher is a university press, or has the word "Press" in its name, just use "U" for "University" and "P" for "Press": "U of Chicago P"; "Oxford UP."

7.   Repeat Steps 5 and 6 for the all remaining publishers except the last.

8.   For the last publisher, repeat Step 5. Then type the name of the publisher, followed by a comma and a space.

9.   Type the copyright year for the current publication, followed by a period.

10.   If your citation continues to a second or subsequent line, double-space that line and indent it one-half inch (five spaces on a typewriter).

See Appendix B for a sample Works Cited list.

```
Johnson, Martha. The Master Spy. 1948. New York:

   Doubleday; London: Ace; Englewood Cliffs:

   Collins, 1997.
```

Figure 104. Example Citation of a Book With Multiple Publishers.

Citing a Book Without Stated Publication Information or Pagination

Sometimes, a book will not list all the information you need to cite it; for example, the publisher's name, location, or copyright year may be missing, or all of this information may be missing. If the author is still living, you may be able to call him or her for the missing information. If the publisher's name is included and it is still in business, try calling it for the information you need.

Table 24 shows the abbreviations you can use in your citations to substitute for the missing information.

Table 24. Abbreviations for Citations With Missing Information.

EXPLANATION	ABBREVIATION
No place of publication given	n.p.
No publisher given	n.p.
No date of publication given	n.d.
No pagination given	n. pag.

Follow the regular instructions for the type of book and number of authors, but substitute the missing information abbreviation in the location where that information would have appeared. Figure 105 shows examples.

NOTE: When the abbreviation begins a new phrase (follows a phrase that ends with a period), the "N" is capitalized.

Date Accurate But From Another Source

If you know the date the book was published, but you got the information from source other than the book itself, put it in brackets to indicate that: [1985]. (See the first example in Figure 106).

Date Accuracy in Question

If you aren't sure that the date is accurate, add a question mark and place the date in brackets (see the second example in Figure 106.

Date Approximated

If you can only approximate the date, enclose it in brackets to show that the information did not come from the original source (see first example in Figure 105). You can also add a "c.," which means "circa" (around): [c. 1920]. (See the third example in Figure 106).

Kennedy, Mary Ann. The Loving Years. N.p.: Barrows,
1935.

Kennedy, Mary Ann. The Loving Years. New York: n.p.,
1935.

Kennedy, Mary Ann. The Loving Years. New York:
Barrows, n.d.

Kennedy, Mary Ann. Photos From the Rooftops.
New York: Barrows, 1938. N. pag.

Figure 105. Example Citations With Missing Information.

Kennedy, Mary Ann. The Loving Years. New York:
Barrows, [1935].

Kennedy, Mary Ann. The Loving Years. New York:
Barrows, [1935?].

Kennedy, Mary Ann. The Loving Years. New York:
Barrows, [c. 1935].

Figure 106. Example Citations With an Approximated Date.

Citing a Book in a Language Other Than English

You may have to cite a book written in a foreign language. Use the rules for citing the type of book and the number of authors just as you would a book written in English. The publication information may be at the back of the book on the last page, however, rather than on the front and back of the inside title page.

If you think your readers will be confused by the foreign title of the book, place its English translation in brackets after the foreign title per the example shown in Figure 107. In addition, translate the name of the city, as shown in Figure 108, if you think this will help your reader better understand the citation. You may leave out the foreign name of the city and use the English version by itself, if you wish (see Figure 109).

```
Saint-Exupéry, Antoine de. Le Petit Prince [The

    Little Prince]. 1946. Paris: Gallimard, 1964.
```

Figure 107. Example Citation of a Book in a Foreign Language With the Title Translated into English for Clarification.

NOTE: Since the above book was originally published in 1946, this citation follows the rules for citing a republished book.

```
Dupont, Jean Pierre. Gaie Paris. Bruxelles [Brussels]:

    Joie, 1983.
```

Figure 108. Example Citation of a Book in a Foreign Language With the City of Publication Translated into English for Clarification.

```
Dupont, Jean Pierre. Gaie Paris. Brussels: Joie, 1983.
```

Figure 109. Example Citation of a Book in a Foreign Language With the English Name of the City of Publication Substituted for Clarification.

Citing a Book Published Before 1900

Since the publishers of books published before 1900 are probably no longer in business, you may leave out the publisher's name for such a citation.

Type the city of publication, followed by a comma, a space, and the year of publication as shown in Figure 110.

```
Danson, Gerald. Mythology in Ancient Greece. New

    York, 1894.
```

Figure 110. Example Citation of a Book Published Before 1900.

Citing a Brochure or Pamphlet

To cite a brochure or pamphlet, follow the rules for book citations with the same type of information; i.e., to cite a brochure or pamphlet with no author, follow the rules for citing a book with no author; to cite a brochure or pamphlet with a group author, follow the rules for citing a book with a group author, etc.

Citing a Translated Book

Many foreign books are translated into English. The book will then list a translator, and possibly an editor, in addition to the author. Figure 111 shows an example of a citation for a translated book with one author and a translator and Figure 112 an example of a translated book with one author, a translator, and an editor. List the translator and editor in the order in which their names appear on the book.

A citation for a translated book with one author consists of the following elements:

- Author's last name

- Author's first name or initial (and middle name or initial, if available)

- Title of book

- Abbreviation "Trans." for "Translated by"

- Translator's first name or initial (and middle name or initial, if available)

- Translator's last name

- Abbreviation "Ed." for "Edited by" (if applicable)

- Editor's first name or initial (and middle name or initial, if available) (if applicable)

- Editor's last name (if applicable)

- City where publisher is located

- Name of publisher

- Year book was copyrighted

To create this citation, follow these steps:

1. At the left margin, type the author's last name, followed by a comma and a space.

2a. If only the first name or initial is available, follow it with a period and a space.

b. If the author's middle name or initial is available, however, type the first name, followed by a space. Then type the middle name or initial, followed by a period and a space.

3. Type and underline the book title. Capitalize the first letter of all words except prepositions and articles (unless the first word is a preposition or an article). Type a space.

4. Type the abbreviation "Trans." followed by a space.

5. Type the translator's first name, and middle name, if available, following the rules in Step 2. Follow it with a space.

6. Type the translator's last name, followed by a period and a space. If there is no editor, skip to Step 10. If there is an editor, however, go to Step 7.

7. Type the abbreviation "Ed." and follow it with a space (see Figure 112).

8. Type the editor's first name, and middle name, if available, following the rules in Step 2. Follow the name with a space.

9. Type the editor's last name, followed by a period and a space.

10. Type the city of publication, followed by a colon and a space.

11. Type the name of the publisher, followed by a period. Shorten the publisher's name, if possible; for instance, if the publisher is Harcourt, Brace, Jovanovich, just put "Harcourt."

12. Then type the copyright year, followed by a period and a space.

13. If your citation continues to a second or subsequent line, double-space that line and indent it one-half inch (five spaces on a typewriter).

See Appendix B for a sample Works Cited list.

Saint-Exupéry, Antoine de. <u>The Little Prince</u>. Trans.

Judy Applegate. New York: Duo, 1984.

Figure 111. Example Citation of a Translated Book With a Translator.

Androvsky, Yuri. <u>Letters From Moscow</u>. Trans. Judy

Smith. Ed. Gerald Jensen. New York: Duo, 1992.

Figure 112. Example Citation of a Translated Book With a Translator and an Editor.

Citing a Multivolume Work

When citing a multivolume work, be sure to include the volume number and the page numbers. Figure 113 shows an example of a multivolume work with one author. Figure 114 shows an example citation for a multivolume work with an editor, and Figure 115 shows an example with an author and an editor.

A citation for a multivolume work with one author consists of the following elements:

- Author's last name

- Author's first name or initial (and middle name or initial, if available)

- Title of book

- Number of volumes

- City where publisher is located

- Name of publisher

- Year book was copyrighted

To create this citation, follow these steps:

1. Referring to Figure 113, at the left margin, type the author's last name, followed by a comma and a space.

2a. If only the first name or initial is available, follow it with a period and a space.

 b. If the author's middle name or initial is available, however, type the first name, followed by a space. Then type the middle name or initial, followed by a period and a space.

3a. Type and underline the book title. Capitalize the first letter of all words except prepositions and articles (unless the first word is a preposition or an article). Follow it with a space.

 b. If you are using two or more volumes, go to Step 4. If you are using only one volume, skip to Step 6.

4. If you are using two or more volumes from the set, use an arabic numeral to type the number of volumes you have cited, followed by a space.

5.   Type the abbreviation "vols." followed by a space. Be sure the "v" is lowercase.

6.   Type the city of publication, followed by a colon and a space.

7.   Type the name of the publisher, followed by a comma and a space. Shorten the publisher's name, if possible; for instance, if the publisher is Harcourt, Brace, Jovanovich, just put "Harcourt."

8.   Type the copyright year, followed by a period and a space.

9.   If your citation continues to a second or subsequent line, double-space that line and indent it one-half inch.

See Appendix B for a sample Works Cited list.

Lopez, Anthony. The Illustrated Shakespeare. 3 vols.

New York: Random House, 1993.

Figure 113. Example Citation of a Multivolume Work With One Author.

Simpson, Jane, ed. The Collected Works of Mark

Twain. 3 vols. New York: Random House, 1993.

Figure 114. Example Citation of a Multivolume Work With One Editor.

Lopez, Anthony. The Collected Works of Edgar Allan

Poe. Ed. Jane Simpson. 2nd ed. 3 vols. New

York: Random House, 1993.

Figure 115. Example Citation of a Multivolume Work With One Author and One Editor.

Citing an Introduction, Preface, Foreword, or Afterword

The author of the work may also write the introduction, preface, foreword, or afterword to the work. Many times, however, one or more of these pieces is written by someone other than the author. This section shows you how to cite an introduction, preface, foreword, or afterword:

- Written by the author

- Written by someone other than the author

Written by the Author

Figure 116 shows an introduction written by the author and consists of the following elements:

- Author's last name

- Author's first name or initial (and middle name or initial, if available)

- Title of the piece

- Title of book

- The word "By" and the author's last name

- City where publisher is located

- Name of publisher

- Year book was copyrighted

- Page numbers of piece

1. Referring to the first example in Figure 116, at the left margin, type the author's last name, followed by a comma and a space.

2a. If only the first name or initial is available, follow it with a period and a space.

b. If the author's middle name or initial is available, however, type the first name, followed by a space. Then type the middle name or initial, followed by a period and a space.

   NOTE: *Type the author's name exactly as listed on the work; i.e., if the work lists the name in full, you should, too. If the work lists initials, use those.*

> *NOTE:*   *For citations with more than one author, see the instructions for citing authors' names on pages 89-93.*

3.   Type the title of the piece, followed by a period and a space.

> *NOTE: Do not underline the title of the piece, nor enclose it in quotation marks.*

4.   Type and underline the book title. Capitalize the first letter of all words except prepositions and articles (unless the first word is a preposition or an article). Type a period and a space.

5.   Type the word "By," followed by a space.

6.   Type the author's last name, followed by a period and a space.

7.   Type the city of publication, followed by a colon and a space.

8.   Type the name of the publisher, followed by a comma and a space. Shorten the publisher's name, if possible; for instance, if the publisher is Harcourt, Brace, Jovanovich, just put "Harcourt."

   If the original publisher is a university press, or has the word "Press" in its name, just use "U" for "University" and "P" for "Press": "U of Chicago P"; "Oxford UP."

9.   Type the copyright year, followed by a period and a space.

10.   Type the page numbers, followed by a period.

11.   If your citation continues to a second or subsequent line, double-space that line and indent it one-half inch (five spaces on a typewriter).

   See Appendix B for a sample Works Cited list.

```
Johnson, Sarah. Introduction. The Illustrated

Shakespeare. By Johnson. New York: Doubleday,

1993. iv-v.
```

Figure 116. Example Citation of an Introduction Written by the Author of the Work.

Written by Someone Other Than the Author

Figure 117 shows an introduction written by someone other than the author and consists of the following elements:

- Last name of author of the piece

- First name or initial (and middle name or initial, if available) of the author of the piece

- Title of the piece

- Title of book

- The word "By" and the author of the work's first name or initial (and middle name or initial, if available) and last name

- City where publisher is located

- Name of publisher

- Year book was copyrighted

- Page numbers of piece

1. At the left margin, type the last name of the author of the piece, followed by a comma and a space.

2a. If only the first name or initial is available, follow it with a period and a space.

b. If the middle name or initial is available for the author of the piece, however, type the first name, followed by a space. Then type the middle name or initial, followed by a period and a space.

   NOTE: *Type the author's name exactly as listed on the work; i.e., if the work lists the name in full, you should, too. If the work lists initials, use those.*

   NOTE: *For citations with more than one author, see the instructions for citing authors' names on pages 89-93.*

3. Type the title of the piece, followed by a period and a space.

   NOTE: *Do not underline the title of the piece, nor enclose it in quotation marks.*

4. Type and underline the book title. Capitalize the first letter of all words except prepositions and articles (unless the first word is a preposition or an article). Type a period and a space.

5. Type the word "By," followed by a space.

6a. Type the first name of the author of the work, followed by a space. If only the first initial is available, follow it with a period and a space.

   b. If the author's middle name is available, follow it with a space. If only the middle initial is available, however, type it, followed by a period and a space.

7. Type the author's last name, followed by a period and a space.

8. Type the city of publication, followed by a colon and a space.

9. Type the name of the publisher, followed by a comma and a space. Shorten the publisher's name, if possible; for instance, if the publisher is Harcourt, Brace, Jovanovich, just put "Harcourt."

   If the original publisher is a university press, or has the word "Press" in its name, just use "U" for "University" and "P" for "Press": "U of Chicago P"; "Oxford UP."

10. Type the copyright year, followed by a period and a space.

11. Type the page numbers, followed by a period.

12. If your citation continues to a second or subsequent line, double-space that line and indent it one-half inch (five spaces on a typewriter).

See Appendix B for a sample Works Cited list.

Derrick, David. Introduction. <u>The Illustrated</u>

<u>Shakespeare</u>. By Sarah Johnson. New York:

Doubleday, 1993. ii-iii.

Figure 117. Example Citation of an Introduction Written by Someone Other Than the Author of the Work.

Citing a Second or Subsequent Edition of a Book

The first publication of a book is the first edition, although the title page will never state these words. Only subsequent editions of the work will specify its edition. A book may be reprinted many times if none of the content changes. When the content does change, however, the book must be published as a new edition (2nd edition, 3rd edition, etc.).

A citation for a book with one author published in a second or subsequent edition is shown in Figure 118 and consists of the following elements:

- Author's last name

- Author's first name or initial (and middle name or initial, if available)

- Title of book

- Edition number

- City where publisher is located

- Name of publisher

- Year book was copyrighted

To create this citation, follow these steps:

1. At the left margin, type the author's last name, followed by a comma and a space.

2a. If only the first name or initial is available, follow it with a period and a space.

 b. If the author's middle name or initial is available, however, type the first name, followed by a space. Then type the middle name or initial, followed by a period and a space.

   NOTE: *Type the author's name exactly as listed on the work; i.e., if the work lists the name in full, you should, too. If the work lists initials, use those.*

   NOTE: *For citations with more than one author, see the instructions for citing authors' names on pages 89-93.*

3. Type and underline the book title. Capitalize the first letter of all words except prepositions and articles (unless the first word is a preposition or an article). Then type a period and a space.

4. Type the edition number in abbreviated format (i.e., 2nd, 3rd, 4th, etc.) followed by a space. Then type the abbreviation "ed.," followed by a space.

5. Type the city of publication, followed by a colon and a space.

6. Type the name of the publisher, followed by a comma and a space. Shorten the publisher's name, if possible; for instance, if the publisher is Harcourt, Brace, Jovanovich, just put "Harcourt."

    If the publisher is a university press, or has the word "Press" in its name, just use "U" for "University" and "P" for "Press": "U of Chicago P"; "Oxford UP."

7. Then type the copyright year, followed by a period.

8. If your citation continues to a second or subsequent line, double-space that line and indent it one-half inch (five spaces on a typewriter).

See Appendix B for a sample Works Cited list.

Parris, Crawley A. <u>Mastering Executive Arts and
    Skills</u>. 2nd ed. New York: Atheneum, 1975.

Figure 118. Example Citation of a Second Edition of a Book.

Citing Cross-References

If you are citing several pieces in an anthology or other collection, you can cite the entire reference once under the editor's or editors' name(s), then use a shortened form of the reference, called a "cross-reference," when citing the individual pieces.

A citation for a cross-reference with one author and one editor is shown in Figure 119 and consists of the following elements:

- Last name of author of the piece

- First name or initial (and middle name or initial, if available) of the author of the piece

- Title of the piece

- Editor's last name

- Page numbers of the piece

1. At the left margin, type the last name of the author of the piece, followed by a comma and a space.

2a. If only the first name or initial is available, follow it with a period and a space.

b. If the middle name or initial is available for the author, however, type the first name, followed by a space. Then type the middle name or initial, followed by a period and a space.

3a. Type the title of the piece, followed by a period and a space.

b. If it is an article, poem, essay, or other work, however, enclose it in quotation marks (see Figure 119).

c. If it is the introduction, preface, foreword, or afterword, do not underline the piece, nor enclose it in quotation marks. (See Figure 120).

4. Type the author's last name, followed by a space.

5. Type the page numbers, followed by a period.

6. If your citation continues to a second or subsequent line, double-space that line and indent it one-half inch (five spaces on a typewriter).

Figure 121 shows other examples of cross-references with their companion full reference. See Appendix B for a sample Works Cited list.

NOTE: *If you cite two or more works for the same editor, add the complete or a shortened version of the title to the cross-reference (see Figure 121 for an example).*

Everett, Susan. "Early One Sunday." Pierson 133-34.

Figure 119. Example Citation of a Cross-Reference of a Piece in a Work With an Editor.

Derrick, David. Foreword. Pierson ii-iii.

Figure 120. Example Citation of a Cross-Reference of a Foreward.

Derrick, David. Foreword. Johnson ii-iii.

Everett, Susan. "Early One Sunday." Pierson, <u>Seren-dipity</u> 133-34.

Johnson, Dylan W. <u>Shades of Gray</u>. Baltimore: Dove, 1997.

Kennedy, Jeremy T. "Another Life." Pierson, <u>Authors</u> 87-88.

Pierson, Louise, ed. <u>Authors of the 90s</u>. New York: Doubleday, 1993.

---, ed. <u>Sweet Serendipity</u>. New York: Doubleday, 1995.

Figure 121. Example Citation of Cross-References With Their Companion Full Reference.

Citing Proceedings From a Conference

Whenever a professional association holds a conference, it usually publishes "proceedings" from the conference—a book containing all the abstracts and/or papers that were presented at the conference. Cite the proceedings like a book, but add the information about the conference itself.

You can cite proceedings in two ways depending upon how the title is structured:

- Proceedings title gives all the information about the conference.

- Proceedings title does not give information about the conference.

NOTE: *If you are citing a presentation in the proceedings, cite it as you would a work in an anthology (see pages 146-147).*

Proceedings Title Gives All the Information About the Conference

A citation for a proceedings with one editor and whose title gives all the information about the conference is shown in Figure 122 and consists of the following elements:

- Editor's last name

- Editor's first name or initial (and middle name or initial, if available)

- Abbreviation "ed."

- Title of proceedings

- City where publisher is located

- Name of publisher

- Year proceedings were copyrighted

To create this citation, follow these steps:

1. At the left margin, type the editor's last name, followed by a comma and a space.

2a. If only the first name or initial is available, follow it with a period and a space.

b. If the middle name or initial is available, however, type the first name, followed by a comma and a space. Then type the middle name or initial, followed by a period, a comma, and a space.

> *NOTE:*   *Type the editor's name exactly as listed on the work; i.e., if the work lists the name in full, you should, too. If the work lists initials, use those.*

> *NOTE:*   *For citations with more than one editor, see the instructions for citing editors' names on page 96.*

3. Type the abbreviation "ed." followed by a space.

4. Type and underline the proceedings title. Capitalize the first letter of all words except prepositions and articles (unless the first word is a preposition or an article). Type a period and a space.

5. Type the city of publication, followed by a colon and a space.

6. Type the name of the publisher, followed by a comma and a space. Shorten the publisher's name, if possible; for instance, if the publisher is Harcourt, Brace, Jovanovich, just put "Harcourt."

   If the publisher is a university press, or has the word "Press" in its name, just use "U" for "University" and "P" for "Press": "U of Chicago P"; "Oxford UP."

7. Then type the copyright year, followed by a period and a space.

8. If your citation continues to a second or subsequent line, double-space that line and indent it one-half inch (five spaces on a typewriter).

See Appendix B for a sample Works Cited list.

```
Amato, Carol J., ed. Proceedings of the Third National

Conference on Excellence in Education, November 3,

1997. Costa Mesa: U of Phoenix, 1997.
```

Figure 122. Example Citation of Proceedings of a Conference in Which the Proceedings Title Contains Information About the Conference.

Proceedings Title Does Not Provide Information About the Conference

A citation for a proceedings with one editor whose title does not provide information about the conference is shown in Figure 123 and consists of the following elements:

- Editor's last name

- Editor's first name or initial (and middle name or initial, if available)

- Abbreviation "ed."

- Title of proceedings

- Abbreviation "Proc. of" (for "Proceedings of")

- Title of conference

- Date of conference

- Name of sponsoring organization

- City where publisher is located

- Name of publisher

- Year proceedings were copyrighted

To create this citation, follow these steps:

1. At the left margin, type the editor's last name, followed by a comma and a space.

2a. Type the editor's first name, followed by a comma and a space. If only the first initial is available, follow it with a period, a comma, and a space.

  b. If the editor's middle name or initial is available, however, type the first name, followed by a space. Then type the middle name, followed by a comma, or the middle initial, followed by a period, a comma, and a space.

3. Type the abbreviation "ed." followed by a space.

4. Type and underline the proceedings title. Capitalize the first letter of all words except prepositions and articles (unless the first word is a preposition or an article). Follow the title with a period and a space.

5. Type the abbreviation "Proc. of" followed by a space.

6. Type the title of the conference, followed by a comma and a space.

7. Type the date of the conference in day, month (abbreviated per Table 5 on page 22), year format. Follow the abbreviation with a comma and a space.

8. Type the year of the conference, followed by a comma and a space.

9. Type the name of the sponsoring organization, followed by a period and a space. If the sponsoring organization is a university, abbreviate "University" as "U."

10. Type the city of publication, followed by a colon and a space.

11. Type the name of the publisher, followed by a comma and a space. Shorten the publisher's name, if possible; for instance, if the publisher is Harcourt, Brace, Jovanovich, just put "Harcourt."

    If the publisher is a university press, or has the word "Press" in its name, just use "U" for "University" and "P" for "Press": "U of Chicago P"; "Oxford UP."

12. Then type the copyright year, followed by a period and a space.

13. If your citation continues to a second or subsequent line, double-space that line and indent it one-half inch (five spaces on a typewriter).

    See Appendix B for a sample Works Cited list.

Nelson, Lars, ed. <u>Techniques for Teaching Phonics</u>.

Proc. of Tenth Annual Meeting of the Society

for Elementary Education, 15 Nov. 1996, Bayside

U. San Francisco: Perkins, 1997.

Figure 123. Example Citation of Conference Proceedings in Which the Proceedings Title Does Not Contain Information About the Conference.

Citing a Presentation in the Proceedings

A citation for a presentation in the proceedings is shown in Figure 124 and consists of the following elements:

- Presenter's last name

- Presenter's first name or initial (and middle name or initial, if available)

- Title of presentation

- Title of proceedings

- Abbreviation "Ed."

- Editor's first name or initial (and middle name or initial, if available)

- Editor's last name

- City where publisher is located

- Name of publisher

- Year proceedings were copyrighted

- Page numbers of presentation

To create this citation, follow these steps:

1. At the left margin, type the presenter's last name, followed by a comma and a space.

2a. If only the first name or initial is available, follow it with a period and a space.

  b. If the middle name or initial is available, however, type the first name, followed by a comma and a space. Then type the middle name or initial, followed by a period, a comma, and a space.

   NOTE: *Type the persenter's name exactly as listed on the work; i.e., if the work lists the name in full, you should, too. If the work lists initials, use those.*

   NOTE: *For citations with more than one presenter, see the instructions for citing authors' names on pages 90-93.*

3. Type an opening presenthesis, the title of the presentation, a period, a closing parenthesis, and a space.

4. Type and underline the proceedings title. Capitalize the first letter of all words except prepositions and articles (unless the first word is a preposition or an article). Type a period and a space.

5. Type the abbreviation "Ed." followed by a space.

6a. Type the editor's first name, followed by a space. If only the first initial is available, follow it with a period and a space.

b. If the editor's middle name is available, follow it with a space. If only the editor's middle initial is available, follow it with a period and a space.

c. Type the editor's last name, followed by a period and a space.

7. Type the city of publication, followed by a colon and a space.

8. Type the name of the publisher, followed by a comma and a space. Shorten the publisher's name, if possible; for instance, if the publisher is Harcourt, Brace, Jovanovich, just put "Harcourt."

    If the publisher is a university press, or has the word "Press" in its name, just use "U" for "University" and "P" for "Press": "U of Chicago P"; "Oxford UP."

9. Then type the copyright year, followed by a period and a space.

10. Type the page number(s) of the presentation, followed by a period.

11. If your citation continues to a second or subsequent line, double-space that line and indent it one-half inch (five spaces on a typewriter).

See Appendix B for a sample Works Cited list.

```
Slobodzian, Kurt. "Expanded Access." Proceedings of

    the Third National Conference on Excellence in

    Education, November 3, 1997. Ed. Carol J. Amato.

    Costa Mesa: U of Phoenix, 1997. 49-54.
```

Figure 124. Example Citation of a Presentation from the Proceedings of a Conference.

Citing Encyclopedias, Dictionaries, and Reference Books

Cite articles in encyclopedias, dictionaries, or reference books as you would a work from an anthology. The elements needed for a citation for an encyclopedia set, dictionary, or reference book with one author appear as shown in the examples in Figure 125. If it is a well-known source, not all the elements below are necessary per Step 5. If it is not a well-known source, however, use as many of the following elements as are relevant:

- Author's last name

- Author's first name or initial (and middle name or initial, if available)

- Title of piece

- Title of encyclopedia set, dictionary, or reference book

- Edition number, if applicable

- Number of volumes used, if applicable, and the abbreviation "vols."

- City where publisher is located

- Name of publisher

- Year book was copyrighted

To create this citation, follow these steps:

NOTE: If there is no author, begin at the left margin with Step 3.

1. At the left margin, type the author's last name, followed by a comma and a space.

2a. If only the first name or initial is available, follow it with a period and a space.

 b. If the author's middle name or initial is available, however, type the first name, followed by a space. Then type the middle name or initial, followed by a period and a space.

  NOTE: *Type the author's name exactly as listed on the work; i.e., if the work lists the name in full, you should, too. If the work lists initials, use those.*

  NOTE: *For citations with more than one author, see the instructions for citing authors' names on pages 89-93.*

3. Type an opening quotation mark, the article title, a period, and a closing quotation mark, followed by a space.

4. Type and underline the encyclopedia, dictionary, or reference book title. Capitalize the first letter of all words except prepositions and articles (unless the first word is a preposition or an article). Follow it with a period and a space.

5. Type the edition number, if applicable, in abbreviated format (i.e., 2nd, 3rd, 4th, etc.) followed by a space. Then type the abbreviation "ed," followed by a period and a space.

6. If the book you are citing is well-known, skip to Step 9. If it is not, type the number of volumes you used (if two or more), then a space, then the abbreviation "vols." in lower case, followed by a space.

7. Type the city of publication, followed by a colon and a space.

8. Type the name of the publisher, followed by a comma and a space. Shorten the publisher's name, if possible; for instance, if the publisher is Harcourt, Brace, Jovanovich, just put "Harcourt."

9. Type the copyright year, followed by a period and a space.

10. If your citation continues to a second or subsequent line, double-space that line and indent it one-half inch (five spaces on a typewriter).

See Appendix B for a sample Works Cited list.

Smith, Ronald. "The Dying Rain Forests." <u>The New Encyclopedia Britannica</u>. 16th ed. 1994.

Jones, Thomas. "Bits, Bytes, and Megabytes." <u>Dictionary of Computer Terms</u>. 2nd ed. 2 vols. New York: Times Books, 1997.

Figure 125. Example Citations From a Well-Known and Not Well-Known Encyclopedia Set and Dictionary With One Author.

Citing Academic Material

This section shows you how to cite published and unpublished doctoral dissertations and abstracts and abstracts from professional journals.

Citing Abstracts

An abstract is a short summary that gives an overview of an article's content so that professionals or students can see quickly whether the article is relevant to their needs. Readers can then look up the full text. Abstracts usually are for published dissertations or published articles from professional journals.

Citing an Abstract for a Published Dissertation

A citation for an abstract from a dissertation is shown in Figure 126 and consists of the following elements:

- Author's last name

- Author's first name or initial (and middle name or initial, if available)

- Title of dissertation

- The abbreviation "Diss."

- University for which dissertation was written

- Year of publication

- Title of abstracts journal

- Volume number

- Year of publication

- Page or item number(s)

To create this citation, follow these steps:

1. At the left margin, type the author's last name, followed by a comma and a space.

2a. If only the first name or initial is available, follow it with a period and a space.

b. If the author's middle name or initial is available, however, type the first name, followed by a space. Then type the middle name or initial, followed by a period and a space.

3. Type an opening quotation mark, the title of the article the abstract is from, a period, a closing quotation mark, and then a space. Capitalize the first letter of all words except for articles and prepositions (unless the first word is an article or preposition).

4. Type the abbreviation "Diss." for "Dissertation," followed by a space.

5. Type the name of the university for which the dissertation was written. Use the abbreviation "U" for "University." Then type a comma and a space.

6. Type the year of the dissertation's publication, followed by a period and a space.

   NOTE: Do not enclose the year in parentheses.

7. Type and underline the abstracts journal title, followed by a space. Capitalize the first letter of all words except for articles and prepositions. (Delete the first word if it is an article; e.g., "The.")

   NOTE: If the publication is Dissertation Abstracts *or* Dissertation Abstracts International, *you may abbreviate the title as DA or DAI.*

8. Type the volume number, followed by a space.

9. Type an opening parenthesis, the year of publication, a closing parenthesis, then a colon and a space.

10. Type the item number or page number(s), followed by a period.

11. If your citation continues to a second or subsequent line, double-space that line and indent it one-half inch (five spaces on a typewriter).

See Appendix B for a sample Works Cited list.

```
Jones, James T. "The Effects of Bottom-up Management

    Techniques on Clerical Employees in Five High-tech

    Companies." Diss. U of California, Berkeley, 1996.

    DA 54 (1998): 2456B.
```

Figure 126. Example Citation of an Abstract From a Published Dissertation.

Citing an Abstract for an Article From a Professional Journal

A citation for an abstract for an article that originally appeared in a professional journal is shown in the first example in Figure 127 and consists of the following elements:

- Author's last name

- Author's first name or initial (and middle name or initial, if available)

- Title of article abstract is from

- Title of original source

- Volume number

- Year of publication

- Page number(s)

- Title of abstracts journal

- Volume number

- Year of publication

- Page or item number(s)

To create this citation, follow these steps:

1. At the left margin, type the author's last name, followed by a comma and a space.

2a. If only the first name or initial is available, follow it with a period and a space.

b. If the author's middle name or initial is available, however, type the first name, followed by a space. Then type the middle name or initial, followed by a period and then a space.

3. Type an opening quotation mark, the title of the article the abstract is from, a period, a closing quotation mark, and then a space. Capitalize the first letter of all words except for articles and prepositions (unless the first word is an article or preposition).

4. Type and underline the title of the journal in which the article originally appeared. Capitalize the first letter of all words except for articles and prepositions. (Delete the first word if it is an article; e.g., "The.") Then type a space.

5. Type the volume number followed by a space.

6. Type an opening parenthesis, the year of publication, a closing parenthesis, a colon, and a space.

7. Type the page number(s), followed by a period and a space.

8. Type and underline the title of the original publication in which the work appeared, followed by a space. Capitalize the first letter of all words except for articles and prepositions. (Delete the first word if it is an article; e.g., "The.")

9. Type and underline the title of the abstracts journal, followed by a space.

   NOTE: If the title of the abstracts journal or periodical itself does not include the word "abstracts," type "Abstract," followed by a period and a space, then the title of the abstracts journal as shown in the second example in Figure 127.

10. Type the volume number, followed by a space.

11. Type an opening parenthesis, the year of publication, a closing parenthesis, a colon, and a space.

12. Type the page number(s) or the word "item" and the item number, followed by a period.

13. If your citation continues to a second or subsequent line, double-space that line and indent it one-half inch (five spaces on a typewriter).

See Appendix B for a sample Works Cited list.

Smith, Herbert N. "Five prehistoric sites in Orange

County, California." Southwest Archeologist 24

(1996): 245. Southwest Archaelogist Abstracts 36

(1997): 178.

Smith, Herbert N. "Five prehistoric sites in Orange

County, California." Southwest Archaeologist 24

(1996): 245. Abstract. Index to Journals in South-

western Archaeology 18 (1996): item 4578.

Figure 127. Example Citations of Abstracts From Professional Journals.

Citing a Published Dissertation

University Microfilms International (UMI) is keeps microfilm copies of all dissertations created in the United States. UMI is the major supplier of copies of dissertations to interested parties. You can check with them to see what other students have done on 'your topic and then order copies of the relevant disserations.

A citation of a published dissertation appears in Figure 128 and consists of the following elements:

- Author's last name

- Author's first name or initial (and middle name or initial, if available)

- Title of dissertation

- The abbreviation "Diss." For "Dissertation"

- Name of degree-granting institution

- Year dissertation was copyrighted by the degree-granting institution

- City of publication

- Publisher's name

- Year dissertation was copyrighted by the publisher

- University Microfilms order number, if dissertation published by UMI

To create this citation, follow these steps:

1. At the left margin, type the author's last name, followed by a comma and a space.

2a. If only the first name or initial is available, follow it with a period and a space.

b. If the author's middle name or initial is available, however, type the first name, followed by a space. Then type the middle name or initial, followed by a period and then a space.

3. Type and underline the dissertation title. Follow it with a period and a space.

4. Type the abbreviation "Diss." followed by a space.

5. Type the name of the degree-granting institution, using a "U" to represent "University." Follow it with a comma and a space.

6. Type the year the university granted the degree, followed by a period and a space.

7. Type the city of publication, followed by a colon and a space.

8. Type the name of the publisher, followed by a comma and a space. Use an acronym or a shortened form of the name, if possible. For example, if the publisher is University Microfilms International, use the acronym "UMI."

NOTE: If the dissertation was privately printed, type the words "privately printed" where the publisher's name would go. Use a lower-case "p" on both words.

9a. Type the year the publisher published the dissertation, followed by a period. If the publisher is not UMI, go to Step 11.

b. If the publisher is UMI, follow the copyright year with a period and a space and go to Step 10.

10. Type the University Microfilms order number, followed by a period.

11. If your citation continues to a second or subsequent line, double-space that line and indent it one-half inch (five spaces on a typewriter).

See Appendix B for a sample Works Cited list.

```
Jones, James T. The Effects of Bottom-up Management

     Techniques on Clerical Employees in Five

     High-tech Companies. U of California, 1997.

     Ann Arbor: UMI, 1997. AAD93-12345.
```

Figure 128. Example Citation of a Published Dissertation Obtained From University Microfilms International.

Citing an Unpublished Dissertation

You might get some material from a dissertation on which some-one is currently working. A citation of a unpublished dissertation appears in Figure 129 and consists of the following elements:

- Author's last name

- Author's first name or initial (and middle name or initial, if available)

- Title of dissertation

- The abbreviation "Diss." For "Disseration"

- Name of degree-granting institution

- Year dissertation was copyrighted by the degree-granting institution

To create this citation, follow these steps:

1. At the left margin, type the author's last name, followed by a comma and a space.

2a. If only the first name or initial is available, follow it with a period and a space.

b. If the author's middle name or initial is available, however, type the first name, followed by a space. Then type the middle name or initial, followed by a period and a space.

> *NOTE:* *Type the author's name exactly as listed on the work; i.e., if the work lists the name in full, you should, too. If the work lists initials, use those.*

> *NOTE:* *For citations with more than one author, see the instructions for citing authors' names on pages 89-93.*

3. Type an opening quotation mark, the dissertation title, a period, a closing quotation mark, and a space.

4. Type the abbreviation "Diss." followed by a space.

5. Type the name of the degree-granting institution, using a "U" to represent "University." Follow it with a comma and a space.

6. Type the year the dissertation was written, followed by a comma and space.

7. If your citation continues to a second or subsequent line, double-space that line and indent it one-half inch (five spaces on a typewriter).

See Appendix B for a sample Works Cited list.

```
Jones, James T. "The Effects of Bottom-up Management

     Techniques on Clerical Employees in Five

     High-tech Companies." Diss. U of California,

     1997.
```

Figure 129. Example Citation of an Unpublished Dissertation.

Citing Government Publications

Federal, state, and local governments print documents that you may find helpful in your research. The Government Printing Office (GPO) prints all the publications from federal agencies. Many are available free or at a low-cost.

NOTE: *For information on citing congressional documents, see the section on Citing Legislative Materials.*

A citation of a government publication appears in Figure 130 and consists of the following elements:

- Issuing government's name

- Issuing agency's name

- Title of report

- City of publication

- Publisher's name

- Year publication was copyrighted

NOTE: *Be sure to follow the rules in the other sections for citing a multivolume work, republished work, etc., if these apply to your government publication.*

To create this citation, follow these steps:

1. At the left margin, type the issuing government's name, followed by a period and a space.

2. Type the issuing agency's name, then a period and a space.

3. Type and underline the report title. Capitalize the first letter of all words except articles and prepositions (unless the first word is an article or preposition). Type a period and a space.

4. Type the city of publication, a colon, and a space.

5. Type the name of the publisher, followed by a comma and a space. Abbreviate the name if possible; e.g., abbreviate Government Printing Office as "GPO," or the British version, Her (or His) Majesty's Stationery Office as "HMSO."

6. Type the year of publication, followed by a period.

7. If your citation continues to a second or subsequent line, double-space that line and indent it one-half inch (five spaces on a typewriter).

See Appendix B for a sample Works Cited list.

United States. Small Business Administration.

Checklist for Going into Business. Washington:

GPO, 1976.

Figure 130. Example Citation of a Government Publication.

Citing Reviews

Many types of materials get reviewed, such as books, movies, videos, plays, concerts, etc. Reviews can appear in different types of periodicals. This section shows how to cite reviews that appear in magazines. If your review is in a newspaper, for instance, refer to the section in this chapter on citing newspaper articles.

A citation of a review with one author in a magazine appears as shown in Figure 131 and consists of the following elements:

- Reviewer's last name and first name or initial (and middle name or initial, if available)

- Title of review

- Abbreviation "Rev. of" for "Review of"

- Title of work reviewed

- The word "by" or the abbreviation "ed."

- Author's/editor's last name and first name or initial (and middle name or initial, if available)

- Name of publication in which the review appeared

- Day, month, and year of review

- Page number(s) of review

To create this citation, follow these steps:

NOTE: If there is no reviewer, skip Step 1 and begin at the left margin with Step 3.

1. At the left margin, type the reviewer's last name, followed by a comma and a space.

2a. If only the first name or initial is available, type it, followed by a period and a space.

b. If the reviewer's middle name or initial is available, however, type the first name, followed by a space. Then type the middle name or initial, followed by a period and a space.

NOTE: If the review has no title, skip Step 3 and go to Step 4.

3. Type an opening parenthesis, the review's title, a period, a closing parenthesis, and a space. Capitalize the first letter of all words in the title, except articles and prepositions (unless the first word is an article or preposition).

4. Type the words "Rev. of" followed by a space.

5. Type and underline the title of the work reviewed. Capitalize the first letter of all words except articles and prepositions (unless the first word is an article or preposition). Type a comma and a space.

6. If the work has an author, type the word "by" and a space, as shown in Figure 131). If the work has an editor, however, type "ed." and a space.

7a. Type the first name of the author/editor of the work reviewed. If only the first name or initial is available, follow it with a period and a space.

b. If the author's/editor's middle name or initial is available, however, type the first name, followed by a space. Then type the middle name or initial, followed by a period and a space.

8. Type the author's/editor's last name, then a period and a space.

9. Type the title of the magazine in which the review appeared and underline it. Capitalize the first letter of all words except for articles and prepositions. Delete the first word if it is an article or preposition (e.g., "The"). After the title, type a space.

10. Type the date in day, month (abbreviated per Table 5 on page 22), year format, followed by a colon and a space.

11. Type the page numbers on which the review appeared, followed by a period.

12. If your citation continues to a second or subsequent line, double-space that line and indent it one-half inch (five spaces on a typewriter).

See Appendix B for a sample Works Cited list.

```
Jones, John T. "Exploring New Management Techniques."

     Rev. of The Bottom-up Approach, by Henry Dawson.

Today's Business 24 Feb. 1984: 25-26.
```

Figure 131. Example Citation of a Review With the Reviewer Named and Appearing in a Magazine.

Citing Manuscripts or Typescripts

A manuscript or typescript is the unpublished version of a document as the author typed it prior to sending it to the publisher. A manuscript for a famous work is sometimes more valuable than a first edition of the work itself. It may contain the author's or editor's handwritten notes in the margins. The manuscript or typescript may be the author's handwritten notes in a notebook or it may not have an identified author at all. Manuscripts are cited differently for articles and essays than for books and notebooks. The exact elements available for any particular manuscript or typescript will vary. Therefore, look at all the examples in this section before deciding which elements your citation must include.

Citing an Unpublished Article or Essay

A citation for an unpublished article or essay with one author appears as shown in Figure 132 and consists of approximately the following elements:

- Author's last name

- Author's first name or initial (and middle name or initial, if available)

- Title or description of the material

- Phrase "Unpublished article" or "Unpublished essay"

- Year the article or essay manuscript was written

To create this citation, follow these steps:

1. At the left margin, type the author's last name, followed by a comma and a space.

2a. If only the first name or initial is available, follow it with a period and a space.

 b. If the author's middle name or initial is available, however, type the first name, followed by a space. Then type the middle name or initial, followed by a period and a space.

> *NOTE:* *Type the author's name exactly as listed on the work; i.e., if the work lists the name in full, you should, too. If the work lists initials, use those.*

> *NOTE:* *For citations with more than one author, see the instructions for citing authors' names on pages 89-93.*

3. Type an opening quotation mark, the title of the article or essay, a period, a closing quotation mark, and a space. Capitalize the first letter of all words except prepositions and articles (unless the first word is an article or a preposition).

4. Type the phrase "Unpublished article" or "Unpublished essay," followed by a comma and a space.

5. Type the year the article or essay was written, followed by a period.

6. If your citation continues to a second or subsequent line, double-space that line and indent it one-half inch (five spaces on a typewriter).

> *NOTE:* *Be sure to check the other examples in this section to see if they display information for your manuscript or typescript that is not shown in the example below.*

See Appendix B for a sample Works Cited list.

```
Jensen, Sara. "Rasputin's Secret." Unpublished

     article, 1996.
```

Figure 132. Example Citation of an Unpublished Article.

Citing an Author's Notebook

A citation for an author's notebook appears as shown in Figure 133 and consists of approximately the following elements:

- Author's last name

- Author's first name or initial (and middle name or initial, if available)

- The word "Notebook"

- Notebook number, if available

- Abbreviation "ms." or "ts."

- Name of the collection to which manuscript or typescript belongs

- Name of the library/institution where manuscript is housed, if available

- City of that library or institution, if available

To create this citation, follow these steps:

1. At the left margin, type the author's last name, followed by a comma and a space.

2a. If only the first name or initial is available, follow it with a period and a space.

  b. If the author's middle name or initial is available, however, type the first name, followed by a space. Then type the middle name or initial, followed by a period and a space.

    NOTE: *Type the author's name exactly as listed on the work; i.e., if the work lists the name in full, you should, too. If the work lists initials, use those.*

    NOTE: *For citations with more than one author, see the instructions for citing authors' names on pages 89-93.*

3. Type the word "Notebook." If it has a number, follow the word with a space, the number, a comma, and another space. If it does not have a number, follow it with a comma and a space.

4. Type "ms." if the notebook is a manuscript (handwritten), "ts." if it is a typescript (typewritten). Follow it with a space.

    NOTE: The "m" and "t" are lower case.

5. Type the collection to which the notebook belongs, if applicable, followed by a period and a space.

6. Type the location of the library/institution housing the manuscript or typescript, followed by a comma and a space.

7. Type the city where the library/institution is located. If it is a well-known city, follow it with a period. If it is not a well-known city, however, follow it with a comma and a space, then the 2-letter state code abbreviation if it is a U.S. state (see Figure 133), or an abbreviation for the country name, followed by a period.

8. If your citation continues to a second or subsequent line, double-space that line and indent it one-half inch (five spaces on a typewriter).

NOTE: Be sure to check the other examples in this section to see if they display information for your manuscript or typescript that is not shown in the example below.

See Appendix B for a sample Works Cited list.

```
Thompson, Blake. Notebook 18, ms. Thompson Papers.

     Billingsley Library, Fullerton, CA.
```

Figure 133. Example Citation of an Author's Notebook.

Citing a Manuscript or Typescript for a Book

A citation for manuscript or typescript for a book with one author appears as shown in Figure 134 and consists of approximately the following elements:

- Author's last name

- Author's first name or initial (and middle name or initial, if available)

- Title or description of the material

- Manuscript/typescript number, if available

- Name of the library/institution where manuscript is housed, if available

- City of that library or institution, if available

To create this citation, follow these steps:

NOTE: If there is no author, begin at the left margin with Step 3.

1. At the left margin, type the author's last name, followed by a comma and a space.

2a. If only the first name or initial is available, follow it with a period and a space.

 b. If the author's middle name or initial is available, however, type the first name, followed by a space. Then type the middle name or initial, followed by a period and a space.

    NOTE: Type the author's name exactly as listed on the work; i.e., if the work lists the name in full, you should, too. If the work lists initials, use those.

    NOTE: For citations with more than one author, see the instructions for citing authors' names on pages 89-93.

3. Type and underline the title or description of the manuscript or typescript, followed by a period and a space. Capitalize the first letter of all the words except prepositions and articles (unless the first word is a preposition or an article).

4. If the manuscript or typescript is catagued by number, type the abbreviation "Ms." or "Ts." followed by a space, the identifying number, a period, and a space. Capitalize the "M" or "T."

5. Type the location of the library/institution housing the manu-
    script or typescript, followed by a comma and a space.

6. Type the city where the library/institution is located, followed by
    a period. If it is located in a city that is not well-known, include
    the two-letter state code per Table 9 on page 24 (or an abbre-
    viation for the country name, if it is located in a foreign country;
    e.g., "Ire." for "Ireland").

7. If your citation continues to a second or subsequent line,
    double-space that line and indent it one-half inch (five spaces
    on a typewriter).

NOTE: *Be sure to check the other examples in this section to see*
if they display information for your manuscript or typescript
that is not shown in the example below.

See Appendix B for a sample Works Cited list.

```
Thompson, Blake. The Underground Tunnel. Ms. 24.

     Billingsley Lib., Fullerton, CA.
```

Figure 134. Example Citation of a Manuscript or Typescript for a Book.

Citing Graphical Materials

This section shows you how to cite:

- Work of art

- Photograph of a work of art

- Map or chart

- Cartoon

- Advertisement

Citing a Work of Art

You can cite a work of art in two ways:

- Citing the work of art itself

- Citing a photograph of the work of art

Citing the Work of Art Itself

Figure 135 shows an example citation of a work of art, which consists of the following elements:

- Artist's last name

- Artist's first name or initial (and middle name or initial, if available)

- Title of painting or sculpture

- Date work was created (optional)

- Name of institution housing the work or, for a private collection, the words "Private collection of" and the name of the owner

- City where the museum or private collection is located

To create this citation, follow these steps:

1. At the left margin, type the artist's last name, followed by a comma and a space.

2a. If only the first name or initial is available, follow it with a period and a space.

b. If the artist's middle name or initial is available, however, type the first name, followed by a space. Then type the middle name or initial, followed by a period and a space.

3. Type and underline the title of the painting or sculpture, followed by a period and a space.

4. If you wish to include the date when the work was created, type it, followed by a period and a space. Otherwise, go to Step 5.

5. Type the name of the museum housing the art (see example 1), or if it is in a private collection, type the words "Private collection of" followed by the name of the owner of the collection (see example 2). Follow these words with a comma and a space.

6. Type the city where the artwork is located, followed by a period.

7. If your citation continues to a second or subsequent line, double-space that line and indent it one-half inch (five spaces on a typewriter).

See Appendix B for a sample Works Cited list.

```
Johnson, James. Bucking Bronco. Carver Museum,

    Los Angeles.
```

or

```
Perry, Charles A. Ice Skating. 1939. Private

    collection of Victor Adamson, Chicago.
```

Figure 135. Example Citations of a Work of Art.

Citing a Photograph of a Work of Art

You may have access to a photograph of a piece of artwork, in a book, for instance. You can cite the photograph rather than the artwork itself. Figure 136 shows an example citation of a photograph of a work of art, which consists of the following elements:

- Artist's first and last name

- Title of painting or sculpture

- Date when work was created (optional)

- Name of institution that houses the work or, for a private collection, the words "Private collection of" and the name of the owner

- City where the museum or private collection is located

- Name of work in which photograph appears

- Author of work in which photograph appears

- City where publisher is located

- Publisher's name

- Year of publication

To create this citation, follow these steps:

1. At the left margin, type the artist's last name, followed by a comma and a space.

2a. If only the first name or initial is available, follow it with a period and a space.

 b. If the artist's middle name or initial is available, however, type the first name, followed by a space. Then type the middle name or initial, followed by a period and a space.

3. Type and underline the title of the painting or sculpture, followed by a period and a space.

4. If you wish to include the date when the work was created, type it, followed by a period and a space. Otherwise, go to Step 5.

5. Type the name of the museum housing the art (see the first example), or if it is in a private collection, type the words "Private collection of" followed by the name of the owner of the collection (see the second example). Follow it with a comma and a space.

6. Type the city where the artwork is located, followed by a period and a space.

7. Type and underline the name of the work in which the painting appears. Follow it with a period and a space.

8. Type the word "By" followed by a space, then the first and last name of the author of the work, followed by a period and a space.

7. Type the city of publication, followed by a colon and a space.

8. Type the publisher's name, followed by a comma and a space.

9. Type the year of publication, followed by a period and a space.

10. Type the page number, followed by a period, or if it is a slide, such as shown in the example, type the word "Slide" followed by a space and then the number of the slide.

11. If your citation continues to a second or subsequent line, double-space that line and indent it one-half inch (five spaces on a typewriter).

See Appendix B for a sample Works Cited list.

```
Lorenzo, Salvatore. Nature's Wish. 1917. Holt Art

     Museum, Los Angeles. Famous Italian Painters. By

     Daniela Arnini. New York: Ace, 1986. Slide 14.
```

```
Lorenzo, Salvatore. Nature's Wish. 1917. Private

     Collection of John Jones, Los Angeles. Famous

     Italian Painters. By Daniela Arnini. New York:

     Ace, 1986. Slide 14.
```

Figure 136. Example Citations of a Photograph of a Work of Art.

Citing a Map or Chart

Cite maps and charts the same way you would a book with no author or editor. This citation appears as shown in Figure 137 and consists of the following elements:

- Title of map or chart

- Word "Map" or "Chart"

- City where publisher is located

- Publisher's name

- Year map or chart was copyrighted

To create this citation, follow these steps:

1. At the left margin, type and underline the map or chart title, followed by a period and a space. Capitalize the first letter of all words except for articles and prepositions (unless the first word is an article or a preposition; i.e., "The").

2. Type the word "Map" or "Chart" to identify the item and follow it with a period and a space.

3. Type the city of publication, followed by a colon and a space.

4. Type the publisher's name, followed by a comma and a space.

5. Type the copyright year, followed by a period.

6. If your citation continues to a second or subsequent line, double-space that line and indent it one-half inch (five spaces on a typewriter).

See Appendix B for a sample Works Cited list.

<u>Greater Los Angeles</u>. Map. Irvine: Thomas, 1998.

<u>Popular Fonts</u>. Chart. New York: Letraset, 1993.

Figure 137. Example Citations of a Map and a Chart.

Citing an Advertisement

You can cite advertisements from magazines, newspapers, television stations, and other sources. This citation appears as shown in Figure 138 and consists of the following beginning elements:

- Name of the product, company, or institution that is the subject of the ad

- Word "Advertisement"

- Name of the source in/on which the ad appeared

- Publication information for the type of source in which the ad appeared

To create this citation, follow these steps:

1. At the left margin, type the name of the product, company, or institution that is the subject of the ad, followed by a period and a space.

2. Type the word "Advertisement," followed by a period and a space.

3. Following the rules for that type of citation, type the name of the source in which the ad appeared, and the rest of the publication information.

4. If your citation continues to a second or subsequent line, double-space that line and indent it one-half inch (five spaces on a typewriter).

See Appendix B for a sample Works Cited list.

```
Holiday Inn. Advertisement. Inc. Nov. 1998: 45.
```

Figure 138. Example Citation of an Advertisement.

Citing a Cartoon

You may wish to cite a cartoon or cartoon strip. A citation for a cartoon is shown in Figure 139 and consists of the following elements:

- Author's last name

- Author's first name

- Title of cartoon, if applicable

- Word "Cartoon"

- Title of publication

- City of publication, if necessary

- Day, month, and year of publication

- Page number(s)

To create this citation, follow these steps:

NOTE: *If the cartoon has more than one cartoonist, cite the number of cartoonists by following the rules for that number of authors.*

1. At the left margin, type the author's last name, followed by a comma and a space.

2a. If only the first name or initial is available, follow it with a period and a space.

  b. If the artist's middle name or initial is available, however, type the first name, followed by a space. Then type the middle name or initial, followed by a period and a space.

3. If the cartoon does not have a title, go to Step 4. Type an opening quotation mark, then the title of the cartoon. Use an initial capital letter on all words except articles and prepositions. End the title with a period, a closing quotation mark, and a space.

4. Type the word "Cartoon," followed by a period and a space.

5. Type and underline the title of the publication, followed by a space. Capitalize the first letter of all words of the title except articles and prepositions. Delete the first word if it is an article (e.g., "The").

6. If the publication is a newspaper whose location is not included in the newspaper title, type an opening bracket, the city where the newspaper is published, and a closing bracket (see example 2).

7. Type the date in day, month order. Abbreviate the month using the accepted three-letter abbreviation (see Table 5 on page 22). Follow the abbreviated month with a period and a space or the unabbreviated month with a space.

8. Type the year of publication followed by a colon and a space.

    NOTE: Do not enclose the year in parentheses.

9. Type the page number(s), followed by a period.

    NOTE: Do not include "p." in the page number.

10. If your citation continues to a second or subsequent line, double-space that line and indent it one-half inch (five spaces on a typewriter).

See Appendix B for a sample Works Cited list.

```
Adams, Scott. "Dilbert." Cartoon. Los Angeles Times

    21 Dec. 1997: B-23.
```

```
Torres, Jose. Cartoon. Register [Costa Mesa] 4 Jan.

    1996: C-14.
```

Figure 139. Example Citations of a Cartoon.

Citing Kits, Models, Globes, Games, Flash Cards, and Dioramas

To cite kits, models, globes, games, flash cards, and dioramas, the MLA suggests using Eugene B. Fleischer's book, *A Style Manual for Citing Microform and Nonprint Media* (Chicago: ALA, 1978).

Citing Letters and Memos

This section shows you how to cite letters and memos, which fall into four types:

- Unpublished letters in archives

- Letters or memos written to the researcher

- Memos written to someone else

- Published letters

Citing an Unpublished Letter in an Archive

Unpublished letters are cited similarly to manuscripts and typescripts (see pages 190-195). Figure 140 shows an example, which consists of the following elements:

- Author's last name

- Author's first name or initial (and middle name or initial, if available)

- Phrase "Letter to" and the name of the recipient

- Day, month, and year letter was written

- Name of the collection to which the letter belongs

- Name of institution or library where letter is located

- City where institution or library is located

To create this citation, follow these steps:

1. At the left margin, type the author's last name, followed by a comma and a space.

2a. If only the first name or initial is available, follow it with a period and a space.

b. If the author's middle name or initial is available, however, type the first name, followed by a space. Then type the middle name or initial, followed by a period and a space.

3. Type the words "Letter to," followed by a space and the first and last names of the person to whom the letter is written. Follow the name with a period and a space.

4. Type the date the letter was written in day, month format. Abbreviate the month using the accepted three-letter abbreviation (see Table 5 on page 22). Follow the abbreviated month with a period and a space or theunabbreviated month with a space.

5. Type the year the letter was written followed by a period and a space.

6. Type the title of the collection, followed by a period and a space.

7. Type the name of the institution housing the letter, followed by a comma and a space. If a library holds the letter, type the name and abbreviate the word "Library" as "Lib." Follow it with a comma and a space.

8. If your citation continues to a second or subsequent line, double-space that line and indent it one-half inch (five spaces on a typewriter.

See Appendix B for a sample Works Cited list.

```
Benton, Thomas Hart. Letter to Charles Fremont. 22

    June 1847. John Charles Fremont Papers. Southwest

    Museum Lib., Los Angeles.
```

Figure 140. Example Citation of an Unpublished Letter in an Archive.

Citing a Letter or Memo Written to the Researcher

During the course of researching your paper, you may receive a letter or memo from someone. Cite a letter you have received as shown in Figure 141. This citation consists of the following elements:

- Letter-writer's last name

- Letter-writer's first name or initial (and middle name or initial, if available)

- Phrase "Letter to the author" or "Memo to the author"

- Day, month, and year letter was written

To create this citation, follow these steps:

1. At the left margin, type the letter-writer's last name, followed by a comma and a space.

2a. If only the first name or initial is available, follow it with a period and a space.

b. If the letter-writer's middle name or initial is available, however, type the first name, followed by a space. Then type the middle name or initial, followed by a period and a space.

3a. If this is a citation of a letter, type the words "Letter to the author" (in this case, you are the author, since you are the writer of the paper in which this citation appears), followed by a period and a space.

b. If this is a citation of a memo, type the words "Memo to the author," followed by a period and a space.

4. Type the day the letter was written, a space, then the month in abbreviated format (see Table 5 on page 22). Then type a space.

5. Type the year the letter was written followed by a period and a space.

6. If your citation continues to a second or subsequent line, double-space that line and indent it one-half inch (five spaces on a typewriter).

See Appendix B for a sample Works Cited list.

```
Roddenberry, Gene. Letter to the author. 3 June 1972.
```

```
Smith, Joe. Memo to the author. 8 Dec. 1998.
```

Figure 141. Example Citations of a Letter and a Memo Written to the Researcher.

Citing a Memo Sent to Someone Else

You may wish to cite a memo sent to someone else. Figure 142 shows a sample, which consists of the following elements:

- Author's last name

- Author's first name or initial (and middle name or initial, if available)

- Title of memo, if applicable

- Phrase "Memo to"

- Recipient's name

- Recipient's professional affiliation

- City and state where the affiliation is located

- Day, month, and year letter was written

To create this citation, follow these steps:

1. At the left margin, type the author's last name, followed by a comma and a space.

2a. If only the first name or initial is available, follow it with a period and a space.

 b. If the author's middle name or initial is available, however, type the first name, followed by a space, or the first initial followed by a period and a space. Then type the middle name or initial, followed by a period and a space.

3a. If the memo does not have a title, go to Step 4. (Refer to the first example in Figure 142.)

 b. If the memo does have a title, however, type an opening quotation mark, the title of the memo, a period, then a closing quotation mark and a space. (Refer to the second example in Figure 142.)

4. Type the phrase "Memo to" followed by a space. Do not enclose it in quotation marks.

5. Type the name of the recipient of the memo, followed by a comma and a space.

6. Type the name of the person, company, agency, committee, etc., with which the recipient is associated, using abbreviations if possible. Follow it with a comma and a space.

7. Type the name of the city where the company, agency, or committee, etc., is located, followed by a comma and a space.

8. Type the state in which the city is located, using the two-letter state code abbreviation (see Table 9 on page 24), followed by a period and a space.

9. Type the day the memo was written, a space, then the month in abbreviated format (see Table 5 on page 22), then a space.

10. Type the year the letter was written, followed by a period.

11. If your citation continues to a second or subsequent line, double-space that line and indent it one-half inch (five spaces on a typewriter).

See Appendix B for a sample Works Cited list.

Harrison, Daniel. Memo to George Brewster, Brewster
    Publishing Co., San Francisco, CA. 8 Aug. 1998.

or

Harrison, Daniel. "New Student Requirements." Memo to
    Edward Davis, Banfield Coll., San Francisco, CA.
    10 Apr. 1998.

Figure 142. Example Citations of a Memo Sent to Someone Else.

Citing a Published Letter

Some letters written by famous people have been published in collections; therefore, cite a published letter as you would a work in a collection. Figure 143 shows an example, which consists of the following elements:

- Author's last name

- Author's first name or initial (and middle name or initial, if available)

- Title of the letter

- Day, month, and year letter was written

- Number of the letter, if applicable

- Name of the collection to which the letter belongs

- Abbreviation "Ed." for "Editor"

- Editor's first name or initial and middle name or initial

- Editor's last name

- City of publication

- Publisher's name

- Year of publication

- Page numbers

NOTE: If you cite more than one letter from the same collection, create one citation for the entire work (see "Citing an Entire Work" on page 56) in the Works Cited list, and cite the letters individually in the text of your paper using the format for citing cross-references (see "Citing Cross-References" on page 170).

To create this citation, follow these steps:

1. At the left margin, type the author's last name, followed by a comma and a space.

2a. If only the first name or initial is available, follow it with a period and a space.

b. If the author's middle name or initial is available, however, type the first name, followed by a space. Then type the middle name or initial, followed by a period and a space.

3.   Type an opening quotation mark, the title of the letter, a period, and a closing quotation mark, followed by a space.

4.   Type the day the letter was written, a space, then the month in abbreviated format (per Table 5 on page 22), then a space.

5.   Type the year the letter was written followed by a period and a space.

6.   Type the word "Letter" followed by the number the editor has given this letter. Follow it with a space, the word "of," and another space.

7.   Type and underline the title of the collection, followed by a period and a space.

8.   Type the abbreviation "Ed." followed by a space.

9.   Type the editor's first name, followed by a space, or the first initial, followed by a period and a space. Repeat for the middle name.

10.   Type the editor's last name, followed by a period.

11.   Type the city of publication, followed by a colon and a space

12.   Type the publisher's name in shortened format, followed by a comma and a space.

13.   Type the year of publication, followed by a period.

14.   Type the page numbers on which the letter appears.

15.   If your citation continues to a second or subsequent line, double-space that line and indent it one-half inch (five spaces on a typewriter).

See Appendix B for a sample Works Cited list.

Madden, Blake. "To Sara Clarke." 10 Dec. 1952. Letter

14 of <u>The Letters of Blake Madden</u>. Ed. Janet

Frank. New York: Ace, 1995. 27-29.

Figure 143. Example Citation of a Published Letter.

Citing Legal Sources

There are several types of legal citations:

- Court cases

- Statutes

- Legislative materials

- Administrative and executive materials

The MLA requires that legal citations be cited with the same information provided in conventional legal formats in legal periodicals. Unlike legal periodicals, however, which list legal citations in footnotes at the bottom of the page, the MLA style guide requires legal citations to be listed in the text of the paper.

For more information on referencing legal sources, please consult *The Bluebook: A Uniform System of Citation* (1991), which the MLA follows for legal citation style.

Citing Court Cases

There are four main types of court cases:

- Court decisions

- Unpublished cases

- Court cases at the trial level

- Court cases at the appellate level

Common abbreviations used in legal citations are shown in Table 16. When using these abbreviations, follow the spacing shown exactly.

Table 25. Abbreviations Used in Court Citations.

ABBREVIATION	MEANING
v.	versus
Cong.	U. S. Congress
H.R.	House of Representatives
S.	Senate
Reg.	Regulation
Res.	Resolution
aff'd	affirmed
F.	*Federal Reporter*
F.2d	*Federal Reporter, Second Series*
F. Supp.	*Federal Supplement*
U.S.C.	*United States Code*
Cong. Rec.	*Congressional Record*
Fed. Reg.	*Federal Register*
WL	Westlaw
Jan.	January
Feb.	February
Aug.	August
Sept.	September
Oct.	October
Nov.	November
Dec.	December

Citing a Court Decision (*Bluebook* Rule 10)

A citation for a court decision appears as shown in Figure 144, and consists of the following elements:

- Name of the decision

- Source volume number

- Source name

- Source page number

- Court name

- Court date

To create this citation, follow these steps:

1. At the left margin, type the name of the decision, followed by a comma and a space. Be sure to use "v." in the decision name.

2. Type the volume number of the published source in which this case is listed, followed by a space.

3a. Type the source name in abbreviated format, followed by a space.

b. Type the source page number, followed by a space.

4. Type an opening parenthesis, then type the court name (in Figure 144, "D. Calif." stands for "District of California"), then type the year of the decision, then a closing parenthesis, a period, and a space.

5. If your citation continues to a second or subsequent line, double-space that line and indent it one-half inch (five spaces on a typewriter).

See Appendix B for a sample Works Cited list.

```
Smith v. Jones, 234 F. Supp. 1394 (D. Calif. 1984).
```

Figure 144. Example Citation of a Court Decision.

Citing an Unpublished Case

There are two types of unpublished cases:

- Filed, but not yet reported

- Unreported decision

Citing a Case That is Filed, But Not Yet Reported

A citation for a case that is filed, but not yet reported, appears as shown in Figure 145, and consists of the following elements:

- Case name

- Docket number

- Court name in which case was filed

- Word "filed"

- Date of filing

1. At the left margin, type the name of the case, followed by a comma and a space.

2. Type the abbreviation "No." (for "Number"), then the docket number, followed by a space.

3a. Type an opening parenthesis, then the name of the court in which the case was filed, followed by a space.

b. Type the word "filed," followed by a space.

c. Type the date of filing. Abbreviate the month, using the three-letter abbreviation per Table 5 on page 22, then type a period and a space. Type the day, followed by a comma and a space, then the year, followed by the closing parenthesis and a period.

4. If your citation continues to a second line, double-space the second line and indent it one-half inch (five spaces on a typewriter).

See Appendix B for a sample Works Cited list.

```
Smith v. Jones, No. 23-1004 (U.S. filed Mar. 3, 1993).
```

Figure 145. Example Citation of a Case That is Filed, But Not Reported.

Citing an Unreported Decision

You can cite an unreported decision from two sources:

- In print

- On LEXIS or Westlaw

CITING AN UNREPORTED DECISION IN PRINT

A citation for an unreported decision in print appears as shown in Figure 146, and consists of the following elements:

- Case name

- Docket number

- Words "slip op."

- Name of the court

- Date of announcement

To create this citation, follow these steps:

1. At the left margin, type the name of the case, followed by a comma, and a space.

2. Type the docket number. Abbreviate "Number" as "No." End with a comma, and a space.

3. Type the words "slip op.," followed by a space. ("Slip op." is short for "slip opinion"—an opinion not published in a case reporter, but printed separately, due to its recency.)

4a. In parentheses, type the name of the court in which the case was filed, followed by a space.

b. Type the word "filed," followed by a space.

c. Type the date of filing. Begin by abbreviating the name of the month and following it with a period and a space. Type the date, followed by a comma, then the year, followed by the closing parenthesis and a period.

5. If your citation continues to a second line, double-space the line and indent it one-half inch (five spaces on a typewriter).

See Appendix B for a sample Works Cited list.

```
Smith v. Jones, No. 23-1004 (U.S. filed Mar. 3, 1993).
```

```
Smith v. Jones, No. 23-1004, slip op. at [10]. (U.S.

    filed Mar. 3, 1993).
```

Figure 146. Example Citations of an Unreported Decision in Print.

CITING AN UNREPORTED DECISION ON LEXIS OR WESTLAW

You can find unreported cases on LEXIS or Westlaw, too. These electronic databases are a tremendous resource for finding legal materials. A citation of an unreported decision found here may or may not have a record number.

Citing an Unreported Decision on LEXIS or Westlaw With a Record Number

A citation with a record number appears as shown in Figure 147, and consists of the following elements:

- Case name

- Docket number

- Decision year

- Court name

- LEXIS or Westlaw record number

- Screen page number

- District name

- Date of decision

To create this citation, follow these steps:

1. At the left margin, type the name of the case, followed by a comma, and a space.

2. Type the docket number, a comma, and a space. Abbreviate "Number" as "No."

3. Type the decision year and court name.

4. Type the LEXIS or Westlaw record number, a comma, and a space.

5. Type the word "at," a space, an asterisk, and the screen page number. (The asterisk is used to distinguish this page number from a slip op page number.)

6a. In parentheses, type the name of the court in which the case was filed.

b. Type the date of filing. Abbreviate the month, if necessary. Follow it with a period and a space. Type the date, a comma, a space, the year, the closing parenthesis, and a period.

7. If your citation continues to a second or subsequent line, double-space that line and indent it one-half inch (five spaces on a typewriter).

See Appendix B for a sample Works Cited list.

```
Gomez v. Sanders Corp., No. 45-1234, 1993 U.S.

Dist. WL 19284, at *4 (D. Kan. Dec. 13, 1993).
```

Figure 147. Example Citation of an Unpublished Case Found on Westlaw With a Record Number.

Citing an Unreported Decision on LEXIS or Westlaw Without a Record Number

A citation without a record number appears as shown in Figure 148, and consists of the following elements:

- Case name

- Docket number

- Court name

- Date of decision

- Source name and other identifying information

To create this citation, follow these steps:

1. At the left margin, type the name of the case, followed by a comma, and a space.

2. Type the docket number and a space.

3a. In parentheses, type the name of the court in which the case was filed, followed by a period and a space.

   b. Type the date of filing. Abbreviate the month, if necessary. Follow it with a period and a space. Type the day, a comma, a space, the year, the closing parenthesis, and a space.

4. In parentheses, type the database name and any other identifying information.

5. If your citation continues to a second or subsequent line, double-space that line and indent it one-half inch (five spaces on a typewriter).

See Appendix B for a sample Works Cited list.

```
Williams v. ABC Manufacturing, No.12-4567 (D. Calif.

      Feb. 25, 1994) (LEXIS, Genfed library, Dist file).
```

Figure 148. Example Citation of an Unpublished Case Found on LEXIS With No Record Number.

Citing a Court Case at the Trial Level

You can cite trials at two levels:

- State trial court

- Federal district court

Citing a State Trial Court Case

A citation of a state trial court case appears as shown in Figure 149, and consists of the following elements:

- Case name

- Source volume number

- Source name

- Source page number

- Court name

- Year of decision

To create this citation, follow these steps:

1. At the left margin, type the name of the case, followed by a comma and a space.

2a. Type the source volume number and a space.

  b. Type the source name and a space.

  c. Type the source page number and a space.

3. In parentheses, type the court name and decision date, followed by a period.

4. If your citation continues to a second or subsequent line, double-space that line and indent it one-half inch (five spaces on a typewriter).

See Appendix B for a sample Works Cited list.

```
Williams v. ABC Manufacturing, 14 Pa. D. & C.4th 136

     (C.P. Washington County 1991).
```

Figure 149. Example Citation of a State Trial Court Case.

Citing a Federal District Court Case

A citation of a federal district court case appears as shown in Figure 150, and consists of the following elements:

- Case name

- Source volume number

- Source name

- Source page number

- Court name

- Year of decision

To create this citation, follow these steps:

1. Indent one-half inch and type the name of the case, followed by a comma and a space.

2a. Type the source volume number and a space.

b. Type the source name and a space.

c. Type the source page number and a space.

3. In parentheses, type the court name and decision date, followed by a period.

4. If your citation continues to a second or subsequent line, double-space that line and indent it one-half inch (five spaces on a typewriter).

See Appendix B for a sample Works Cited list.

```
Williams v. ABC Manufacturing, 456 F. Supp. 234

     (D. Calif. 1989).
```

Figure 150. Example Citation of a Federal District Court Case.

Citing a Court Case at the Appellate Level

Court cases can be appealed to one of two courts:

- State supreme court

- State court of appeals

Citing a Court Case Appealed to a State Supreme Court

A citation of a court case appealed to a state supreme court appears as shown in Figure 151, and consists of the following elements:

- Case name

- Source volume number

- Source name

- Source page number

- Year of decision

To create this citation, follow these steps:

1. At the left margin, type the name of the case, followed by a comma, and a space.

2a. Type the source volume number and a space.

 b. Type the source name and a space.

 c. Type the source page number and a space.

3. In parentheses, type the decision date, followed by a period.

4. If your citation continues to a second or subsequent line, double-space that line and indent it one-half inch (five spaces on a typewriter).

See Appendix B for a sample Works Cited list.

```
Williams v. ABC Manufacturing, 456 Calif. 234 (1989).
```

Figure 151. Example Citation of a Court Case Appealed to a State Supreme Court.

Citing a Court Case Appealed to a State Court of Appeals

A citation of a court case appealed to a state court of appeals appears as shown in Figure 152, and consists of the following elements:

- Case name

- Source volume number

- Source name

- Source page number

- Court name

- Year of decision

To create this citation, follow these steps:

1. At the left margin, type the name of the case, followed by a comma, and a space.

2a. Type the source volume number and a space.

  b. Type the source name and a space.

  c. Type the source page number and a space.

3. In parentheses, type the court name and decision date, followed by a period.

4. If your citation continues to a second or subsequent line, double-space that line and indent it one-half inch (five spaces on a typewriter).

See Appendix B for a sample Works Cited list.

```
Williams v. ABC Manufacturing, 234 S.W.2d 234 (Calif.

   Ct. App. 1989).
```

Figure 152. Example Citation of a Court Case Appealed to a State Court of Appeals.

Citing Statutes

You can cite statutes from two sources:

- State code
- Federal code

Citing a Statute in a State Code

A citation for a statute in a state code appears as shown in Figure 153 and consists of the following elements:

- Name of act
- Volume number
- Source
- Section number
- Any other citations to the act

To create this citation, follow these steps:

1. At the left margin, type the name of the act, followed by a comma and a space.

2. Type the volume number, followed by a space.

3. Type the source name, followed by a space.

4. Type the section symbol(s), followed by a space, and the section number(s), followed by a comma.

5. In parentheses, type any other citations to the act, followed by a period.

6. If your citation continues to a second or subsequent line, double-space that line and indent it one-half inch (five spaces on a typewriter).

See Appendix B for a sample Works Cited list.

```
Mental Care and Treatment Act, 4 Kan. Stat. Ann.

    §§ 59-2901-2941 (1983 & Supp. 1992).
```

Figure 153. Example Citation of a Statute in a State Code.

Citing a Statute in a Federal Code

A citation for a statute in a federal code appears as shown in Figure 154 and consists of the following elements:

- Name of act and year passed

- Volume number

- Source

- Section number

- Publisher of volume, if relevant

- Year volume was published

To create this citation, follow these steps:

1. At the left margin, type the name of the act, followed by a comma and a space.

2. Type the volume number, followed by a space.

3. Type the source name, followed by a space.

4. Type the section symbol, followed by a space, and the section number.

5. In parentheses, type the name of the publisher, if relevant, a space, and the year the volume was published, followed by a period.

6. If your citation continues to a second or subsequent line, double-space that line and indent it one-half inch (five spaces on a typewriter).

See Appendix B for a sample Works Cited list.

```
National Environmental Policy Act of 1969,

     44 U.S.C.A. § 4332 (West 1976).
```

Figure 154. Example Citation of a Statute in a Federal Code.

Citing Legislative Materials (Bluebook Rule 13)

Legislative materials include:

- Testimony at hearings

- Full hearings

- Federal reports and documents

- Unenacted federal bills and resolutions

- Enacted bills and resolutions

Citing Testimony at a Hearing

A citation for testimony at a hearing appears as shown in Figure 155 and consists of the following elements:

- Title of hearing as stated on official pamphlet

- Congressional number and abbreviation "Cong."

- Session number and abbreviation "Sess."

- Page number of pamphlet

- Year testimony was given

- The words "testimony of" and the testifier's name

To create this citation, follow these steps:

1. At the left margin, type the hearing title, followed by a period and a space. Include the bill number, if relevant; the submittee name, if relevant; and the committee name. Underline this entire entry.

2. Type the Congressional number, followed by a comma and a space. Abbreviate "Congress" as "Cong."

3. Type the session number (use just "d" for "second" or "third"), followed by a space. Then type the abbreviation "Sess." for "session," followed by a space.

4. Type the page number in the pamphlet where the testimony is documented.

5. In parentheses, type the year in which the testimony was given.

6. In parentheses, type the name of the person whose testimony you are referencing. End with a period.

7. If your citation continues to a second or subsequent line, double-space that line and indent it one-half inch (five spaces on a typewriter).

See Appendix B for a sample Works Cited list.

RU486: The Import Ban and Its Effect on Medical Research:

Hearings Before the Subcommittee on Regulation,

Business Opportunities, and Energy, of the House

Committee on Small Business. 101st Cong., 2d Sess.

35 (1990) (testimony of Ronald Chesemore).

Figure 155. Example Citation of Testimony at a Hearing.

Citing a Full Hearing

A citation for a full hearing appears as shown in Figure 156 and consists of the following elements:

- Title of hearing as stated on official pamphlet

- Congressional number

- Session number

- Page number of pamphlet

- Year testimony was given

To create this citation, follow these steps:

1. At the left margin, type the hearing name, followed by a period and a space. Include the bill number, if relevant; the subcommittee name, if relevant; and the committee name. Underline this entire entry.

2. Type the Congressional number, followed by a comma and a space. Abbreviate "Congress" as "Cong."

3. Type the session number (use just "d" for "second" or "third"), followed by a space. Then type the abbreviation "Sess." for "session," followed by a space.

4. Type the page number in the pamphlet where the testimony is documented.

5. In parentheses, type the year in which the testimony was given. End with a period.

6. If your citation continues to a second or subsequent line, double-space that line and indent it one-half inch (five spaces on a typewriter).

See Appendix B for a sample Works Cited list.

RU486: The Import Ban and Its Effect on Medical
Research: Hearings Before the Subcommittee on
Regulation, Business Opportunities, and Energy, of
the House Committee on Small Business. 101st Cong.,
2d Sess. 35 (1990).

Figure 156. Example Citation of a Full Hearing.

Citing a Federal Report or Document

A citation for a federal report or document appears as shown in Figure 157 and consists of the following elements:

- Report or document number

- Congressional number and abbreviation "Cong."

- Session number and abbreviation "Sess."

- Year report or document was published

To create this citation, follow these steps:

1. At the left margin, type the source name ("H.R. Rep." or "H.R. Doc." for House of Representatives Report or Document, or "S. Rep." for Senate Report or Document) and the report or document number, followed by a comma and a space.

2. Type the Congressional number, followed by a comma and a space. Abbreviate "Congress" as "Cong."

3. Type the session number (use just "d" for "second" or "third"), followed by a space. Then type the abbreviation "Sess." for "session," followed by a space.

4. Type the year in which the report or document was published.

5. If your citation continues to a second or subsequent line, double-space that line and indent it one-half inch (five spaces on a typewriter).

See Appendix B for a sample Works Cited list.

```
S. Rep. No. 234, 103d Cong., 1st Sess. (1993).
```

or

```
S. Doc. No. 234, 103d Cong., 1st Sess. (1993).
```

Figure 157. Example Citations of a Federal Report or Document.

Citing an Enacted Federal Bill or Resolution

A citation for an enacted federal bill or resolution appears as shown in Figure 158 and consists of the following elements:

- Source and title, if available

- Bill or resolution number

- Congressional or Senate number

- Abbreviation "Cong." or "Sen."

- Session number

- Abbreviation "Sess." for "Session"

- Volume number

- Source

- Page number

- Year bill or resolution was passed

To create this citation, follow these steps:

1. At the left margin, type the source name ("H.R. Res." for House of Representatives Resolution or "S. Res." for Senate Resolution) and the bill or resolution number, followed by a comma and a space.

2. Type the Congressional or Senate number, followed by a comma and a space.

3. Type the abbreviation "Cong." or "Sen.," followed by a space.

4. Type the session number (use just "d" for "second" or "third"), followed by a space. Then type the abbreviation "Sess." for "session," followed by a space.

5. Type the source volume number, followed by a space.

6. Type the source name in abbreviated form, followed by a space.

7. Type the page number, followed by a space.

8. In parentheses, type the year in which the bill or resolution was passed.

9. If your citation continues to a second or subsequent line, double-space that line and indent it one-half inch (five spaces on a typewriter).

See Appendix B for a sample Works Cited list.

```
S. Res. 107, 103d Cong., 1st Sess. 139 Cong. Rec.

    107, 5826 (1993).
```

Figure 158. Example Citation of an Enacted Federal Bill or Resolution.

Citing an Unenacted Federal Bill or Resolution

A citation for an unenacted federal bill or resolution appears as shown in Figure 159 and consists of the following elements:

- Title, if available

- Source name

- Bill or resolution number

- Congressional or Senate number and the abbreviation "Cong." or "Sen."

- Session number and the abbreviation "Sess."

- Section number, if relevant

- Year bill or resolution was introduced

To create this citation, follow these steps:

1. At the left margin, type the bill or resolution name, followed by a comma and a space.

2. Type the source name (H.R. for House of Representatives or S. for Senate), a space, and the bill or resolution number, followed by a comma and a space.

3. Type the Senate or Congressional number (use "d" for "second" or "third"), followed by a comma and a space. Then type "Sen." for "Senate," or "Cong." for Congress, followed by a space.

4. Type the session number (use just "d" for "second" or "third"), followed by a space. Then type the abbreviation "Sess." for "session," followed by a space.

5. Type the section symbol, a space, and the section number.

6. In parentheses, type the year in which the bill or resolution was introduced.

7. If your citation continues to a second or subsequent line, double-space that line and indent it one-half inch (five spaces on a typewriter).

See Appendix B for a sample Works Cited list.

```
Space Memorial Bill, S. 5936, 102d Cong., 2d Sess.

    § 4 (1992).
```

Figure 159. Example Citation of an Unenacted Federal Bill or Resolution.

Citing Administrative and Executive Materials

You can cite two types of administrative and executive materials:

- Federal rules and regulations
- Executive orders

Citing a Federal Rule or Regulation

A citation for a federal rule or regulation appears as shown in Figure 160 and consists of the following elements:

- Title of the rule or regulation
- Number of the rule or regulation
- Volume number
- Source
- Section number
- Year in which the rule or regulation was passed

To create this citation, follow these steps:

1. At the left margin, type the rule or regulation title (and number, if relevant), a comma and a space.

2. Type the volume number, followed by a space.

3. Type the section symbol, followed by a space.

4. Type the section number, followed by a space.

5. Type the year the rule or regulation was passed.

6. If your citation continues to a second or subsequent line, double-space that line and indent it one-half inch (five spaces on a typewriter).

See Appendix B for a sample Works Cited list.

```
FTC Credit Practices Rule, 16 C.F.R. § 444 (1991).
```

Figure 160. Example Citation of a Federal Regulation.

Citing an Executive Order

A citation for an executive order appears as shown in Figure 161 and consists of the following elements:

- Executive order number

- Volume number of the Code of Federal Regulations

- Page number

- Year in which the executive order was passed

To create this citation, follow these steps:

1. At the left margin, type the executive order number, a comma, and a space. Abbreviate as "Exec. Order No."

2. Type the volume number, followed by a space.

3. Type the abbreviation C.F.R., followed by a space.

4. Type the page number, followed by a space.

5. Type the year the executive order was issued, followed by a period.

6. If your citation continues to a second or subsequent line, double-space that line and indent it one-half inch (five spaces on a typewriter).

See Appendix B for a sample Works Cited list.

```
Exec. Order No. 12804, 3 C.F.R. 298 (1992).
```

Figure 161. Example Citation of an Executive Order.

Citing Audio-Visual Materials

This section shows you how to cite a(n):

- Movie, videotape, videodisc, slide program, or filmstrip

- Television or radio program

- Performance

- Personal interview

- Oral presentation

- Sound recording

- Musical composition

Citing Movies

You can cite movies in two ways:

- By its title

- By a contributor's name

Citing a Movie by its Title

A citation of a movie is shown in Figure 162 and consists of the following elements, which you can obtain from the movie's credits:

- Title of the movie

- Phrase "Screenplay by" and the writer's name (optional)

- Abbreviation "Dir." for "Directed by"

- Director's first and last name

- Abbreviation "Prod." for "Produced by" and the producer's first and last name (optional)

- Abbreviation "Perf." for "Performed by" and the first and last names of the performers (optional)

- Distributor's name

- Year released

To create this citation, follow these steps:

1. At the left margin, type and underline the movie's title, followed by a period and a space. Capitalize the first letter of all words except articles and prepositions (unless the first word is an article or a preposition.)

   NOTE: If the title is a translation of a foreign title, type the original title, underline it, and enclose it in brackets per Figure 162.

2. If you do not wish to include the writer's name, go to Step 3. If you wish to include the writer's name, however, type the phrase "Screenplay by," then a space, then the writer's first and last name, followed by a period and a space.

3. Type the abbreviation "Dir." followed by a space.

4. Type the director's first name, followed by a space, then the last name, followed by a period and a space.

5. If you do not wish to include the producer's name, go to Step 6. If you wish to include the producer's name, however, type the abbreviation "Prod.," then a space, then the producer's first and last names, followed by a period and a space.

6a. If you do not wish to include the performers' names, go to Step 7. If you wish to include the performers' names, however, type the abbreviation "Perf.," then a space, then the first performer's first and last name, followed by a comma and a space.

b. Type the second performer's first and last name, followed by comma and a space. Repeat for all performers except the last.

c. When you get to the last performer's name, type the word "and" and then the performer's first and last names, followed by a period and a space.

7. Type the distributor's name, followed by a comma.

8. Type the year in which the movie was copyrighted, followed by a period.

9. If your citation continues to a second or subsequent line, double-space that line and indent it one-half inch (five spaces on a typewriter).

See Appendix B for a sample Works Cited list.

```
October Sky. Screenplay by Lewis Colick and Lewis

     Gordon. Dir. Joe Johnston. Prod. Larry J. Franco

     and Charles Gordon. Perf. Jake Gyllenhaal, Chris

     Cooper, William Lee Scott, Chad Lindberg, and

     Laura Dern. Universal, 1999.
```

Figure 162. Example Citation of a Movie by Title.

Citing a Movie by a Contributor's Name

You can also cite a movie by the name of one of its contributors; i.e., the writer's name, director's name, producer's name, or the name of a performer. Figure 163 shows an example citation of a movie by a contributor's name and consists of the following elements, which you can get from the movie's credits:

- Name of the contributor

- Contributor's title

- Title of the movie

- Original writer's name

- Abbreviation "Dir." for "Directed by"

- Director's first and last name

- Abbreviation "Prod." for "Produced by" and the producer's first and last name (optional)

- Abbreviation "Perf." for "Performed by" and the first and last names of the performers (optional)

- Distributor's name

- Year released

To create this citation, follow these steps:

1. At the left margin, type the last name of the person you wish to cite, followed by a comma and a space. In Figure 163, this person is the writer of the screenplay.

2. Type the person's first name, followed by a comma and a space. The example in Figure 163 includes the writer's maiden name, so the comma and the space follow that.

3. Type the abbreviation of the person's title. Figure 163 shows the writer as the adaptor of a previous work, so the abbreviation "adapt." follows the name. Type a space.

4. Type and underline the movie's title, followed by a period and a space. Capitalize the first letter of all words except articles and prepositions (unless the first word is an article or a preposition.)

5. To include the name of the writer of the original work, type "By," then a space, then the writer's name as listed on the work, followed by a period and a space. Figure 163 shows the writer's first and middle initials and the last name.

6. Type the abbreviation "Dir." followed by a space.

7. Type the director's first name, followed by a space, then the last name, followed by a period and a space.

8. If you do not wish to include the producer's name, go to Step 9. If you wish to include the producer's name, however, type the abbreviation "Prod.," then a space, then the producer's first and last names, followed by a period and a space.

9a. To include the performers' names, type the abbreviation "Perf.," then a space, then the first performer's first and last name, followed by a comma and a space.

b. Type the second performer's first and last name, followed by comma and a space. Repeat for all performers except the last.

c. When you get to the last performer's name, type the word "and" and then the performer's first and last names, followed by a period and a space.

10. Type the distributor's name, followed by a comma.

11. Type the year in which the movie was copyrighted, followed by a period.

12. If your citation continues to a second or subsequent line, double-space that line and indent it one-half inch (five spaces on a typewriter).

See Appendix B for a sample Works Cited list.

```
Schiff, Stephen, adapt. The Deep End of the Ocean. By

    Jacquelyn Mitchard. Dir. Ulu Grosbard. Prod. Frank

    Capra III and Steve Nicolaides. Perf. Michelle

    Pfeiffer, Treat Williams, Whoopi Goldberg,

    Jonathan Jackson, and Ryan Merriman. Columbia,

    1999.
```

Figure 163. Example Citation of a Movie by a Contributor's Name.

Citing Videotapes, Videodiscs, Slide Programs, or Filmstrips

Videotapes, videodiscs, slide programs, or filmstrips are cited like movies, but they have the following added elements before the name of the distributor:

- Original release date (if relevant)

- Medium (videotape, videodisc, slide program, or filmstrip)

To create a citation for a videotape, videodisc, slide program, or filmstrip, first follow Steps 1-6 for *Citing a Movie by its Title*, pages 238-239, or Steps 1-9 for *Citing a Movie by a Contributor's Name*, pages 240-241. Then, referring to Figure 164, follow these additional steps:

1. Type the original release date, if relevant, followed by a period and a space (see the first example in Figure 164).

2. Type the medium in which this item appears: e.g., videotape, videodisc, slide program, or filmstrip, followed by a period and a space.

NOTE: *If the medium has two words, such as "slide program," capitalize only the first letter of the first word.*

NOTE: *If you are citing a filmstrip, type "Filmstrip" if it is silent, or "Sound filmstrip" if it has sound. If using "Sound filmstrip," capitalize only the "S."*

3. Type the distributor's name, followed by a comma.

4. Type the year in which the movie was copyrighted, followed by a period and a space.

5. If your citation continues to a second or subsequent line, double-space that line and indent it one-half inch (five spaces on a typewriter).

See Appendix B for a sample Works Cited list.

One Flew Over the Cuckoo's Nest. Dir. Milos Forman.

    Perf. Jack Nicholson, Louise Fletcher, and

    William Redford. 1975. Videocassette. Republic,

    1993.

Mulligan, Robert, dir. To Kill a Mockingbird. Perf.

    Gregory Peck, John Megna, Frank Overton, and

    Rosemary Murphy. 1962. Videodisc. Banner, 1994.

Reach for the Stars. Prod. Public Relations Depart-

    ment, Rockwell International. Slide program.

    Ad Astra, 1984.

Signal 30. Sound filmstrip. Illinois State Police.

    1960.

Figure 164. Example Citations of a Videotape, Videodisc, Slide Program, and Filmstrip.

Citing Television or Radio Programs

You can cite television or radio programs in two ways:

- By the title of the program

- By a contributor's name

Citing a Television or Radio Program by Its Title

Figure 165 shows examples of citations of television and radio programs cited by their titles. These citations consist of the following elements:

- Title of episode or segment, if applicable

- Title of the program

- Title of the series, if applicable

- Abbreviations "Narr." for "Narrated by," "Writ." for "Written by," "Dir." for "Directed by," "Perf." For "Performed by," and/or "Introd." for "Introduced by," if applicable, and first and last names for those involved

- Name of network

- Call letters and city of local station

- Day, month, and year of broadcast

To create this citation, follow these steps:

1. At the left margin, type an opening quotation mark, the title of the episode or segment, a period, a closing quotation mark, and a space.

   If there is no episode title, begin with Step 2.

2. Type and underline the title of the program, followed by a period and a space. Capitalize the first letter of all words except articles and prepositions (unless the first word is a preposition or an article).

3. Type the title of the series, if applicable. Do not underline it or enclose it in quotation marks. Capitalize the first letter of all words except articles and prepositions (unless the first word is a preposition or an article).

NOTE: *Some program titles and series titles are the same; i.e.,* Star Trek *is the name of the program and the series.*

4a. At this point, you can choose to list the narrator, writer, producer, director, performers, etc. Table 1 on page 20 lists the correct abbreviations.

b. For example, to list the narrator, type the abbreviation "Narr." followed by a period and a space. Then type the narrator's first and last name, followed by a period and a space. Repeat this step for each person you wish to cite.

5. Type the name of the network. Abbreviate words, if possible. Follow the name with a period and a space.

6. Type the call letters of the television or radio station (remember to capitalize them), followed by a comma and a space.

7. Type the name of the city where the station is located, followed by a period and a space.

8. Type the date the episode or segment was broadcast in day, month (abbreviated per Table 5 on page 20), year format, followed by a period.

9. If your citation continues to a second or subsequent line, double-space that line and indent it one-half inch (five spaces on a typewriter).

See Appendix B for a sample Works Cited list.

"A Man of Property." The Forsyte Saga. By John Galsworthy.

 Masterpiece Theatre. Narr. Alistair Cooke. PBS.

 KCET, Los Angeles. 7 June 1973.

Down Home. By Darryl Pace. Dir. Daniel Ross. Perf.

 Thomas Gaines and Patricia Hansen. Hallmark Hall

 of Fame. NBC. KNBC, Los Angeles. 17 Nov. 1995.

"The Pueblo Incident." Narr. Joseph Perry. The Joseph

 Perry Show. Cox. KSJC, Los Angeles. 4 Feb. 1972.

Figure 165. Example Citations of Television and Radio Programs by Title.

Citing a Television or Radio Program by a Contributor's Name

You may wish to cite the program by the name of the director or an actor, for example, to emphasize that person's work. Remember that the exact elements of the citation will depend on how many of the people involved in the production you wish to cite. Figure 166 shows an example that consists of the following elements:

- Name of contributor

- Title of contributor

- Title of program

- Word "By" and the original author of work

- Abbreviation "Adapt." and the name of the scriptwriter

- Name of the program/series

- Name of the network

- Call letters and city of local station

- Day, month, and year of broadcast

The steps to creating the example citation are as follows:

1. At the left margin, type the last name of the contributor, followed by a comma and a space.

2. Type the first name of the contributor, followed by a comma and a space.

3. In the example, the contributor is the director. Therefore, the abbreviation "dir." in lower-case letters follows his name. Follow that with a space.

4. Type and underline the title of the program, followed by a period and a space. Capitalize the first letter of all words except articles and prepositions (unless the first word is a preposition).

5. Since Orson Welles did not write *The War of the Worlds*, the author must be cited. Type the word "By" followed by a space. Type the author's first and last names (the similarity in last names is a coincidence). In this case, the author goes by his initials: H. G. Be sure to put a space between the period following the "H" and the "G." Then type the author's last name, followed by a period and a space.

6. The short story *The War of the Worlds* was adapted into a radio script by someone other than the original author, H. G. Wells. This person's name must be cited, beginning with the abbreviation "Adapt." for "Adapted by." Type a space. Then type the scriptwriter's first and last names—in this case, Howard Koch. Follow the name with a period and a space.

   (At this point in another citation, you could list the narrator, producer, director, performers, etc. Table 1 on page 20 lists the correct abbreviations. See page 245 for an example.

   For example, to list the narrator, type the abbreviation "Narr." followed by a period and a space. Then type the narrator's first and last name, followed by a period and a space. Repeat this step for each person you wish to cite.)

7. Type the name of the program, which in this example, is the same as the series.

8. Type the name of the network. Although it is not necessary in the example in Figure 166, abbreviate words, if possible. Follow the network name with a period and a space.

9. Type the call letters of the television or radio station (remember to capitalize them), followed by a comma and a space.

10. Type the name of the city where the station is located, followed by a period and a space.

11. Type the date the episode or segment was broadcast in day, month (abbreviated per Table 5 on page 22), year format, followed by a period.

12. If your citation continues to a second or subsequent line, double-space that line and indent it one-half inch (five spaces on a typewriter).

See Appendix B for a sample Works Cited list.

```
Welles, Orson, dir. The War of the Worlds. By H. G.

     Wells. Adapt. Howard Koch. Mercury Theatre on

     the Air. CBS Radio. WCBS, New York. 30 Oct. 1938.
```

Figure 166. Example Citation of a Television Show Cited by a Contributor's Name.

Citing Performances

Performances include events such as plays, ballets, concerts, and operas. Cite a performance similarly to a film. Once again, the precise elements you may want to cite will vary from performance to performance. Refer to Table 1 on page 20, which lists all the elements and their abbreviated forms.

Figure 167 shows a sample of a citation for a performance. This sample, as do most performances in general, consists of the following elements:

- Title of the performance

- Word "By" and the writer's name

- Abbreviation "Dir." and the director's name

- Abbreviation "Perf." and the name(s) of the performer(s)

- Location of the performance

- City where the performance was held

- Day, month, and year performance was held

The steps for citing the sample citation are as follows:

1. At the left margin, type and underline the title of the performance, followed by a period and a space. Capitalize the first letter of all words except articles and prepositions (unless the first word is an article or a preposition.)

2. If you do not wish to include the writer's name, go to Step 3. To include the writer's name, type the phrase "By," then a space, then the writer's first and last name, followed by a period and a space.

3. Type the abbreviation "Dir." followed by a space, then type the director's first name, followed by a space, then the last name, followed by a period and a space.

4. To include a performer's name, type the abbreviation "Perf.," then a space, then the performer's first and last names, followed by a period and a space.

    (At this point in another citation, you could list the narrator, producer, director, performers, etc. Table 1 on page 20 lists the correct abbreviations. See page 245 for an example.

For example, to list the narrator, type the abbreviation "Narr." followed by a period and a space. Then type the narrator's first and last name, followed by a period and a space. Repeat this step for each category and person you wish to cite.)

5. Type the location of the performance, followed by a comma and a space.

6. Type the city where the performance was held, followed by a period and a space.

7. Type the date the performance was held in day, month (abbreviated per Table 5 on page 22), year format, followed by a period.

8. If your citation continues to a second or subsequent line, double-space that line and indent it one-half inch (five spaces on a typewriter).

See Appendix B for a sample Works Cited list.

<u>Hamlet</u>. By William Shakespeare. Dir. John Gielgud.

    Perf. Richard Burton. Shubert Theatre, Boston.

    4 Mar. 1964.

<u>Medea</u>. By Euripides. Trans. Alistair Elliot. Dir.

    Jonathan Kent. Perf. Diana Rigg. Longacre Theatre,

    New York. 7 Apr. 1994.

<u>The River</u>. Chor. Alvin Ailey. Dance Theater of Harlem.

    New York State Theater, New York. 15 Mar. 1994.

Figure 167. Example Citations of a Performance.

Citing Oral Presentations

Oral presentations include lectures, speeches, readings, and addresses. You can cite a presentation with a title or without a title. Figure 168 shows both.

The first example in Figure 168 shows a citation of an oral presentation with a title, which consists of the following elements:

- Speaker's last name

- Speaker's first name or initial (and middle name or initial, if available)

- Title or description of the presentation

- Name of the meeting, if applicable

- Name of the sponsoring organization, if applicable

- Location of the meeting

- Day, month, and year of presentation

To create this citation, follow these steps:

1. At the left margin, type the speaker's last name, followed by a comma and a space.

2. Type the speaker's first name, followed by a period and a space.

3. If there is no title, go to Step 4. Otherwise, type an opening quotation mark, the title, a period, then a closing quotation mark. Capitalize the first letter of all words except articles and prepositions (unless the first word is an article or preposition).

4. Type a description of the presentation, such as "Reading of ," followed by the title of the material read, a period, and a space; or "Address," "Keynote speech," "Lecture," etc. followed by a period.

NOTE: *If you use the phrase "Reading of," followed by the title of the material read, underline the title of that material, as shown in the third example in Figure 168.*

5. If applicable, type the name of the meeting, followed by a period and a space. Otherwise, go to Step 5.

6. If applicable, type the name of the sponsoring organization followed by a period and a space. Otherwise, go to Step 7.

7. Type the location of the meeting, followed by a comma and a space.

8. Type city where the presentation was held, followed by a period and a space.

9. Type the date the performance was held in day, month (abbreviated per Table 5 on page 22), year format, followed by a period.

10. If your citation continues to a second or subsequent line, double-space that line and indent it one-half inch (five spaces on a typewriter).

See Appendix B for a sample Works Cited list.

```
Jensen, Sarah. "Timing is Everything." Inspired

     Teaching Session. Excellence in Education

     Conference. University of Phoenix. Hyatt Hotel,

     Long Beach. 7 Nov. 1998.
```

```
Ortega, Raul. Keynote speech. Artist's Forum.

     Amer. Artist's Assoc. Annual Mtg. Hotel

     Mark Hopkins, San Francisco. 15 Mar. 1998.
```

```
Sanderson, Louise. Reading of Poe's The Raven.

     Ctr. for the Performing Arts, Costa Mesa.

     17 Nov. 1998.
```

Figure 168. Example Citations of Oral Presentations With Titles.

Citing Sound Recordings

Sound recordings include CDs, audiocassettes, audiotapes (reel-to-reel tapes), and LPs (long-playing records). This section shows you how to cite a:

- Musical or spoken word recording

- Specific song

- Private or archival recording or tape

- Libretto, booklet, liner notes, or other accompanying materials

You can find the required elements on the box cover or label.

Citing a Musical Recording

When citing a musical recording, decide which contributor to list first—the composer, conductor, or performer. The order of the information included in the citation depends on it. This section shows some examples, but also refer to *Citing a Musical Composition* for symphony citation examples. A citation of musical recording appears in Figure 169 and consists of the following elements:

- Name of contributor

- Abbreviation "Cond." or "cond." for "conducted by," or "Perf." or "perf." for "performed by"

- Name of orchestra, if applicable

- Title of recording

- Name of performer(s) and/or conductor and abbreviations shown above if not already used

- Recording date, if applicable

- Media type

- Name of manufacturer

- Production company name

To create this citation, follow these steps:

1. At the left margin, type the contributor's last name, followed by a comma and a space.

2a. Type the contributor's first name (and/or middle name or initial), followed by a period and a space. Figure 169 shows the composer's name cited.

b. If you cited a performer in Step a, after the first or middle name or initial, add a comma, the abbreviation "perf.," and a space; (e.g., "Jones, John, perf."). If you cited the conductor, add a comma, the abbreviation, "cond.," and a space; (e.g., "Lewis, Simon, cond.").

3. Type and underline the title of the recording, followed by a period and a space.

4. You can cite the orchestra here, using the abbreviation "Orch.," if "Orchestra" is in the name. Follow it with a period and a space. Then type the abbreviation "Cond.," followed by the conductor's name, a period, and a space.

5. If you cited the composer in Step 1, you can cite the performers next, using the abbreviation "Perf." and the names. Follow it with the abbreviation "Cond." and the name of the conductor.

6. If the recording was previously published, type the abbreviation "Rec." for "Recorded," then the date in day, month (per Table 5 on page 22), year format, followed by a period and a space.

7. Type the media type (i.e., Audiocassette, LP, CD, Audiotape, etc.), followed by a period and a space.

8. Type the name of the production company name, followed by a comma and a space.

9. Type the year the current recording was made, followed by a period.

10. If your citation continues to a second or subsequent line, double-space that line and indent it one-half inch (five spaces on a typewriter).

See Appendix B for a sample Works Cited list and other examples of sound recording citations.

```
Smith, Ronald L. Birdsong. City News Orch. Perf. John

    Jones and Perry Adams. Cond. Simon Lewis. Rec.

    4 Dec. 1988. CD. Abco, 1998.
```

Figure 169. Example Citation of a Musical Recording.

Citing a Specific Song

You can cite a specific song from a recording. The elements required will vary according to the type of information available (i.e., whether or not there are performers, a previous recording date, etc.). The first example in Figure 170 shows a citation for a specific song that consists of the following elements:

- Name of singer

- Title of song

- Word "By" and the songwriter's name

- Title of recording on which the song appears

- Name of recording company

- Recording date

To create this citation, follow these steps:

1. Referring to the first example in Figure 170, at the left margin, type the singer's last name, followed by a comma and a space.

2a. If only the first name or initial is available, follow it with a period and a space.

 b. If the singer's middle name or initial is available, however, type the first name, followed by a space. Then type the middle name or the initial, followed by a period and a space.

3. Type an opening quotation mark, the title of the song, a period, a closing quotation mark, and a space.

4. Type the word "By" and the songwriter's name in first name, last name format. Follow it with a period and a space.

5. Type and underline the title of the recording, followed by a period and a space.

6. Type the name of the recording company name, followed by a comma and a space.

7. Type the year the recording was made, followed by a period and a space.

8. If your citation continues to a second or subsequent line, double-space that line and indent it one-half inch (five spaces on a typewriter).

See Appendix B for a sample Works Cited list.

Jeffries, Lance. "Love Song." By Elliott Graves.
Songs From England. New World, 1998.

Peters, Marianne. "My Only Love." Perf. Peters and
Gerald Williams. Rec. 24 June 1989. Taking Charge.
Abco, 1998.

Figure 170. Example Citations of Specific Songs.

Citing a Spoken Word Recording

When citing a spoken word recording, decide which contributor to list first—the speaker, author, or production director. The order of the information included in the citation depends on it. This section shows some examples.

A citation of spoken word recording listing the author first appears in the first example in Figure 171 and consists of the following elements:

- Name of contributor

- Title of recording

- Original publication date, if applicable

- Phrase "Read by"

- Name of speaker

- Media type

- Name of recording house

- Year recorded

To create this citation, follow these steps:

1. At the left margin, type the author's last name, followed by a comma and a space.

2a. If only the first name or initial is available, follow it with a period and a space.

  b. If the author's middle name or initial is available, however, type the first name, followed by a space. Then type the middle name, or the initial followed by a period and a space.

3. Type and underline the title of the recording, followed by a period and a space. Capitalize the first letter of all words except articles and prepositions (unless the first word is an article or preposition).

4. If the recording was previously published, type the date in day, month (abbreviated per Table 5 on page 22), year format, followed by a period and a space.

5. Type the phrase "Read by," followed by a space.

6. Type the name of the speaker in first name, last name format, followed by a period and a space.

7. Type the media type (i.e., audiocassette, LP, CD, audiotape, etc.), followed by a period and a space.

8. Type the recording company name, followed by a comma and a space.

9. Type the year the recording was made, followed by a period.

10. If your citation continues to a second or subsequent line, double-space that line and indent it one-half inch (five spaces on a typewriter).

See Appendix B for a sample Works Cited list.

Barrington, Joseph. <u>The City Lights</u>. 1953. Read by

    Gerald.Rand. Audiocassette. Abco, 1997.

Lewis, Jennifer, narr. <u>Found Alive</u>. LP. Lowell, 1983.

Kendall, Kenneth, dir. <u>Taking Liberties</u>. By Thomas Lind.

    Adapt. Tony Santo. Star Radio Theater. Rec. 5 Jan.

    1973. Audiocassette. Abco, 1998.

Wright, Daniel. <u>Over the Wall</u>. Perf. Janet Sloan,

    Joseph Gaines, and Terence Lloyd. Dir. Barton

    Garrison. CD. Moonlight, 1999.

Figure 171. Example Citations of Spoken Word Recordings.

Citing an Archival or Private Recording or Tape

When citing an archival or private recording or tape, decide which contributor to list first—the speaker, author, or production director. The order of the information included in the citation depends on it.

A citation of spoken word recording listing the author first appears in Figure 172 and consists of the following elements:

- Name of speaker

- Title of recording

- Abbreviation "Rec." and original recording date, if applicable

- Media type

- Name of organization or institution where recording or tape is stored

- City where organization or institution is located

- Identifying number of the recording

To create this citation, follow these steps:

1. At the left margin, type the speaker's last name, followed by a comma and a space.

2a. If only the first name or initial is available, follow it with a period and a space.

  b. If the speaker's middle name or initial is available, however, type the first name, followed by a space. Then type the middle name, or the initial followed by a period and a space.

3. Type the title of the recording and follow it with a period and a space. Capitalize the first letter of all words except articles and prepositions (unless the first word is an article or preposition).

    NOTE: Do not underline the title nor put it in quotation marks.

4a. If you do not know the recording date, go to Step 5.

  b. If you know the recording date, however, type the abbreviation "Rec.," followed by a space.

   c. Type the date in day, month (abbreviated per Table 5 on page 22), year format, followed by a period and a space.

5. Type the media type (i.e., audiocassette, LP, CD, audiotape, etc.), followed by a period and a space.

6. Type the name of the organization or institution where the recording is archived, followed by a comma and a space.

7a. Type the name of the city where the organization or institution is located.

   b. If the archive itself does not have a name, type a period and a space and go to Step 8.

   c. If the archive itself has a name, however, type a comma and a space, then the name of the archive, followed by a period and a space.

8. Type the number of the recording, followed by a period.

9. If your citation continues to a second or subsequent line, double-space that line and indent it one-half inch (five spaces on a typewriter).

See Appendix B for a sample Works Cited.

```
Garrison, Jason. Down the Lonesome Road. Rec. 3 Dec.,

     1984. Audiocassette. Bensen Library, San Francisco,

     Smith Archives. S248.
```

Figure 172. Example Citation of an Archival Recording.

Citing a Libretto, Booklet, Liner Notes, or Other Material Accompanying a Recording

You can also cite information accompanying a recording, such as a libretto, booklet, liner notes, etc. This section shows some examples, but also refer to the other citations in this section for more details on citing the publication information, which will vary from citation to citation. Remember that the exact citation will depend on which one of these items you are citing and whether you choose to cite a performer, the conductor, etc. Also see *Citing a Musical Composition* for symphony citation examples.

The first example in Figure 173 shows a citation for a booklet. It consists of the following elements:

- Name of booklet author

- Title of booklet

- Word "Booklet"

- Title of recording

- Name of writer of music on recording

- Media type

- Name of recording company

- Recording date

To create this citation, follow these steps:

1. At the left margin, type the author's last name, followed by a comma and a space.

2a. If only the first name or initial is available, follow it with a period and a space.

b. If the author's middle name or initial is available, however, type the first name, followed by a space. Then type the middle name, or the initial followed by a period and a space.

3. Type an opening quotation mark, the title of the booklet, a period, and a closing quotation mark, followed by a period and a space.

   NOTE: Underline the title of the recording if it is in the title of the booklet.

4. Type the word "Booklet," followed by a period and a space.

5. Type and underline the name of the recording that the booklet accompanies, followed by a period and a space.

6. Type the word "By" and the name of the writer of the music on the recording, followed by a period and a space.

7. Type the media type (i.e., Audiocassette, LP, CD, Audiotape, etc.), followed by a period and a space.

8. Type the name of the recording company, followed by a comma and a space.

9. Type the year the recording was made, followed by a period.

10. If your citation continues to a second or subsequent line, double-space that line and indent it one-half inch (five spaces on a typewriter).

See Appendix B for a sample Works Cited list.

```
Randall, George. "Ronald Smith's Birdsong." Booklet.

     Birdsong. By Ronald Smith. CD. Abco, 1998.
```

```
D'Angelo, Maria. Libretto. Un Uomo e Una Dama. Music

     by Luigi Santori. Orch. Nazionale Napoli. Cond.

     Giorgio Giovanni. CD. Musica d'Italia, 1997.
```

```
Thompson, Sandra. Liner Notes. Music of the Mountains.

     By Gerry Robinson. LP. Ace, 1983.
```

Figure 173. Example Citations of Materials Accompanying a Recording.

Citing Musical Compositions

Musical compositions include operas, ballets, symphonies, etc. This citation assumes you are citing the actual piece of sheet music itself. If you are citing a musical composition presented in a sound recording, television or radio program, or performance, see *Citing a Television or Radio Program* on pages 244-247, *Citing a Performance* on page 248-249, or *Citing a Sound Recording* on page 252-253.

Figure 174 shows an example citation of a musical composition, which consists of the following elements:

- Composer's last name

- Composer's first name or initial (and middle name or initial, if available)

- Title of the piece, opera, ballet, etc.

- Abbreviation "op." and number, if applicable

and, for published scores:

- Date piece was originally written, if available

- City of publication

- Name of publisher

- Year of publication

To create this citation, follow these steps:

1. At the left margin, type the composer's last name, followed by a comma and a space.

2a. If only the first name or initial is available, follow it with a period and a space.

 b. If the author's middle name or initial is available, however, type the first name, followed by a space. Then type the middle name or initial, followed by a period and a space.

3. Type and underline the title of the composition. Capitalize the first letter of all words except articles and prepositions (unless the first word is an article or a preposition). Follow the title with a period and a space.

> **EXCEPTION:** *If the composition is identified only by form, number, and key, do not underline it nor enclose it in quotation mark. (See the second example in Figure 174.)*

4. If applicable, type the abbreviation "op." followed by a space, then the number, followed by a period.

5. If the piece is not a published score, go to Step 11. If the piece is a published score, however, refer to the third example in Figure 174, and complete Steps 6 through 11:

6. Ensure that "No." and "Op." in the title start with capital letters. Type a space.

7. Type the year the piece was originally written, if available, followed by a period and a space.

8. Type city where the publisher is located, followed by a colon and a space.

9. Type the publisher's name, followed by a comma and a space.

10. Type the year of publication, followed by a period.

11. If your citation continues to a second or subsequent line, double-space that line and indent it one-half inch (five spaces on a typewriter).

See Appendix B for a sample Works Cited list.

```
Jones, Steven. Symphony of the Woods, op. 2.
```

```
Jones, Steven. Symphony no. 6 in C, op. 47.
```

```
Jones, Steven. Symphony No. 5 in D, Op. 25. 1954.

     Los Angeles: Castle, 1992.
```

Figure 174. Example Citations of Musical Compositions.

Citing Personal Interviews

You can cite four kinds of interviews:

- Published interviews

- Interviews you conduct

- Recorded interviews

- Interviews broadcast on television or radio

Citing a Published Interview

Published interviews are those in which the author or editor includes an interview with someone else in the work. The elements included will vary according to what is available for any particular work. Figure 175 shows an example citation of a published interview. This one consists of the following elements:

- Interviewee's last name and first name or initial (and middle name or initial, if available)

- Title of interview

- Title of work

- Abbreviation "Ed."

- Editor's first name or initial (and middle name or initial, if available) and last name

- City of publication

- Publisher's name

- Year of publication

- Page number(s) of interview

To create this citation, follow these steps:

1. At the left margin, type the interviewee's last name, followed by a comma and a space.

2a. If only the first name or initial is available, follow it with a period and a space.

   b. If the author's middle name or initial is available, however, type the first name, followed by a space. Then type the middle name or initial, followed by a period and a space.

3. Type an opening quotation mark, then the title of the interview. Capitalize the first letter of all words except articles and prepositions (unless the first word is an article or preposition). End the title with a period, a closing quotation mark, and a space.

    NOTE: If the interview does not have a title, type the word "Interview" instead; e.g., "Di Pietro, Giovanni. Interview. Touring Tuscany," etc.

4. Type and underline the title of the work, followed by a period. Capitalize the first letter of all words except articles and prepositions (unless the first word is a preposition).

5. Type the abbreviation "Ed." followed by a space.

6. Type the editor's first name, followed by a space, then the editor's last name, followed by a period.

7. Type the city of publication, followed by a colon.

8. Type the publisher's name, followed by a comma and a space.

9. Type the year of publication, followed by a period and a space.

10. Type the page number(s), followed by a period.

    NOTE: Do not include "p." or "pp." in the page number.

    NOTE: If you are including a range of page numbers that has three digits or more, include only two digits in the second half of the range, as shown in Figure 175.

11. If your citation continues to a second or subsequent line, double-space that line and indent it one-half inch (five spaces on a typewriter).

    See Appendix B for a sample Works Cited list.

```
Di Pietro, Giovanni. "Old Memories." Touring Tuscany.
    Ed. Mary Ellen Frank. New York: Time/Life. 1998.
    170-76.
```

Figure 175. Example Citation of a Published Interview.

Citing an Interview Published Independently

An interview may be conducted and published independently; i.e., it does not appear in a magazine or book of other materials but is published as the interview itself or in a series of interviews. Figure 176 shows an example citation of an interview published independently, which consists of the following elements:

- Interviewee's last name

- Interviewee's first name or initial (and middle name or initial, if available)

- Word "Interview"

- Title of interview

- Word "By"

- Interviewer's first name or initial (and middle name or initial, if available) and last name

- City of publication

- Publisher's name

- Year of publication

- Page number(s) of interview

To create this citation, follow these steps:

1. At the left margin, type the interviewee's last name, followed by a comma and a space.

2a. If only the first name or initial is available, follow it with a period and a space.

 b. If the interviewee's middle name or initial is available, however, type the first name, followed by a space. Then type the middle name or initial, followed by a period and a space.

3. Type the word "Interview," followed by a period and a space.

4. Type and underline the title of the interview. Capitalize the first letter of all words except articles and prepositions (unless the first word is an article or preposition). Follow the title with a period and a space.

5. Type the word "By" followed by a space.

6. Type the interviewer's first name, followed by a space, then the interviewer's last name, followed by a period and a space.

7. Type the city of publication, followed by a colon and a space.

8. Type the publisher's name, followed by a comma and a space.

9. Type the year of publication followed by a period and a space.

10. Type the page number(s), followed by a period.

    NOTE: Do not include "p." or "pp." in the page number.

    NOTE: If you are including a range of page numbers that has three digits or more, include only two digits in the second half of the range.

11. If your citation continues to a second or subsequent line, double-space that line and indent it one-half inch (five spaces on a typewriter).

See Appendix B for a sample Works Cited list.

```
Miller, Craig. Interview. Assault on the Presidency.
     By John Winters. New York: Doubleday. 1998.
     24-26.
```

Figure 176. Example Citation of an Interview Published Independently.

Citing an Untitled Interview

Figure 177 shows an example citation of an untitled interview in a magazine. This citation consists of the following elements:

- Interviewee's last name

- Interviewee's first name or initial (and middle name or initial, if available)

- Phrase "Interview"

- Name of publication

- Rest of elements for the citation for that type of publication

To create this citation, follow these steps:

1. At the left margin, type the interviewee's last name, followed by a comma and a space.

2a. If only the first name or initial is available, follow it with a period and a space.

 b. If the interviewee's middle name or initial is available, however, type the first name, followed by a space. Then type the middle name or initial, followed by a period and a space.

3. Type the phrase "Interview" followed by a period and a space.

4. Follow the instructions for the type of publication in which this material appears. For instance, if it is a newspaper, follow the instructions for citing a newspaper. If it is a magazine, following the instructions for citing a magazine. Figure 177 shows an example citation of an untitled interview in a magazine.

5. If your citation continues to a second or subsequent line, double-space that line and indent it one-half inch (five spaces on a typewriter).

See Appendix B for a sample Works Cited list.

```
Jones, Thomas. Interview. Business Talk 21 June

     1997: 23-24.
```

Figure 177. Example Citation of an Untitled Interview in a Magazine.

Citing an Interview the Researcher Conducted

During the course of your research, you may interview some subject-matter experts. Figure 178 shows an example of such a citation, which consists of the following elements:

- Interviewee's last name

- Interviewee's first name or initial (and middle name or initial, if available)

- Description of type of interview

- Day, month, and year of interview

To create this citation, follow these steps:

1. At the left margin, type the interviewee's last name, followed by a comma and a space.

2a. If only the first name or initial is available, follow it with a period and a space.

  b. If the interviewee's middle name or initial is available, however, type the first name, followed by a space. Then type the middle name or initial, followed by a period and a space.

3. Type the type of interview you conducted; i.e., "Personal interview," "Telephone interview," etc., followed by a period and a space.

4. Type the date of the interview in day, month (abbreviated per Table 5 on page 22), year format, followed by a period.

5. If your citation continues to a second or subsequent line, double-space that line and indent it one-half inch (five spaces on a typewriter).

See Appendix B for a sample Works Cited list.

```
Angelou, Maya. Personal interview. 25 Nov. 1997.
```

Figure 178. Example Citation of an Interview the Researcher Conducted.

Citing a Recorded Interview

Recorded interviews are those in which a host interviews someone and makes the interview available on audio- or videocassette. Figure 179 shows an example citation of a recorded interview, which consists of the following elements:

- Interviewee's last name and first name or initial (and middle name or initial, if available)

- Title of interview

- Title of audio- or videocassette

- Abbreviation "Dir." for "Directed by"

- Director's first name or initial (and middle name or initial, if available) and last name

- Phrase "Audiocassette" or "Videocassette"

- Publisher's name

- Year of publication

To create this citation, follow these steps:

1. At the left margin, type the interviewee's last name, followed by a comma and a space.

2a. If only the first name or initial is available, follow it with a period and a space.

 b. If the interviewee's middle name or initial is available, however, type the first name, followed by a space. Then type the middle name or initial, followed by a period and a space.

3. Type an opening quotation mark, then the title of the interview. Capitalize the first letter of all words except articles and prepositions (unless the first word is an article or a preposition). End the title with a period, a closing quotation mark, and a space.

   NOTE: *If the interview does not have a title, type the word "Interview" instead; e.g., "Morrison, Howard. Interview. <u>Events of the Century</u>," etc.*

4. Type underline the title of the audio- or videocassette. Capitalize the first letter of all words except articles and prepositions (unless the first word is an article or preposition). Follow the title with a period and a space.

5. Since the source is a videocassette, you must include the director's name. Type the abbreviation "Dir." followed by a space.

6. Type the director's first name, followed by a space, then the director's last name, followed by a period and a space.

7. Type the phrase "Videocassette," followed by a period and a space.

8. Type the publisher's name, followed by a comma and a space.

9. Type the year of publication, followed by a period and a space.

10. If your citation continues to a second or subsequent line, double-space that line and indent it one-half inch (five spaces on a typewriter).

See Appendix B for a sample Works Cited list.

Morrison, Howard. "The Gulf War." <u>Events of the</u>

<u>Century</u>. Dir. John Jones. Videocassette.

New World, 1998.

Figure 179. Example Citation of a Recorded Interview.

Citing an Interview Broadcast on Radio or TV

Figure 180 shows an example citation of an interview broadcast on radio or TV, which consists of the following elements:

- Interviewee's last name

- Interviewee's first name or initial (and middle name or initial, if available)

- Phrase "Interview with"

- Name(s) of interviewer(s)

- Name of show

- Name of network

- Call letters of station

- City where station is located

- Day, month, and year of interview

To create this citation, follow these steps:

1. At the left margin, type the interviewee's last name, followed by a comma and a space.

2a. If only the first name or initial is available, follow it with a period and a space.

   b. If the interviewee's middle name or initial is available, however, type the first name, followed by a space. Then type the middle name or initial, followed by a period and a space.

3. Type the phrase "Interview with" followed by a space.

4. Type the name(s) of the interviewer(s). If there is one, follow the last name with a period and a space. If there are two, follow the surname of the first interviewer with a space, then type "and," then type the first and last name of the second interviewer, followed by a period and a space.

5. Type and underline the title of the program. Capitalize the first letter of all words except articles and prepositions (unless the first word is an article or a preposition). Follow the title with a period and a space.

6. Type the name of the network. Abbreviate words, if possible. Follow the name with a period and a space.

7. Type the call letters of the television or radio station (remember to capitalize them), followed by a comma and a space.

8. Type the name of the city where the station is located, followed by a period and a space.

9. Type the date of the interview in day, month (abbreviated per Table 5 on page 22), year format, followed by a period.

10. If your citation continues to a second or subsequent line, double-space that line and indent it one-half inch (five spaces on a typewriter).

See Appendix B for a sample Works Cited list.

```
Powell, Colin. Interview with Jane Pauley and

     Stone Phillips. Dateline. NBC. WNBC, New York.

     7 June 1997.
```

```
Clancy, Tom. Interview with Michael Jackson.

     Michael Jackson Show. ABC. KABC, Los Angeles.

     18 Dec. 1997.
```

Figure 180. Example Citations of Television and Radio Interviews.

Citing Electronic Media

You are not limited to using physical books and periodicals as source material for expert opinion for the papers you write; you can do research on the Internet, too. These online sources must be cited, but be careful: while physical books and magazines are generally reputable sources, anyone can publish on the Internet. Just because an article or book appears online does not mean it is accurate or reputable. Be sure you seek out sources from respected authors and publishers.

This section shows you how to cite the following:

- Software program that you have downloaded

- Publication on CD-ROM, diskette, or magnetic tape

- Scholarly project, reference database

- Professional or personal website

- E-mail message and online posting

- Chat

- Book

- Article

- Review

- Abstract

- Editorial

- Letter to the editor

- Work of art, map, cartoon, and advertisement

- Television or radio program, film or film clip

- Sound recording or sound clip

- Interview

- Manuscript

Citing Downloaded Computer Software

A citation of computer software with an author appears as shown in Figure 181 and consists of the following elements:

- Title of program

- Abbreviation "Vers."

- Version number

- Date of download

- Online address

To create this citation, follow these steps:

1. Type and underline the software title, followed by a period and a space.

2. Type the abbreviation "Vers." followed by a space.

3. Type the version number, followed by a period and a space.

4. Type the day you downloaded the software, followed by a space. Then type the month in abbreviated format (see Table 5 on page 22), followed by a space. Then type the year, followed by a space.

5. Type the complete online address, being sure to include opening and closing carats (i.e., < >).

6. If your citation continues to a second or subsequent line, double-space that line and indent one-half inch (five spaces on a typewriter).

See Appendix B for a sample Works Cited list.

```
Legal+. Vers. 2.0. 24 Jan. 1999 <http://www.

        advancedpro.com/software/legal+>.
```

Figure 181. Example Citation of Downloaded Computer Software.

Citing Publications on CD-ROM, Diskette, or Magnetic Tape

Many publications are issued on CD-ROM, diskette, or magnetic tape. These citations must include the added description of the type of medium used (CD-ROM, diskette, or magnetic tape). These publications may have editors, translators, compilers, etc., so if your publication does not appear in the examples given here, look in the section on *Citing Books* for the proper way to cite the beginning part of the publication information. If some of the information is missing, cite what is available. If information for a previously printed version is available, cite that first. Then return to this section for instructions on citing the type of medium.

Citing a Non-Periodical on CD-ROM, Diskette, or Magnetic Tape

Some books and other non-periodicals (publications not revised regularly) are produced on CD-ROM, diskette, or magnetic tape, rather than in print form. These are cited similar to a printed book. Remember to cite any information regarding a previously printed version.

A citation for a non-periodical with one author that has not been previously published appears as shown in Figure 182 and consists of the following elements:

- Author's last name

- Author's first name or initial (and middle name or initial, if available)

- Title of book

- Publication medium

- Edition, release, or version number, if relevant

- City where the publisher is located

- Name of publisher

- Date of publication

To create this citation, follow these steps:

1. At the left margin, type the author's last name, followed by a comma and a space.

2a. If only the first name or initial is available, follow it with a period and a space.

    b. If the author's middle name or initial is available, however, type the first name, followed by a space. Then type the middle name or initial, followed by a period and a space.

3. Type and underline the book title. Capitalize the first letter of all words except articles and prepositions (unless the first word is an article or a preposition). Follow it with a period and a space.

4a. Type the publication medium (CD-ROM, diskette, or magnetic tape), followed by a period and a space.

    b. If the publication has more than one CD-ROM, cite the total number of discs in the set by typing the number followed by the word "discs," a period, and a space. (i.e., "CD-ROM. 4 discs.").

    c. To cite only the number of the disc you use, type the word "Disc," followed by the number of the disc you used, a period, and a space (see the second example in Figure 182).

5. Type the edition, release, or version (if relevant), followed by a period and a space.

6. Type the city of publication, followed by a colon and a space.

7. Type the name of the publisher, followed by a comma and a space. Shorten the publisher's name, if possible; for instance, if the publisher is Harcourt, Brace, Jovanovich, just put "Harcourt."

8. Type the copyright year, followed by a period.

9. If your citation continues to a second or subsequent line, double-space that line and indent it one-half inch (five spaces on a typewriter).

See Appendix B for a sample Works Cited list.

```
Thompson, Joan T. Authors of the Victorian Age. CD-ROM.

     Vers. 1.0. Santa Clara: Artworks, 1998.
```

```
Patterson, Ruth. 19th Century Spanish Writers. CD-ROM.

     Disc 3. Vers. 2.0. Santa Clara: Artworks, 1996.
```

Figure 182. Example Citations of a Nonperiodical With One Author on CD-ROM.

Citing Material From a Periodically Published Database on CD-ROM

Many journals, magazines, newspapers, reference works, etc., are not only published in print form, but also on CD-ROM. Begin by citing the information for the printed version. This section shows an example of a periodically published database on CD-ROM that has one author. If your citation is different, be sure to look up the information for the print version first elsewhere in this chapter, then return to this page for the CD-ROM citation instructions.

A citation for a periodically published database on CD-ROM with one author appears as shown in Figure 183 and consists of the following elements:

- Author's last name

- Author's first name or initial (and middle name or initial, if available)

- Title of printed version

- City of publisher of printed version

- Name of publisher of printed version

- Date of publication of printed version

- Title of CD-ROM version

- Word "CD-ROM"

- Name of vendor of CD-ROM version

- Date of publication of CD-ROM version

To create this citation, follow these steps:

1. At the left margin, type the author's last name, followed by a comma and a space.

2. If only the first name or initial is available, follow it with a period and a space. If the author's middle name or initial is available, however, type the first name, followed by a space. Then type the middle name or initial, followed by a period and a space.

3. Type and underline the title of the printed version. Capitalize the first letter of all words except prepositions and articles (unless the first word is a preposition or an article). Follow the title with a period and a space.

4. Type the city of publication of the printed version, followed by a colon and a space.

5. Type the name of the publisher of the printed version, followed by a period and a space.

6. Type the year of publication of the printed version, followed by a period and a space. (Include the day and month, if relevant.)

7. Type the title of the CD-ROM version and underline it. Follow it with a period and a space. Capitalize the title per Step 3.

8a. Type the word "CD-ROM," followed by a period and a space.

b. If the publication has more than one CD-ROM, cite the total number of discs in the set by typing the number followed by the word "discs," a period, and a space. (See the second example in Figure 183).

c. To cite only the number of the disc you use, type the word "Disc," followed by the number of the disc you used, a period, and a space (i.e., "CD-ROM. Disc 1.").

9. Type the name of the publisher of the CD-ROM version, followed by a period and a space.

10. Type the copyright year, followed by a period and a space.

11. If your citation continues to a second or subsequent line, double-space that line and indent it one-half inch (five spaces on a typewriter).

See Appendix B for a sample Works Cited list.

```
Johnson, Dylan W. The Writer's Sourcebook. New York:

     Ames, 1998. The Writer's Sourcebook. CD-ROM. Vers.

     2.0. Writer's Reference Shelf. 1998.
```

```
Johnson, Dylan W. The Writer's Sourcebook. New York:

     Ames, 1998. The Writer's Sourcebook. CD-ROM.

     2 discs. Vers. 2.0. Writer's Reference Shelf. 1998.
```

Figure 183. Example Citations of a Periodically Published Database With One Author on CD-ROM.

Citing Online Scholarly Projects or Reference Databases

Scholarly projects and reference databases are good sources for your paper; you can also find these online. A citation for a scholarly project or reference database with one editor appears as shown in Figure 184 and consists of the following elements:

- Title of the project or database

- Abbreviation "Ed."

- Editor's first name or initial (and middle name or initial, if available)

- Editor's last name

- Version number, if applicable and not part of title

- Date of electronic publication or of latest version

- Name of sponsoring institution or organization

- Date of access

- Online address

To create this citation, follow these steps:

NOTE: *If you cannot find some of this information, cite what is available.*

1. At the left margin, type the title of the project or database and underline it. Capitalize the first letter of all words except prepositions and articles (unless the first word is a preposition or an article). Follow the title with a period and a space.

2. Type the abbreviation "Ed.," followed by a space.

3a. Type the editor's first name, followed by a space, or the first initial followed by a period and a space.

 b. If the editor's middle name is available, follow it with a space, or type the middle initial, followed by a period and a space.

 c. Type the editor's last name, followed by a period and a space.

4a. If this citation is for an online project, go to Step 5.

 b. If this citation is for a database with a version number that is not part of the title, type the abbreviation "Vers." followed by the number and a period and a space (see the second example in Figure 184).

5. Type the date of electronic publication or of the latest version in day, month (abbreviated per Table 5 on page 22), year format, followed by a period and a space.

6. Type the name of the sponsoring organization or institution, followed by a period and a space. Abbreviate, if possible.

7. Type the date you accessed this source in day, month (abbreviated per Table 5 on page 22), year format, followed by a space.

8. Type an opening karat, the electronic address, and a closing karat, followed by a period.

9. If your citation continues to a second or subsequent line, double-space that line and indent it one-half inch (five spaces on a typewriter).

See Appendix B for a sample Works Cited list.

```
The Alyssium Project. Ed. John K. Mitchell. 1997.

     Dept. of English, South Coast U. 9 Mar. 1999

     <http://www.southcoastuniv.edu/alyssium/>.
```

```
Latin American Literature Database. Ed. Eva Bradshaw.

     Vers. 2.0. 1997. Dept. of English, South Coast U.

     9 Mar. 1999 <http://www.southcoastuniv.edu/laldb/>.
```

Figure 184. Example Citations of an Online Scholarly Project and a Reference Database With One Author.

Citing Works Within Scholarly Projects or Reference Databases

You may wish to cite a poem, short story, other short work, or a book contained in a scholarly project or an article in a reference database. This section shows you how.

Citing a Short Work in a Scholarly Project

A citation for a short work with one author in a scholarly project appears as shown in Figure 185 and consists of the following elements:

- Author's last name

- Author's first name or initial (and middle name or initial, if available)

- Title of short work

- Title of the project

- Abbreviation "Ed."

- Name of editor of project

- Date of electronic publication

- Name of sponsoring institution or organization

- Date of access

- Online address

To create this citation, follow these steps:

1. At the left margin, type the author's last name, followed by a comma and a space.

2a. If only the author's first name or initial is available, follow it with a period and a space.

  b. If the author's middle name or initial is available, however, type the first name, followed by a space. Then type the middle name or initial, followed by a period and a space.

3. Type an opening quotation mark, the title of the short work, a period, a closing quotation mark, and a space.

4. Type and underline the title of the project. Capitalize the first letter of all words except articles and prepositions (unless the first word is an article or a preposition). Follow the title with a period and a space.

5. Type the abbreviation "Ed.," followed by a space.

6a. Type the editor's first name, followed by a space, or the first initial followed by a period and a space.

b. If the editor's middle name is available, follow it with a space, or type the middle initial, followed by a period and a space.

c. Type the editor's last name, followed by a period and a space.

7. Type the year of publication, followed by a period and a space.

8. Type the name of the sponsoring organization or institution, followed by a period and a space. Abbreviate, if possible.

   NOTE: *If the sponsoring organization or institution is in a foreign country, type the name, a comma, a space, then the city in which the organization or institution is located.*

9. Type the date you accessed this source in day, month (abbreviated per Table 5 on page 22), year format, followed by a space.

10. Type an opening karat, the electronic address, and a closing karat, followed by a period. List the URL of the short work if it is different from that of the entire work.

11. If your citation continues to a second or subsequent line, double-space that line and indent it one-half inch (five spaces on a typewriter).

   See Appendix B for a sample Works Cited list.

```
Rivera, José. "El Sombrero Negro." Latin American

    Literature Database. Ed. Eva Bradshaw. 1997.

    Dept. of Spanish, South Coast U. 9 Mar. 1999

    <http://www.southcoastuniv.edu/span/laldb/>.
```

Figure 185. Example Citation of a Short Work With One Author in an Online Scholarly Project.

Citing an Anonymous Article or Short Work in a Reference Database

A citation for an anonymous article or other short work with one author in a reference database appears as shown in Figure 186 and consists of the following elements:

- Title of article or short work

- Title of the project

- Abbreviation "Ed." (if relevant)

- Name of editor of database (if relevant)

- Date of electronic publication

- Name of sponsoring institution or organization

- Date of access

- Online address

To create this citation, follow these steps:

1. Type an opening quotation mark, the title of the article or short work, a period, a closing quotation mark, and a space.

2. Type and underline the title of the database. Capitalize the first letter of all words except articles and prepositions (unless the first word is an article or a preposition). Follow the title with a period and a space.

3a. If the work does not have an editor, go to Step 6 and refer to the first example in Figure 186.

  b. If it does have an editor, however, type the abbreviation "Ed.," followed by a space. (Refer to the second example in Figure 186.)

4. Type the editor's last name, followed by a comma and a space.

5a. If only the editor's first name or initial is available, follow it with a period and a space.

  b. If the editor's middle name or initial is available, however, type the first name, followed by a space. Then type the middle name or initial, followed by a period and a space.

6. Type the date of electronic publication or of the latest version in day, month (abbreviated per Table 5 on page 22), year format, followed by a period and a space.

7. Type the name of the sponsoring organization or institution, followed by a period and a space. Abbreviate, if possible.

    NOTE: *If the sponsoring organization or institution is in a foreign country, type the name, a comma, a space, then the city in which the organization or institution is located.*

8. Type the date you accessed this source in day, month (abbreviated per Table 5 on page 22), year format, followed by a space.

9. Type an opening karat, the electronic address, and a closing karat, followed by a period.

10. If your citation continues to a second or subsequent line, double-space that line and indent it one-half inch (five spaces on a typewriter).

See Appendix B for a sample Works Cited list.

"Telling Tales." <u>Modern English Writers</u>. 1997.

Northern State U. 9 Mar. 1999 <http://www.

northernstate.edu/mod/>.

"The Lonesome Soul." <u>Modern American Literature</u> Database.

Ed. Eva Bradshaw. 1997. Dept. of English, South

Coast U. 9 Mar. 1999 <http://www.southcoastuniv.

edu/laldb/>.

Figure 186. Example Citations of an Anonymous Short Work in an Online Scholarly Project and Reference Database.

Citing a Book in a Scholarly Project

Books found online also may be included in scholarly projects and may have been published before. Online books are cited just like their physical counterparts, but you must also include the online access information. Therefore, if the book you wish to cite has a translator, compiler, etc., follow the rules for those citations in the section on *Citing Books* that begins on page 130. Then return to this page for the steps to creating the online access information.

A citation for a book with one author found online in a scholarly project and previously published appears as shown in Figure 187 and consists of the following elements:

- Author's last name and first name or initial (and middle name or initial, if available)

- Title of book

- City where original publisher is located

- Year book was originally copyrighted

- Name of scholarly project

- Abbreviation "Ed."

- Name of editor of scholarly project

- Date of electronic publication

- Name of sponsoring institution or organization

- Date of access

- Online address

To create this citation, follow these steps:

1. At the left margin, type the author's last name, followed by a comma and a space.

2. If only the first name or initial is available, follow it with a period and a space. If the author's middle name or initial is available, however, type the first name, followed by a space. Then type the middle name or initial, followed by a period and a space.

3. Type and underline the book title. Capitalize the first letter of all words except articles and prepositions (unless the first word is an article or a preposition). Follow it with a period and a space.

4a. If the book has not been previously published, go to Step 7.

 b. If the book has been previously published, however, type the city of original publication, followed by a colon and a space.

5. Type the name of the original publisher, followed by a comma and a space.

6. Type the year of original publication, followed by a period and a space.

7. Type and underline the title of the scholarly project. Then follow it with a period and a space.

8. Type the abbreviation "Ed.," followed by a space.

9. Type the editor's first name, followed by a space, then the middle name, if available, followed by a space. (If using initials, be sure to add periods.) Then type the last name, followed by a period and a space.

10. Type the date of electronic publication, followed by a period and a space.

11. Type the name of the sponsoring institution or organization, followed by a period and a space.

12. Type the date you accessed the book in day, month (abbreviated per Table 5 on page 22), year format, followed by a space.

13. Type an opening karat, then the complete online address, followed by a closing karat and a period. If the URL for the book is different from that of the project itself, cite the URL for the book.

14. If your citation continues to a second or subsequent line, double-space that line and indent it one-half inch (five spaces on a typewriter).

See Appendix B for a sample Works Cited list.

```
Kennedy, David. The Life of Roald Dahl. New York: Ace,

1994. 20th Century English Writers. Ed. John

Daniels. 1997. Northern State U. 9 Mar. 1999

<http://www.northernstate.edu/mod/>.
```

Figure 187. Example Citation of a Book with One Author Found Online in a Scholarly Project and Previously Published.

Citing Professional or Personal Websites

You may find information on professional or personal websites. A citation for such a source having one author appears as shown in Figure 188 and consists of the following elements:

- Title of the person who created the site, if available

- Title of the site or, if there is no title, description "Home page"

- Version number, if applicable and not part of title

- Name of associated institution or organization, if any

- Date of access

- Online address

To create this citation, follow these steps:

NOTE: *If you cannot find some of this information, cite what is available.*

NOTE: *If the website creator is not listed on the website, go to Step 3 and refer to the third example in Figure 188.*

1. At the left margin, type the website creator's last name, followed by a comma and a space.

2a. If only the website creator's first name or initial is available, follow it with a period and a space.

b. If the website creator's middle name or initial is available, however, type the first name, followed by a space. Then type the middle name or initial, followed by a period and a space.

3a. Type and underline the title of the website. Capitalize the first letter of all words except articles and prepositions (unless the first word is an article or a preposition). Follow the title with a period and a space. See the first example in Figure 188.

b. If the website has no title, type the phrase "Home page" followed by a period and a space. See the second example in Figure 188.

4. If there is a sponsoring organization or institution, type the name, followed by a period and a space. Abbreviate, if possible.

5. Type the date you accessed this website in day, month (abbreviated per Table 5 on page 22), year format, followed by a space.

6. Type an opening karat, the electronic address, and a closing karat, followed by a period.

7. If your citation continues to a second or subsequent line, double-space that line and indent it one-half inch (five spaces on a typewriter).

See Appendix B for a sample Works Cited list.

```
Jones, Jerry. Mark Twain Page. 1997. South Coast U.

     19 Nov. 1999 <http://www.southcoastuniv.edu/

     jjones/mtwain.html>.
```

```
Samuel, L. K. Home page. 1998. 9 Oct. 1999 <http://www.

     southcoastuniv.edu/lsamuel>.
```

```
Science Fiction Authors' Page. U of North Bayview. 9 Oct.

     1999 <http://www.univnorthbayview.edu/>.
```

Figure 188. Example Citations of Professional or Personal Websites.

Citing Online Communications

You may receive information for your paper via e-mail, the Internet, online postings on bulletin boards, etc. This section shows you how to cite these sources.

Citing E-mail Communications

A citation for an e-mail message appears as shown in Figure 189 and consists of the following elements:

- Author's last name

- Author's first name or initial (and middle name or initial, if available)

- Subject of e-mail message, if available

- Phrase "E-mail to" and the receiver's complete name

- Date of e-mail

To create this citation, follow these steps:

1. At the left margin, type the author's last name, followed by a comma and a space.

2a. If only the first name or initial is available, follow it with a period and a space.

 b. If the author's middle name or initial is available, however, type the first name, followed by a space. Then type the middle name or initial, followed by a period and a space.

3. If there is no subject line, go to Step 4. Otherwise, type an opening quotation mark, the subject of the e-mail, a period, a closing quotation mark, and a space. Capitalize the first letter of all words except articles and prepositions (unless the first word is an article or a preposition).

4. Type the phrase "E-mail to," followed by the name of the recipient, followed by a period and a space (see the first example in Figure 189). If you are the recipient, type "the author," followed by a period and a space (see the second example in Figure 189).

5. Type the day of the message, followed by a space; then type the month in abbreviated format (see Table 5 on page 22), followed by a space. Then type the year, followed by a space.

6. If your citation continues to a second or subsequent line, double-space that line and indent it one-half inch (five spaces on a typewriter).

See Appendix B for a sample Works Cited list.

```
Jeffries, Mason L. "Re: The Lost Boys." E-mail to

Sandra Smith. 14 Aug. 1999.
```

```
Kellogg, J. S. E-mail to the author. 15 Apr. 1999.
```

Figure 189. Example Citations of E-mail Messages.

Citing Online Postings

Your source may be a posting to an Internet source. This section shows you how to cite the following:

- Online posting in an e-mail discussion list or World Wide Web forum

- Onlineline posting to a Usenet user group

- Document forwarded within a posting

Citing an Online Posting in an E-mail Discussion List or on a World Wide Web Forum

A citation for an online posting in an e-mail discussion list or on a World Wide Web forum appears as shown in Figure 190 and consists of the following elements:

- Author's last name

- Author's first name or initial (and middle name or initial, if available)

- Title of the document (from the subject line)

- Phrase "Online Posting"

- Date material was posted

- Name of the forum, if known

- Date of access

- Online address of the discussion list's Internet site, or if not available, the e-mail address of the list's moderator or supervisor, or the online address of the World Wide Web forum

To create this citation, follow these steps:

1. At the left margin, type the author's last name, followed by a comma and a space.

2a. If only the first name or initial is available, follow it with a period and a space.

b. If the author's middle name or initial is available, however, type the first name, followed by a space. Then type the middle name or initial, followed by a period and a space.

3. Type an opening quotation mark, the title of the document as listed in the e-mail's subject line, a period, a closing quotation mark, and a space. Capitalize the first letter of all words except articles and prepositions (unless the first word is an article or a preposition).

4. Type the phrase "Online posting," followed by a period and a space.

5. Type the day the message was posted, followed by a space; then type the month in abbreviated format (see Table 5 per page 22), followed by a space; then type the year, followed by a period and a space.

6. Type the name of the discussion group, if known, followed by a period and a space.

7. Type the day you accessed the posting, followed by a space; then type the month in abbreviated format (see Table 5 per page 22), followed by a space; then type the year, followed by a space.

8a. Type an opening karat, the online address of the list's Internet site, a closing karat, and a period.

  b. If you don't know the Internet site, type an opening karat, the e-mail address of the list's moderator or supervisor, a closing karat, and a period.

  c. If this is a World Wide Web forum, type an opening karat, the address for that forum, a closing karat, and a period.

    NOTE: If possible, cite the address for a stored (archival) version of the posting for easier finding.

9. If your citation continues to a second or subsequent line, double-space that line and indent it one-half inch (five spaces on a typewriter).

See Appendix B for a sample Works Cited list.

```
Jeffries, Mason L. "Dealing With Difficult People."

    Online posting. 24 Aug. 1998. Buslist. 4 Mar.

    1999. <http://www.todaysbusiness.com/buslist/

    people/diff.html/>.
```

Figure 190. Example Citation of an Online Posting to an E-mail Discussion List.

Citing an Online Posting to a Usenet News Group

A citation for an online posting to a Usenet News Group appears as shown in Figure 191 and consists of the following elements:

- Author's last name

- Author's first name or initial (and middle name or initial, if available)

- Title of the document (from the subject line)

- Phrase "Online Posting"

- Date material was posted

- Date of access

- Prefix "News" and the name of the newsgroup

To create this citation, follow these steps:

1. At the left margin, type the author's last name, followed by a comma and a space.

2a. If only the first name or initial is available, follow it with a period and a space.

  b. If the author's middle name or initial is available, however, type the first name, followed by a space. Then type the middle name or initial, followed by a period and a space.

3. Type an opening quotation mark, the title of the posting as listed in the subject line, a period, a closing quotation mark, and a space. Capitalize the first letter of all words except articles and prepositions (unless the first word is an article or a preposition).

4. Type the phrase "Online posting," followed by a period and a space.

5. Type the day the message was posted, followed by a space. Then type the month in abbreviated format (see Table 5 on page 22), followed by a space. Then type the year, followed by a period and a space.

6. Type the day you accessed the posting, followed by a space. Then type the month in abbreviated format (see Table 5 on page 22), followed by a space. Then type the year, followed by a space.

7. Type an opening karat, the prefix "news" followed by a colon, then the newsgroup address, a closing karat, and a period.

8. If your citation continues to a second or subsequent line, double-space that line and indent it one-half inch (five spaces on a typewriter).

See Appendix B for a sample Works Cited list.

```
Sherland, Joan L. "Re: Proper English Usage."

    Online posting. 24 Aug. 1998. 4 Mar. 1999

    <news:lang.edu.english.usage>.
```

Figure 191. Example Citation of an Online Posting to a Usenet Newsgroup.

Citing a Document Forwarded in an Online Posting

A citation for a document forwarded in an online posting appears as shown in Figure 192 and consists of the following elements:

- Author's last name

- Author's first name or initial (and middle name or initial, if available)

- Title of the document (from the subject line)

- Date material was posted

- Phrase "Fwd. by" ("Forwarded by") and the name of the person who forwarded the material

- Phrase "Online posting"

- Date on which the material was forwarded

- Name of the discussion list, online forum, or news-group

- Date of access

- Online address

To create this citation, follow these steps:

1. At the left margin, type the author's last name, followed by a comma and a space.

2a. If only the first name or initial is available, follow it with a period and a space.

b. If the author's middle name or initial is available, however, type the first name, followed by a space. Then type the middle name or initial, followed by a period and a space.

3. Type an opening quotation mark, the title of the document, a period, a closing quotation mark, and a space. Capitalize the first letter of all words except articles and prepositions (unless the first word is an article or a preposition).

4. Type the day the message was originally posted, followed by a space. Then type the month in abbreviated format (see Table 5 on page 22), followed by a space. Then type the year, followed by a period and a space.

5.   Type the phrase "Fwd. by," followed by the name of the person who forwarded the material in first name, last name format. Follow the name with a period and a space.

6.   Type the phrase "Online posting," followed by a period and a space.

7.   Type the day the document was forwarded, followed by a space. Then type the month in abbreviated format (see Table 5 on page 22), followed by a space. Then type the year, followed by a period and a space.

8.   Type the name of the discussion list, online forum, or news-group, followed by a period and a space.

9.   Type the day you accessed the posting, followed by a space. Then type the month in abbreviated format (see Table 5 on page 22), followed by a space. Then type the year, followed by a space.

10.   Type an opening karat, the online address of the discussion list, online forum, or newsgroup, a closing karat, and a period.

11.   If your citation continues to a second or subsequent line, double-space that line and indent it one-half inch (five spaces on a typewriter).

See Appendix B for a sample Works Cited list.

```
Sherland, Joan L. "Proper English Usage." 12 June

    1998. Fwd. by John Smith. Online posting. 24

    Aug. 1998. English Language Discussion. 4 Mar.

    1999 <http://sgu.edu/~englang/sherland.txt>.
```

Figure 192. Example Citation of a Document Forwarded in an Online Posting to a Discussion List.

Citing an Online Chat

You may take part in an online chat that is posted in a forum such as a MUD (multi-user domain) or MOO (multiuser domain, object-oriented). For example, an author may invite the public to converse online with him or her at a specific time. You can cite this communication as a source, too (see Figure 193), although if you can cite a stored copy of the transcript, it will be easier for your readers to check your source (see Figure 194).

A citation for an online chat appears in Figure 193 and consists of the following elements:

- Speaker's last name

- Speaker's first name or initial (and middle name or initial, if available)

- Description of the event

- Date of the event

- Forum name

- Date of access

- Online address with the prefix "telnet://"

To create this citation, follow these steps:

1. At the left margin, type the speaker's last name, followed by a comma and a space.

2a. If only the speaker's first name or initial is available, follow it with a period and a space.

 b. If the speaker's middle name or initial is available, however, type the first name, followed by a space. Then type the middle name or initial, followed by a period and a space.

3. Type a description of the event, followed by a period and a space. (See the first example in Figure 193). If part of the description is a title, put the title in quotation marks, with the closing quotation mark outside the period. Follow with a space. (See the second example in Figure 193.)

4. Type the date of the event in day, month (abbreviated per Table 5 on page 22), year format, followed by a period and a space.

5. Type the name of the forum, followed by a period and a space.

6. Type the date you accessed this source in day, month (abbreviated per Table 5 on page 22), year format, followed by a space.

7a. If this is a citation for a realtime communication, type an opening karat, the word "telnet," a colon and two forward slashes, the rest of the electronic address, and a closing karat, followed by a period.

b. If this is a citation for an archival copy of a realtime communication, type an opening karat, then the web address, a closing karat, and a period (see Figure 194).

8. If your citation continues to a second or subsequent line, double-space that line and indent it one-half inch (five spaces on a typewriter).

See Appendix B for a sample Works Cited list.

```
Silver, Daniel. Online discussion with fans. 13 Feb.

     1999. ScifiMOO. 13 Feb. 1999 <telnet://scifi.

     ucbayview.edu:4444>.
```

```
Silver, Daniel. Online discussion of "The Time Runners."

     13 Feb. 1999. ScifiMOO. 13 Feb. 1999 <telnet://

     scifi.ucbayview.edu:4444>.
```

Figure 193. Example Citations of an Online Chat.

```
Silver, Daniel. Online discussion of "The Time Runners."

     13 Feb. 1999. ScifiMOO. 22 June 1999 <http://

     www.ucbayview.edu/scifi/silver/timerunner.html>.
```

Figure 194. Example Citation of an Archival Copy of an Online Chat.

Citing Online Books

Books found online may or may not have been published in a physical form. Online books are cited just like their physical counterparts, but you must also include the online access information. Therefore, if the book you wish to cite has an editor, translator, compiler, etc., follow the rules for those citations in the section on *Citing Books* that begins on page 128. Then return to this page for the steps to creating the online access information.

A citation for a book with one author found online and previously published appears as shown in Figure 195 and consists of the following elements:

- Author's last name

- Author's first name or initial (and middle name or initial, if available)

- Title of book

- City where original publisher is located

- Name of original publisher

- Year book was originally copyrighted

- Date of electronic publication

- Electronic address

NOTE: For citations with more than one author, see the instructions for citing authors' names on pages 89-93.

To create this citation, follow these steps:

1. At the left margin, type the author's last name, followed by a comma and a space.

2a. If only the first name or initial is available, follow it with a period and a space.

b. If the author's middle name or initial is available, however, type the first name, followed by a space. Then type the middle name or initial, followed by a period and a space.

NOTE: Type the author's name exactly as listed on the work; i.e., if the work lists the name in full, you should, too. If the work lists initials, use those.

3. Type and underline the book title. Capitalize the first letter of all words except articles and prepositions (unless the first word is an article or a preposition). Follow it with a period and a space.

4a. If the book has not been previously published, go to Step 7.

b. If the book has been previously published, however, type the city of original publication, followed by a colon and a space.

5. Type the name of the publisher, followed by a comma and a space. Shorten the publisher's name, if possible; for instance, if the publisher is Harcourt, Brace, Jovanovich, just put "Harcourt."

    If the publisher is a university press, or has the word "Press" in its name, just use "U" for "University" and "P" for "Press": "U of Chicago P"; "Oxford UP."

6. Type the copyright year, followed by a period and a space.

7. Type the date of electronic publication in day, month (abbreviated per Table 5 on page 22), year format, followed by a space.

8. Type an opening karat, then the complete online address, followed by a closing karat and a period.

    NOTE: If you are citing part of an online book, include the online address for that part of the book, not for the book itself.

9. If your citation continues to a second or subsequent line, double-space that line and indent it one-half inch (five spaces on a typewriter).

    See Appendix B for a sample Works Cited list.

Parris, Crawley A. <u>Mastering Executive Arts and</u>

   <u>Skills</u>. New York: Atheneum, 1969. 3 Feb. 1998

   <http://businessbooks.com/management/>.

Figure 195. Example Citation of a Book With One Author Found Online and Previously Published

Citing Articles in Online Publications

Just as with online books, online articles are cited like their physical counterparts. This section shows some examples, but be sure to check *Citing Periodicals*, starting on page 97, for detailed instructions on citing the publication information for sources not shown here.

Citing an Article in an Online Scholarly Journal

To create a citation for an article with one author in an online scholarly journal, follow the steps for citing the original publication information in *Citing Journal Articles* on pages 97-105. Then come to this page for the instructions for adding the following:

- Date of access

- Online address

Figure 196 shows an example.

1. At the end of the original citation, type the date you accessed the article in day, month (abbreviated per Table 5 on page 22), year format, followed by a space.

2. Type an opening karat, then the complete online address, followed by a closing karat and a period.

3. If your citation continues to a second or subsequent line, double-space that line and indent it one-half inch (five spaces on a typewriter).

See Appendix B for a complete sample works cited list.

```
Matthews, Yolanda S. "Racism in Contemporary Novels."

    Journal of Higher Education 39 (1993): 360-65.

    24 Sept. 1998 <http://www.ufbc.edu/journal/>.
```

```
Matthews, Yolanda S. "Racism in Contemporary Novels."

    Journal of Higher Education 39 (1993): 19 pars.

    24 Sept. 1998 <http://www.ufbc.edu/journal/>.
```

Figure 196. Example Citations of an Article With One Author in an Online Scholarly Journal.

Citing an Article in an Online Newspaper or on an Online Newswire

Cite an online newspaper article with an author just as you would a physical newspaper article with one author. Cite the original newspaper's publication information per the instructions in *Citing Newspaper Articles* on pages 120-123. Then come to this page for the instructions for adding the following:

- Date of access

- Online address

Figure 197 shows an example.

1. At the end of the original citation, type the date you accessed the publication in day, month (abbreviated per Table 5 on page 22), year format, followed by a space.

2. Type an opening karat, then the complete online address, followed by a closing karat and a period.

3. If your citation continues to a second or subsequent line, double-space that line and indent it one-half inch (five spaces on a typewriter).

See Appendix B for a sample Works Cited list.

```
Jones, John T. "The truth about Y2K." Los Angeles

     Times Online 5 Feb. 1998. 10 Dec. 1998. <http://

     www.latimes.com/business/y2k/article28.html>.
```

Figure 197. Example Citation of a Newspaper Article With an Author and Found in an Online Newspaper.

Citing an Article in an Online Magazine

Cite an article with one author in an online magazine just as you would a physical magazine article with one author. Cite the original magazine's publication information per the instructions in *Citing Magazine Articles* on pages 106-111. Then come to this page for instructions for adding the following:

- Date of access

- Online address

Figure 198 shows an example.

1. At the end of the original citation, type the date you accessed the publication in day, month (abbreviated per Table 5 on page 22), year format, followed by a space.

2. Type an opening karat, then the complete online address, followed by a closing karat and a period.

3. If your citation continues to a second or subsequent line, double-space that line and indent it one-half inch (five spaces on a typewriter).

See Appendix B for a sample Works Cited list.

```
Morrison, H. A. "The paperless office." Business

    Talk 21 Dec. 1992. 5 Mar. 1998 <http://bustalk.

    com/officetips/article38>.
```

Figure 198. Example Citation of an Article in an Online Magazine.

Citing a Review in an Online Magazine

To cite a review in an online magazine, follow the steps for citing the original publication information in *Citing Reviews* on pages 190-191. Then come to this page for the instructions for adding the following:

- Date of access

- Online address

Figure 199 shows an example.

1. At the end of the original citation, type the date you accessed the publication in day, month (abbreviated per Table 5 on page 22), year format, followed by a space.

2. Type an opening karat, the online address, and a closing karat, followed by a period.

3. If your citation continues to a second or subsequent line, double-space that line and indent it one-half inch (five spaces on a typewriter.

See Appendix B for a sample Works Cited list.

```
Jones, John T. "Exploring New Management Techniques."

    Rev. of The Bottom-up Approach, by Henry Dawson.

    Today's Business 10 (1994). 8 Pars. 9 Apr. 1997

    <http://businesslib.com/todaysbusiness/management/

    techniques.html>.
```

Figure 199. Example Citation of a Review in an Online Magazine.

Citing an Abstract in an Online Journal

To create a citation for an abstract in an online journal, follow the steps for citing the original publication information in *Citing Abstracts* on pages 180-182. Then come to this page for the instructions for adding the following:

- Date of access

- Online address

Figure 200 shows an example.

1. At the end of the original citation, type the date you accessed the article in day, month (abbreviated per Table 5 on page 22), year format, followed by a space.

2. Type an opening karat, the online address, and a closing karat, followed by a period.

3. If your citation continues to a second or subsequent line, double-space that line and indent it one-half inch (five spaces on a typewriter).

See Appendix B for a sample Works Cited list.

```
Johnson, Donald W. "Twelve Facts About King Arthur."

    English World 8 (1993): 25. Abstract. 14 June

    1997. <http://www.englishworld.org/arthur/12facts.

    html>.
```

Figure 200. Example Citation of an Online Abstract.

Citing an Editorial in an Online Newspaper

To create a citation for an editorial in an online newspaper, follow the steps for citing the original publication information in *Citing a Newspaper Editorial* on pages 124-125. Then return to this page for the instructions for adding the following:

- Date of access

- Online address

Figure 201 shows an example.

1. At the end of the original citation, type the date you accessed the article in day, month (abbreviated per Table 5 on page 22), year format, followed by a space.

2. Type an opening karat, the online address, and a closing karat, followed by a period.

3. If your citation continues to a second or subsequent line, double-space that line and indent it one-half inch (five spaces on a typewriter).

See Appendix B for a sample Works Cited list.

```
Thompson, John. "To Sue or Not to Sue." Editorial.

Los Angeles Times 2 Mar. 1998. 5 Mar. 1998

<http://www.latimes.com/editorial/sue.html>.
```

Figure 201. Example Citation of an Online Newpaper Editorial With an Author.

Citing a Letter to the Editor in an Online Newspaper

To create a citation for a letter to the editor in an online newspaper, follow the steps for citing the original publication information in *Citing a Letter to the Editor in a Newspaper* on pages 126-127. Then return to this page for the instructions for adding the following:

- Date of access

- Online address

Figure 202 shows an example.

1. At the end of the original citation, type the date you accessed the article in day, month (abbreviated per Table 5 on page 22), year format, followed by a space.

2. Type an opening karat, the online address, and a closing karat, followed by a period.

3. If your citation continues to a second or subsequent line, double-space that line and indent it one-half inch.

See Appendix B for a sample Works Cited list.

```
Jones, John T. Letter. Los Angeles Times, 10 Dec.

    1998. 11 Dec. 1998 <http://www.latimes.com/

    letters/december/11.html>.
```

Figure 202. Example Citation of a Letter to the Editor in an Online Newspaper.

Citing Graphical Materials Found Online

Graphical materials from online sources are cited just like their print counterparts, but the online address must be included. Some examples are shown in this section, but be sure to reference back to the *Citing Graphical Materials* section, beginning on page 198, for more detailed instructions (for instance, if your citation is for a photograph of a work of art, a work of art included in a book with an editor, a slide, etc., follow those instructions first, then add the online address information as shown in examples in this section).

Citing a Work of Art Found Online

To create a citation for a work of art found online, follow the steps for citing the original publication information on pages 198-201. Then return to this page for instructions for adding the following:

- Date of access

- Online address

Figure 203 shows an example.

1. At the end of the original citation, type the date you accessed the article in day, month (abbreviated per Table 5 on page 22), year format, followed by a space.

2. Type an opening karat, the online address, and a closing karat, followed by a period.

3. If your citation continues to a second or subsequent line, double-space that line and indent it one-half inch (five spaces on a typewriter).

See Appendix B for a sample Works Cited list.

```
Smith, Sandra. The Dust Bowl. 1937. Logan Art Museum,

    San Diego. 13 May 1999 <http://www.loganart.com/

    depression/smith.html>.
```

Figure 203. Example Citation of a Work of Art Found Online.

Citing a Work of Art on CD-ROM

To create a citation for a work of art on CD-ROM, follow the steps for citing the original publication information in *Citing a Work of Art* on pages 198-201, the return to this page for the instructions for adding the following:

- Phrase "CD-ROM"

- City where publisher is located

- Name of publisher

- Year software was published

Figure 204 shows an example.

1. At the end of the original citation, type the phrase "CD-ROM," followed by a period and a space.

2. Type the city where the publisher is located, followed by a colon and a space.

3. Type the name of the publisher, followed by a comma and a space.

4. Type the year of publication, followed by a period.

5. If your citation continues to a second or subsequent line, double-space that line and indent it one-half inch (five spaces on a typewriter).

See Appendix B for a sample Works Cited list.

```
Smith, Sandra. The Dust Bowl. 1937. Logan Art Museum,

     San Diego. CD-ROM. Santa Clara: Artworks, 1996.
```

Figure 204. Example Citation of a Work of Art on CD-ROM.

Citing a Map Found Online

A citation for a map or chart found online appears as shown in Figure 205 and consists of the following elements:

- Title of map or chart

- Word "Map" or "Chart"

- Name of publication

- Publisher's name

- Date of access

- Online address

To create this citation, follow these steps:

1. At the left margin, type and underline the map or chart title, followed by a period. Capitalize the first letter of all words except for articles and prepositions (unless the first word is an article or a preposition; i.e., "The").

2. Type the word "Map" or "Chart" to identify the item and follow it with a period and a space.

3. Type and underline the name of the publication in which you found the map, followed by a period and a space.

4. Type the publisher's name, followed by a period and a space.

5. Type the date you accessed the map or chart in day, month, year format, followed by a space.

6. Type an opening karat, the online address, and a closing karat, followed by a period.

7. If your citation continues to a second or subsequent line, double-space that line and indent it one-half inch.

See Appendix B for a sample Works Cited list.

<u>Greater Los Angeles</u>. Map. <u>Thomas Guides</u>. Thomas

    Brothers. 24 Oct. 1999 <http://www.thomasbros.

    com/california/la.html>.

Figure 205. Example Citation of a Map Found Online.

Citing an Online Advertisement

You can cite advertisements from magazines, newspapers, television stations, and other sources. This citation appears as shown in Figure 206 and consists of the following beginning elements:

- Name of the product, company, or institution that is the subject of the ad

- Word "Advertisement"

- Name of the source in/on which the ad appeared

- Publication information for the type of source in which the ad appeared

To create this citation, follow these steps:

1. At the left margin, type the name of the product, company, or institution that is the subject of the ad, followed by a period and a space.

2. Type the word "Advertisement," followed by a period and a space.

3. Type the date you accessed the advertisement in day, month, year format, followed by a space.

4. Type an opening karat, the online address, and a closing karat, followed by a period.

5. If your citation continues to a second or subsequent line, double-space that line and indent it one-half inch.

See Appendix B for a sample Works Cited list.

```
Holiday Inn. Advertisement. 13 Nov. 1998 <http://

     www.holidayinn.com/california/losangeles>.
```

Figure 206. Example Citation of an Online Advertisement.

Citing a Cartoon Found Online

To create a citation for a cartoon found online, follow Steps 1-8 in *Citing a Cartoon* on pages 204-205. Then return to this page for instructions for adding the following:

- Date of access

- Online address

Figure 207 shows an example.

1. After the date of publication, type a space, then type the date you accessed the article in day, month(abbreviated per Table 5 on page 22), year format, followed by a space.

2. Type an opening karat, the online address, and a closing karat, followed by a period.

3. If your citation continues to a second or subsequent line, double-space that line and indent it one-half inch (five spaces on a typewriter).

See Appendix B for a sample Works Cited list.

NOTE: *If the cartoon has more than one cartoonist, cite that number of cartoonists by following the rules for that number of authors.*

```
Torres, Jose. "The Great Escape." Cartoon. Register

     Online. 4 Jan. 1999. 6 Jan. 1999 <http://www.

     ocregister/1999/january/cartoons>.
```

Figure 207. Example Citation of a Cartoon Found Online

Citing Audio-Visual Materials Found Online

Citing a Television or Radio Program Found Online

Figure 208 shows an example citation for a transcript of a television or radio program found online. First follow the steps in the section on *Citing a Television or Radio Program* on pages 246-249, then return to this page for instructions for adding the following:

- Word "Transcript"

- Date of access

- Online address

1. At the end of the citation, type the word "Transcript," followed by a period and a space.

2. Type the date you accessed the program in day, month (abbreviated per Table 5 on page 22), year format, followed by a space.

3. Type an opening karat, the online address, and a closing karat, followed by a period.

4. If your citation continues to a second or subsequent line, double-space that line and indent it one-half inch (five spaces on a typewriter).

See Appendix B for a sample Works Cited list.

```
Welles, Orson. "The War of the Worlds." Mercury Theatre.

    CBS Radio. WCBS, New York. 30 Oct. 1938. Tran-

    script. 29 Jan. 1999 <http://www.mercurytheatre.

    com/welles/warworld.html>.
```

Figure 208. Example Citation of an Online Transcript of a Television or Radio Program.

Citing a Sound Recording or Sound Clip Found Online

Citing a sound recording or sound clip online involves a lot of the same elements as citing a sound recording on tape, CD, etc. The order of the information included in the citation depends on whether the recording has been previously recorded, whether you cite a specific song or speech, or include the conductor, performer(s), orchestra, etc. This section shows some examples, but first refer to *Citing a Sound Recording* on pages 254-261 and to *Citing a Musical Composition* on pages 264-265 for the correct way to cite the original source. Then return to this page for instructions on adding the following:

- Date of access

- Online address

Figure 209 shows examples.

1. At the end of the original citation, type the date you accessed the recording in day, month (abbreviated per Table 5 on page 22), year format, followed by a space.

2. Type an opening karat, the online address, and a closing karat, followed by a period.

3. If your citation continues to a second or subsequent line, double-space that line and indent it one-half inch.

See Appendix B for a sample Works Cited list and other examples of sound recording citations.

```
Franklin, Georgia. "Loyalty: A Dying Trait?" Great

    American Speakers. Natl. Public Radio, 17 Nov.

    1996. 25 Mar. 1999 <http://www.npr.org/speakers/

    franklin/47350.gas.23.spk>.
```

```
Smith, Ronald L. "The Whipporwill." 1958. Birdsong.

    Abco, 1995. 3 July 1999 <http://www.abco.com/

    Smith/03459093.bdc.24>.
```

Figure 209. Example Citations of Sound Recordings Found Online.

Citing a Film or Film Clip Found Online

You can cite a film or film clip found online. First check the section on *Citing Movies* pages 240-243 for instructions on citing the original source. Then return to this page for information on adding the following:

- Date of access

- Online address

Remember that different elements are required depending on whether or not the film was adapted from another work. Figure 210 shows an example of a movie listed by the director's name.

1. At the end of the citation for the original source, type the date you accessed the program in day, month, year format, followed by a space.

2. Type an opening karat, the online address, and a closing karat, followed by a period.

3. If your citation continues to a second or subsequent line, double-space that line and indent it one-half inch (five spaces on a typewriter).

See Appendix B for a sample Works Cited list.

```
Johnston, Joe, dir. October Sky. Universal, 1999.

    24 Aug. 1999 <http://www.octobersky.com/credits.

htm.
```

Figure 210. Example Citation of a Film Found Online and Listed by the Director's Name.

Citing a Manuscript or Working Paper on Online

To cite a manuscript or working paper found online, first refer to *Citing a Manuscript or Typescript for a Book* on pages 196-197 for instructions on citing the original source. Then return to this page for instructions for adding the:

- Date of access

- Online address

Figure 211 shows examples of a manuscript or working paper found online.

1. At the end of the citation for the original source, type the date you accessed the program in day, month (abbreviated per Table 5 on page 22), year format, followed by a space.

2. Type an opening karat, the online address, and a closing karat, followed by a period.

3. If your citation continues to a second or subsequent line, double-space that line and indent it one-half inch (five spaces on a typewriter).

See Appendix B for a sample Works Cited list.

```
Jensen, Sara. "Shakespeare's Secret." Ms. 23, 1996.

     19 Sept. 1998 <http://www.unc.edu/classics/

     shakespeare/jensen1.html>.
```

```
Jensen, Sara. "The Truth About Shakespeare." Working

     paper, 1998. 19 Sept. 1998 <http://www.unc.edu/

     classics/shakespeare/jensen2.html>.
```

Figure 211. Example Citations of a Manuscript and Working Paper Found Online.

Citing an Interview Found Online

To cite an interview found online, first refer to *Citing Personal Interviews* on pages 266-274 or instructions on citing the original source information, the return to this page for instructions on adding the following:

- Date of access

- Online address

- Published interview found online

- Untitled published interview found online

Citing a Published Interview Found Online

Figure 212 shows an example of a published interview found online.

1. At the end of the original citation, type the date you accessed the program in day, month (abbreviated per Table 5 on page 22), year format, followed by a space.

2. Type an opening karat, the online address, and a closing karat, followed by a period.

3. If your citation continues to a second or subsequent line, double-space that line and indent it one-half inch.

See Appendix B for a sample Works Cited list.

```
Jason, John. "The Battle of Gettysburg." Historical

    Weekly. 25 Nov. 1997. 8 Feb. 1999 <http://www.

    histweek.com/Nov98>.
```

Figure 212. Example Citation of a Published Interview Found Online.

Citing an Untitled Interview Found Online

Figure 213 shows an example of an untitled interview found online:

1. At the end of the original citation, type the date you accessed the program in day, month (abbreviated per Table 5 on page 22), year format, followed by a space.

2. Type an opening karat, the online address, and a closing karat, followed by a period.

3. If your citation continues to a second or subsequent line, double-space that line and indent it one-half inch.

See Appendix B for a sample Works Cited list.

```
Jason, John. Interview. Historical Weekly. 25 Nov. 1997.

     8 Feb. 1999 <http://www.histweek.com/Nov98>.
```

Figure 213. Example Citation of an Untitled Published Interview Found Online.

Citing Works Published in More Than One Media Format

Some works may be available on multiple media, such as CD-ROM, 3.5" diskette, videodisc, and as a printed book. You can cite all the media or just the one(s) you used. Figure 214 shows examples of both.

A citation for a work with one author and published in more than one medium appears as shown in Figure 214 and consists of the following elements:

- Author's last name

- Author's first name or initial (and middle name or initial, if available)

- Title of work

- Type(s) of medium or media

- City where publisher is located

- Name of publisher

- Year work was published

To create this citation, follow these steps:

1. At the left margin, type the author's last name, followed by a comma and a space.

2a. If only the first name or initial is available, follow it with a period and a space.

 b. If the author's middle name or initial is available, however, type the first name, followed by a space. Then type the middle name or initial, followed by a period and a space.

3. Type and underline the title of the workt. Capitalize the first letter of all words except prepositions and articles (unless the first word is a preposition or an article). Follow the title with a period and a space.

4. At this point, you have a choice to cite all the media for which this title is available, or just the one you used. The first example in Figure 214 lists all the media, while the second example shows just the medium used. Be sure to put a period and a space at the end of your list.

5. If there is a version number, type the abbreviation "Vers." followed by a space, then the number, followed by a period and a space.

6. Type the city of publication, followed by a colon and a space.

7. Type the name of the publisher, followed by a comma and a space.

8. Type the year of publication, followed by a period and a space. (Include the day and month, if relevant.)

9. If your citation continues to a second or subsequent line, double-space that line and indent it one-half inch (five spaces on a typewriter).

See Appendix B for a sample Works Cited list.

```
Johnson, Dylan W. The Writer's Sourcebook. Book,

     CD-ROM, diskette. Vers. 2.0. New York: Writer's

     Reference Shelf, 1998.
```

```
Johnson, Dylan W. The Writer's Sourcebook. CD-ROM.

     Vers. 2.0. New York: Writer's Reference Shelf,

     1998.
```

Figure 214. Example Citations of a Periodically Published Database With One Author on CD-ROM.

Citing Works When the Medium Format is Unknown

Perhaps you have found a source on the Internet, but you don't know whether it is now available on CD-ROM or only on a website. The medium type, therefore, is unknown. In this case, you can use the word "Electronic" as the medium type. Cite whatever publication information is available, including network names, sponsoring organizations, etc., and the date you accessed the source. Remember to look in the other sections of this chapter for the directions on citing the particular type of publication informa-tion, then return to this page for the online information instructions.

A citation for a work with one author for which the publication medium is unknown appears as shown in Figure 215 and consists of the following elements:

- Author's last name

- Author's first name or initial (and middle name or initial, if available)

- Title of work

- Any relevant publication information for the original version, if applicable

- City where current publisher is located

- Name of current publisher

- Year of current publication

- Word "Electronic"

- Name of network or sponsoring organization

- Date of access

To create this citation, follow these steps:

1. At the left margin, type the author's last name, followed by a comma and a space.

2a. If only the first name or initial is available, follow it with a period and a space.

b. If the author's middle name or initial is available, however, type the first name, followed by a space. Then type the middle name or initial, followed by a period and a space.

3. Type and underline the title of the work. Capitalize the first letter of all words except articles and prepositions (unless the first word is an article or a preposition). Follow it with a period and a space.

4. Type the publication information for the original version, if relevant. Figure 215 shows the city where the publisher is located, followed by a colon and a space; the publisher's name, followed by a comma and a space; and the date of publication, followed by a period and a space.

5. Type the city where the current publisher is located, followed by a colon and a space.

6. Type the name of the current publisher, followed by a comma and a space.

7. Type the copyright year of the current work, followed by a period and a space.

8. Type the word "Electronic" followed by a period and a space.

9. Type the name of the network or sponsoring organization, followed by a period and a space.

10. Type the date you accessed this source in day, month (abbreviated per Table 5 on page 22), year format, followed by a period.

11. If your citation continues to a second or subsequent line, double-space that line and indent it one-half inch (five spaces on a typewriter).

See Appendix B for a sample Works Cited list.

```
Daniels, Susan. The Author's Companion. New York:

    Ames, 1988. New York: Writers' Resource Network,

    1998. Electronic. WriteNet. 3 Mar. 1999.
```

Figure 215. Example Citation of a Work When the Format is Unknown.

Alphabetizing Citations

To alphabetize citations, follow the rules in Table 26.

Table 26. Rules for Alphabetizing Citations in the List of Works Cited.

RULE	EXAMPLES
1. List names in alphabetical order by last name of the first author using letter-by-letter system.	Gold, Thomas M. Golding, Sandra. Golding, Terence.
2. Alphabetize the prefixes M', Mc, and Mac literally	MacIntyre, Peter L. McGill, Brian R. M'Connell, Thomas.
3. Alphabetize foreign last names containing articles and prepositions as follows: *Italian names* - Names of people who lived before or during the Renaissance are alphabetized by first name. All others are alphabetized by last name. "De," "Del," "Della," and "Di" go first. *Spanish* - "de" goes after first name, but "Del" is alphabetized first. Paternal surname always goes first, despite how author is known. *French names* - Do not use the word "de" with the last name unless the last name has only one syllable. If "Du" or "Des" is capitalized, list it first. *Latin* - When citing Roman names, use the form most common in English, even if the person's original name is not of Latin origin. Consult the <u>Oxford Classical Dictionary</u> for more detail. *German* - "Von" goes first; "von" goes after the first name. *All:* Treat foreign letters with diacritical marks (à, á, â, ä, ò, ó, ö, ü, etc.) like their English counterparts.	Aldenbruck, Peder von Brutus. Cicero. Copernicus. D'Angelo, T. L. de Gaulle, Charles. De La Salandra, Mary G. Della Vedova, Nick. Del Signore, Calogero. Desforges, duc de Desjarvins, Girard. Des Rosiers, Robert. Di Stefano, Philip. Du Bois, Jean J. Fröding, Gustav. Frost, Robert. Horace. García Lorca, Federico Maupassant, Guy de Michelangelo Buonnaroti Rios, Carlos R. de Van Handel, Sandra L. Von Richtofen, Peter D.
4. Alphabetize multiple works by the same author(s) by the title of each work. Use three dashes in place of the author's name for all entries but the first.	Garrison, John T. <u>Bountiful Lessons</u>. - - -. <u>Road to Nowhere</u>.
5. Alphabetize one-author works before multiple author works with that same author.	Garrison, John T. Garrison, John T. and Taylor, Bruce R.
6. Alphabetize works with the same first author and different second or third authors by the name of the second (then third) author.	Garrison, John T. and Luis N. Marcos. Garrison, John T. and Bruce R. Taylor. Garrison, John T. , Bruce R. Taylor, and Salvador Javier.
7. Alphabetize works with group authors or no authors by the first significant word of the name or of the title, if no name is listed. Treat legal citations likewise. Ignore "A," "An," and "The."	American Medical Association. Arthur, Allen D. "As the Millenium Turns." Barstow's Rules for Management. Barrett, Allen. "A Bottle Full of Miracles." National Endowment for the Arts. <u>The National Road to Recovery</u>. Peterson, Janet. Public Resource Council.
8. Alphabetize citations beginning with numbers as if the numbers were spelled out.	5 Rules for Good Management. Forbes, Martin T.

Chapter 6

Punctuation and Spelling

This chapter explains grammar requirements peculiar to the MLA for:

- Commas, quotation marks, brackets, underlines, slashes, and hyphens

- Spelling

- Numbering

Punctuation Requirements and Exceptions

Table 27 shows the punctuation requirements; Table 28 shows the exceptions to those requirements. Be consistent throughout your paper.

Table 27. Punctuation Requirements.

PUNCTUATION	HOW USED	EXAMPLE
Comma	Between elements in a series of three or more items	. . . two managers, three employees, and five clients.
	In dates written as month, day, year	July 4, 1776,
Double quotation marks	To introduce a word or phrase used as an ironic comment, slang, or as an invented or coined expression.	Dawson referred to the man as "hip."
	To set off the title of an article in a magazine or chapter in a book when mentioned in the text.	Smith's article, "The Paperless Office," focuses on the use of . . . .
Brackets	To enclose parenthetical material within parentheses.	<u>Huckleberry Finn</u> (by Mark Twain [Samuel Clemens]) dealt with racism.
Underline	To show a word or letter referred to as such.	Donegan said the word <u>cool</u> first became a popular slang term in the 1950s. Many English words end with a silent <u>e</u>.
Slash	Avoid use except when dividing lines in poetry (see *Citing Quotes From Poetry*, p. 42) or when pairing two terms as opposites	Toffler states that as global conflicts fade in the East/West and North/South, and society continues to undergo rapid technological change, the world will . . . .
Hypen	Use instead of slash when two terms paired as opposites or alternatives modify a noun.	The nature-nurture controversy continues to this day.

Table 28. Punctuation Exceptions.

PUNCTUATION	DO NOT USE	TYPE AS
Comma	In dates written as day, month, year	4 July 1776
	In dates written as month, year	July 1776
Slash	In these phrases: Monday and/or Tuesday pretest/posttest	Monday, Tuesday, or both pretest and posttest

Spelling Requirements

1. Do not divide words at ends of lines. Let wordwrap just take the whole word to the next line.

2. Reproduce all diacritical marks (à, á, â, è, etc.) If you are using a typewriter, write the marks in by hand.

Numbering Requirements

Table 29 shows numbering requirements when listing pages in the references and names in the text. List full numbers through 99. When listing numbers from 100 and up, list only two digits in the second half of the reference.

Table 29. Numbering Requirements.

PAGE NUMBERS	NAMES IN TEXT
6-7	Henry VIII
32-67	Elizabeth I
125-27	Elizabeth II
1145-49	Pope Pius XII

Table 30 shows the exceptions to these rules. These apply when using the rules in Table 29 would prove confusing.

Table 30. Numbering Exceptions.

CORRECT	CORRECT
85-108	984-1025

Percentages and Currency Requirements

Table 31 shows the MLA requirements when typing percentages and currency. You can spell the words out if there are three words or less. Be consistent throughout your paper.

Table 31. Percentages and Currency Requirements.

PERCENTAGES	CURRENCY
5%	25¢
20%	$50
100%	$4.50

Works Cited

Abrams, M. H., et al., ed. *The Norton Anthology of English Literature.* 2 vols. New York: Norton, 1962.

Alarcón, Pedro Antonio de. *El Sombrero de Tres Picos [The Three-Cornered Hat].* Boston: Ginn, 1952.

Clark, William George and William Aldis Wright. *The Unabridged William Shakespeare.* Phildelphia, Courage, 1997.

Drucker, Peter. *Innovation and Entrepreneurship: Practice and Principles.* New York: Harper, 1985.

Ewing, Anne. "Eulogy." *The Write Stuff.* Whittier: Writers' Club of Whittier, 1997.

Gibaldi, Joseph. *Handbook for Writers of Research Papers.* 4th ed. New York: MLA, 1995.

- - -. *Handbook for Writers of Research Papers.* 5th ed. New York: MLA, 1999.

- - -. *MLA Style Manual and Guide to Scholarly Publishing.* 2nd ed. New York: MLA, 1998.

Gleeson, Kerry. *The Personal Efficiency Program: How to Get Organized to Do More Work in Less Time.* New York: Wiley, 1994.

Harvard Law Review Association. *The Bluebook: A Uniform System of Citation.* 15th ed. Cambridge: HLRA, 1991.

Hofstadter, Douglas R. *Gödel, Escher, Bach: An Eternal Golden Braid.* New York: Vintage, 1979.

Interagency Arctic Research Policy Committee. *United States Artic Research Plan.* Washington: National Science Foundation, 1987.

Stine, G. Harry. *The Third Industrial Revolution.* New York: G. P. Putnam's Sons, 1975.

Teacher, Lawrence, ed. *The Unabridged Mark Twain.* Vol. 1. Philadelphia: Courage, 1997.

Toffler, Alvin. *Future Shock.* New York: Random, 1970.

Tolkien, J. R. R. *The Fellowship of the Rings.* The Lord of the Rings. Boston: Houghton, 1981.

Appendix A

Sample Report

NOTE: *The paper in this example uses headings to break it up into sections. These headings are not necessary for very short papers nor is the length of each section in this example an indication of the length your sections should be; these sections are abbreviated due to space limitations. For complete information on using headings, see* Using Headings *on page 29.*

Barbara Bond

Bus 450

Ms. Elliott

October 3, 1998

Alternative Dispute Resolution

The benefit of using an alternative dispute resolution
(ADR) process in a workplace setting all depends on the people
involved and the circumstances surrounding the dispute. ADR, as
part of a conflict management system within an organization, is
"any method of dispute resolution other than formal adjudication
such as court litigation or administrative proceedings"
(Costantino 33). This is broad enough to include employer-
supported options such as open door policies, peer review, or
internally trained mediators through a non-binding process.

Some proponents of ADR believe that the "A" in ADR might be
better stand for "appropriate" rather than alternative. They go
on to say that ADR is not a process that will work for every
dispute (Costantino 41).

Authors Costantino and Merchant discuss a downside to ADR
in this way: "In many organizations, the people who control
selection of the dispute resolution process and the resolution
of disputes have both power (the ability to influence) and
authority (the ability to decide). As a result, they may have a
personal stake in preserving the status quo dispute resolution

process and may be potential sources of resistance to any change effort" (Constantino 33).

Pros and Cons of ADR

Generally, complicated cases are more difficult in an ADR situation because the parties involved want to win, neither will offer room for compromise, and there are high dollars at risk. There is, however, a more positive side to ADR than this introduction might conclude.

ADR is a form of negotiation that takes place on a continual basis - inside of the work environment as well as outside of it. ADR is a faster process than court litigation and is far less expensive. Additionally, ADR generally produces a choice of remedies that the court system does not provide and is far more accessible.

ADR Language

Accessibility to a process does not mean that the process is good, however. An organization needs to "test" its ability to set up an ADR system properly before attempting to move forward. Language supported by the American Arbitration Association (AAA) includes statements such as "complaints heard by an impartial person" of joint selection by the employer and employee and "due process." "Fair in fact and perception" is another part of a clause that is recommended by the AAA (Johnson 34).

Binding resolution takes on a serious tone. Once arbitration of the dispute begins, an organization must have the process well enough established so that everyone understands the steps involved and enters the conversation with a minimum of trust that the process is meant to work. Regardless of the process selected and the language used, no one program is meant to meet every need of every situation. ADR should be part of the overall conflict management system within the organization that is provided to employees as an effort to manage the inevitable.

Conclusion

As both employers and employees are asked to do more with less in large organizations, there will continue to be conflict. Continual change through downsizing, mergers, and colliding cultures demand that an organization develop dispute resolution options that all parties perceive to be fair, fast, and final. Knowing all of this, however, does not make the task of bringing conflict management systems into the forefront of the business priority any easier.

Works Cited

Costantino, Cathy A., and Christina Sickles Merchant. <u>Designing</u>

<u>Conflict Management Systems: A Guide to Creating Healthy</u>

<u>Organizations</u>. San Francisco: Jossey-Bass, 1996.

Johnson, Dylan W. "The American Arbitration Association and

ADR." Dispute Resolution Journal (June 1997): 34-36.

Appendix B

Sample Works Cited List

Works Cited

Bernstein, T. M. The Careful Writer: A Modern Guide to English Usage. New York: Atheneum, 1965.

Harrison, Paul R. The Manager's World. Los Angeles: Business Press, 1989.

Jones, John. Ed. Time Management for Executives. New York: Doubleday, 1992.

Lopez, Tomás L. "The Workplace in the Year 2000." Management in the New Millenium. Ed. Susan L. Graves. New York: Acme Press, 1992. 201-210.

Skills for Tomorrow's Manager. New York: American Management Association, 1992.

Morrison, Howard A. "The Paperless Office." Business Talk (Dec. 1992): 70-76.

Parris, Crawley A. Mastering Executive Arts and Skills. New York: Atheneum, 1969.

RU486: The Import Ban and Its Effect on Medical Research: Hearings Before the Subcommittee on Regulation, Business Opportunities, and Energy, of the House Committee on Small Business. 101st Cong., 2d Sess. 35 (1990) (Testimony of Ronald Chesemore).

S. 5936, 102d Cong., 2d Sess. § 4(1992).

Sanders, Martin L., and Donald M. Wilkie. How to Bullet-Proof Your Management Techniques. New York: Atheneum, 1983.

The Wallace Dictionary. 4th ed. New York: Wallace, 1992.

Index